Great Family Collections

Great

Family Collections

Edited and with an Introduction by Douglas Cooper

The Macmillan Company New York

Copyright © 1965 by George Weidenfeld and Nicolson Ltd

Designed by George Mayhew for George Weidenfeld and Nicolson Ltd

Library of Congress Catalog Card Number 65-10731

Printed in Switzerland by Conzett & Huber, Zürich

Contents

Acknowledgements

The editor and publishers wish to thank the owners of the collections for giving permission for their collections to be described in this book. They also wish to express their appreciation of the help given by the owners of the collections and the authors of the articles in assembling the illustrative material.

The publishers are indebted to the following for permission to reproduce photographs and wish to acknowledge photographic credits as indicated.

All numbers refer to pages

THE PRINCES COLONNA
23 photo Gabinetto Fotografico Nazionale, Rome; 24–27, 29, 31, 32, 33, 34 right, 35, 38 left, 43, 46 photo De Antonis; 30, 34 left, 36, 37, 38 right, 39, 40, 41, 45 photo Anderson; 44 reproduced by courtesy of Prince Colonna

THE PRINCES DORIA PAMPHILI
All photographs by Gabinetto Fotografico Nazionale, Rome, except 50 left, 51 right, 68, 69 Fototeca Berenson, Florence; 51 left photo Anderson; 55, 56, 60 top, 61 right, 65, 66, 73 photo De Antonis, Rome; 60 bottom Foto Villani, Bologna

THE COUNTS WRANGEL AND BRAHE
77 left, 91 left photo Erik Andrén; 83 top and bottom, 87, 94, 95, 96 by courtesy of the Nordiska Museet, Stockholm, photos by M. Clarens; 88 top right, 88 bottom left, 88 bottom right, 90 top and bottom, 92 bottom, 93 top left and right, 93 bottom by courtesy of the Nordiska Museet, Stockholm; 77 right Svenska Portrattarkivet, National-museum; 79, 80, 84 top and bottom, 85, 86, 88 top left 94 bottom photo Hans Hammarskiöld; 78, 81, 91 right, 92 top photo Ulf Fredrik Wahlström

THE COUNTS HARRACH
All photographs by Photo Meyer, Vienna

THE PRINCES PALLAVICINI
All photographs by Gabinetto Fotografico Nazionale, Rome, except 135–7, 138 top and bottom photo De Antonis

Introduction

Douglas Cooper

The urge to collect – be it works of art, gems, weapons, furniture, books, medals or something else – has revealed itself throughout man's history as a fundamentally human phenomenon. Stimulated by motives of many kinds, some good, some bad, the collector's passion has taken many different forms just as the scale of its gratification has inevitably varied greatly. Since we are here to be concerned with the accumulated legacies of a great many eager and famous collectors, it would seem appropriate to begin by saying something about the different types of human mentality – as well as the more material factors – which have helped to produce them. But before doing so I must emphasise that the uniqueness of the collections which are described and explained in this book lies in the fact that none of them represents the expression of any one man's personal choice but all are the result of an interplay between the taste and interests of individuals with the fortunes and misfortunes which constitute the historical continuity of a family's life story. These are essentially collections of a type which I would designate as 'historical'. That is to say, they have built up over a long period of time, without any preconceived notions of creating a unity, and have been added to by successive generations of some great family amongst the members of which perhaps only a few have shown any real taste for or love and understanding of things artistic. For the rest, these collections have formed themselves in the sense that much of what they contain has come together through marriages, bequests, the fortunes of war, the liberality of sovereigns, or diplomatic and political triumphs. Yet, despite the share which the workings of history have had in their making, it is in the end to man-made fortunes and personal choice that much of the distinctive character of these collections is due. So to man let us forthwith return.

Collectors, as I have said, are of many different types. To begin with there are the true lovers of things artistic, like Pope Julius II, King Charles I, Cardinal Mazarin, the Archduke Leopold of Austria, the Duc d'Orléans, the Marquis de Marigny, Pierre Crozat, the second Duke of Devonshire, Sir Robert Walpole, Carl Gustaf Tessin, the Duc d'Aumale or Lord Hertford, who choose carefully and with enlightened discrimination the finest examples of the various schools or individual artists whom they most admire. That is to say, such men are primarily inspired as collectors by aesthetic considerations and personal taste, and the fact that their mind and eye have been formed through contact with the art of past times can give them a selective insight into the art of their contemporaries. Against this type of collector-amateur we may set the great artist-collectors such as Mantegna, Rubens, Rembrandt, Lely, Lankrink or Lawrence, for whom practical considerations weigh at least as heavily as the aesthetic ones. That is to say, the artist-collector acquires works of art not merely to look at and to enjoy them, but to learn more about his own profession from the examples of others, thereby nourishing his own inventive gifts and spurring himself on to higher creative achievements. Another type of collector is represented by an artist-historiographer like Vasari, who set out to assemble, on a systematic and historical basis, a collection of drawings which would illustrate stage by stage the progressive stylistic evolution of those artists whose biographies he was compiling. Then of course there have been the predatory collectors, men like Napoleon and Hitler, who rapaciously amassed vast quantities of works of art not because they loved or admired them but because the act of assembling them would appear symbolical of their worldly might and spiritual glorification.

This is only a brief *résumé* of some of the types of collector who are to be encountered. But already it must be apparent that, as an activity, collecting is an outward expression of incentives of many (and often conflicting) kinds, because among them we must reckon with creativity, curiosity, self-instruction, concupiscence, self-glorification, or the promotion of culture and learning.

Sometimes – and there are numerous outstanding examples in the present book – the urge to collect has been allied with an active patronage of contemporary artists and artisans, though this has not by any means always been the case. Here taste, vanity, financial possibilities and the desire to promote new things all play a determining role. But so of course do the availability of creative artists, the possibility of employing them and the chances that the current style will be adaptable to a specific purpose. However, many collectors take no interest in actuality. These men do not want to create a monument to the artistic glories of their own time and choose instead to create an imaginary present through the vestiges of a glorious past. Still others prefer to cultivate antiquarian interests for personal or political reasons. Thus 'when the new cities founded by Alexander the Great and his generals were being built,' Francis Taylor tells us (*The Taste of Angels*, New York and London, 1948), 'they were eager to acquire the reputation for a culture which hitherto they had not possessed. Already art was destined to be the handmaiden of political and military conquest. Alexander at Pella, moved by a nostalgia for the purity of ancient Athenian civilisation, became a collector of antiquities. The Hellenistic monarchs began systematically and reverently to collect the ruins and the fragments of the classic age and Sicyon became the gathering place for the art dealers of the empire. Mahaffy has described this city as "a Renaissance Florence of the Hellenistic age". No king or satrap of Alexander's empire, he pointed out, would overlook the fashionable necessity of having works of art, particularly bronzes from Sicyon, brought to his collection.'

A strangely decisive role in arousing a collector's instinct has also been played on some occasions by felicitous historical accidents. Neither the Emperor Charles V nor King Henry VIII of England seems to have been inclined by nature to distinguish himself as an art collector, nor for that matter as a patron of the arts. Yet when Titian was presented to the

Emperor during his Italian campaign he took a liking to him as a man, decided to appoint him his Court Painter, soon discovered the pleasure to be had from cultivating his friendship, and ended up by acquiring an important group of his works – eight in number – which he came to regard as being among his most treasured possessions. 'Wherefore,' wrote Aretino, 'Titian has achieved what is the miracle of his style in satisfying at the same time the body and soul of the stupendous Emperor.' With Henry VIII things happened the other way round: the great artist chose the great sovereign for whom he wished to work. Holbein, writes Ellis Waterhouse (*Painting in Britain 1530–1790*, London 1953), 'was driven by economic necessity to seek fortune in what seemed a hopeful and prosperous kingdom as a change from the meagre prospects for a great artist in a city, such as Basel, torn by the religious disturbances of the Reformation,' moved over to London 'as a speculation' and duly managed to impose his services on the king. So far as Holbein himself was concerned this development meant renouncing his aspirations to becoming a great religious painter, but he turned himself instead into not only one of the greatest portraitists of his age, but indeed of all time. The king, on the other hand, perhaps without fully realising what he was doing, thereby became the sponsor of a great human and artistic record of the notabilities of the period, while at the same time laying the foundations of a major royal collection. And, in fact, it is thanks to Holbein that these people come to life before our eyes with such vividness that we receive a clear image of that famous Tudor court and are thus granted an unexpected insight into the dramas of history in which they were all caught up.

Such encounters as these drive home once again the important point that the acquisition of works of art is not only determined by personal taste. As soon as one begins to look into the history of art patronage and collecting one learns how great the part played by chance has been in stimulating both the creation of great art and the willingness to acquire it. Would the Sistine ceiling, of which the decoration had been completed only twenty years earlier, ever have been repainted by Michelangelo but for the determination of Pope Julius II to prevent the Florentine master accepting employment under a rival patron while he waited for a favourable moment to continue the work on his own mausoleum?

Now, having considered some of the motives for collecting and various material factors which affect the outcome, we may well ask where the history of collecting begins, and also what form the earliest collections assumed. 'The plunder of war and the tangible fruits of industry,' says Francis Taylor, 'have always passed from one generation to the next, and works of art, being constantly associated with power, served as a medium of exchange; at the same time, by virtue of their intrinsic worth, based primarily upon the precious metals and rare stones of which they were composed, they served as a reserve of public wealth and a symbol of the nation's credit.' The earliest collections of works of art consisted of objects which were displayed, yet also served a function in everyday life. They were generally associated on the one hand with religious practices, and on the other with state functions, so they were housed in temples or treasure-houses which, says Mr Taylor again, 'were neither actually museums nor theoretical creations for cultural delectation'. We must then understand that, originally, the objects which we now prize as works of art (or museum specimens) had a utility value, and considered in the mass represented the power, wealth and splendour of the community which possessed them. Yet even in the earliest recorded periods it seems that the taste and enterprise of certain individuals soon began to show itself. Here for example is what Francis Taylor has to say about the Pharaohs of the New Empire (c 1500 BC):

The most spectacular collection, because it is the largest ever found intact, that of Tutankhamen, has been described as a 'dynastic museum established possibly for political reasons'. It was a collection, said Howard Carter, 'of the art of various periods and even of various nations – in short a collection of the Palace heirlooms gathered by Pharaoh after Pharaoh over a considerable period' . . . Despite their awesome majesty, the Pharaohs were prone to human weaknesses and, like the more mortal monarchs of a later day, indulged in fantasy. The young Tutankhamen, it appears, was an amateur collector of walking sticks and staves, for in the annex to his tomb and its antechamber were found a great number. His predecessor, Amenhotep III, was something of a collector and had a passion for blue enamel. Thutmose III was interested in nature and brought back from his campaigns a series of rare and exotic plants, ordering a catalogue of his botanical and biological specimens to be carved upon the walls of the Temple at Karnak. With this interest in natural philosophy it followed that there should be awakened an intellectual curiosity in regard to books and the accumulated knowledge of mankind. Thus at Thebes, and up and down the Valley of the Nile, the great new buildings of the Pharaohs contained as part of the palace enclosures vast libraries and treasure rooms where historical works began to find a logical and quite natural setting.

Now this pattern of things is not only true in regard to the Pharaohs but, as we can discover in the various essays that follow, has been repeated subsequently with variations in century after century. All that distinguishes the Pharaohs from later collectors is their belief that whatever they had amassed and loved in this life would accompany them into some life hereafter if it was packed with them into the tomb-chamber. It is amusing to speculate on the consequences to the history of the development of styles in art if this belief had gained universal acceptance. But for having thus saved from destruction (by time, the hand of man and other misfortunes) such a complete record of the material achievements and aesthetic concepts of early Egyptian civilisation we owe a special debt of gratitude to the Pharaohs. Of how many later rulers and their *fondés de pouvoir* must we not say, alas, that they allowed (when they did not actively order or encourage destruction) collections of great works of art, whole libraries and major pieces of architecture to perish through envy, fear, incomprehension or neglect? Do we fully realise how tremendously the world is indebted to private collectors of many periods and races for their unselfish efforts to guard and preserve things of value, of beauty and of human interest for future generations? We must beware of being blinded by majesty and millions, for in fact many true *amateur* collectors, especially during the last two hundred years, have been impecunious bourgeois like François Marcille or Victor Chocquet who, as a gesture of love, were ready to sacrifice all that they had in order to acquire on a considerable scale works of art – in these particular cases French eighteenth- and nineteenth-century paintings – which had no aesthetic appeal for their contemporaries.

Private collections seem to have been unknown in classical Greece, an austere civilisation in which artists and artisans were regarded as a low order of citizen while works of art, created as the need arose and admired only as perfect realisations, were, writes Francis Taylor, 'essentially public property and were displayed, if not in the religious shrines themselves, in the agorae or pinacothecae and in the gymnasia'. In Rome, on the other hand, with the whole conquered world at its feet and money circulating plentifully, public collections were established in the temples and baths, and these, in turn, set the pattern for great private collections of antique sculpture and paintings which were established in villas and palaces throughout the length and breadth of the Empire. But the transfer of the capital to Byzantium in the fourth century AD, the invasions of the barbarians and the increasing hold gained by the fanatically communizing early Christians transformed the social and economic structure of the world, brought in its wake destruction of the classical civilization and put an end to the possibility of collecting. For almost a thousand years, until the arrival on the scene of a new and wealthy bourgeoisie, only a few powerful rulers like Charlemagne and great ecclesiastics like Abbot Suger of St Denis were in a position to indulge in personal patronage of the arts. During that millenium art was essentially made by and enjoyed as the fruit of communal activity. No one collected remnants of past artistic achievements because they had no place in the hierarchy of ideas. The new Church represented the power and glory of the present; to it all artistic creation automatically belonged, because not only did it have to be embellished, but also its beliefs had to be visually propagated to an illiterate, struggling mass. It is, however, significant that out of this commanding attitude were created some of the greatest monuments of all time, whose artistic embellishment – for the major part anonymous – was of the highest order and whose treasuries and libraries were stocked with the finest products that the hand of contemporary man could produce.

The mid-fifteenth century witnessed at last a change in this situation and the history of private collecting, in the modern sense, may be said to have originated when a new bourgeois class assumed power in some of the

Italian republics. It is the bankers and men of commerce in Florence and Venice, the Falieris, the Mocenigos, the Dandolos and the Medicis, who ventured to break with the custom prevailing till then of accumulating all works of art in libraries and treasuries controlled by the Church or the ruling house. These men, whose wealth was newly earned and who certainly liked to display it, began to form collections of gems and works of art for their personal delectation in the privacy of their homes. From that time on the collecting bug has afflicted all manner of men, as power and riches have changed hands across the continent of Europe during the last five hundred years. 'The trumpet of art,' said Louis XIV, 'blows louder through time and space than any other trumpet.' Certainly there has been plenty of obvious evidence to support this thesis in the manoeuvres which have led to Popes, Emperors, Kings, Queens, great nobles, men of letters, artists and ultimately the bourgeois successively vying with each other to accumulate a greater and more impressive display of treasures.

Most of the great collections of the past have been dispersed long ago and can only be imagined today in some uncertain form through the interpretation of contemporary inventories, where they exist. Some of these collections lingered on in an identifiable form because either they were selectively absorbed (like that of Crozat by Mariette) into a later collection, or (like that of Queen Christina of Sweden) were acquired *en masse* by the Vatican and by representatives of a few reigning houses, whose possessions have subsequently been distributed through different departments of great museums. Nevertheless, even if we summon to our aid our fullest powers of imagination, it is virtually impossible to conjure up visually and intellectually any true conception of how they looked and what they must have signified for their time. Even such comparatively recent accumulations as the Musée Napoléon, the Galérie Louis Philippe or the collection of Marshal Soult are beyond the ability of our mind's eye to envisage properly. And no attempted reconstruction, in the form of a temporary exhibition, can adequately recapture the look and feel of the original. So much of the meaning of a collection depends on the *ambiance* which surrounds it. And that is really the principal motive for undertaking the present book. Of course, there are others too, though they are of a more specifically professional nature. But the real interest of this book, it seems to me, lies in the enormously colourful picture it gives of how we have come by so much of our cultural heritage and in the repeated evidence it offers of how art thrives and assumes a fuller significance when it is closely integrated with life.

There is no need for me here to recapitulate the careful historical and descriptive analyses by the eminent contributors to this book of the twelve family collections which it records. They have been chosen as outstanding examples of a type which, under economic and other pressures, has been disappearing rapidly in our own time. It may seem, from the way these few collections are spread geographically across the map of Europe, as though many others still exist. Such is not the case. Only in Great Britain and Italy, indeed, can they still be found in any numbers. In France, for instance, there are no great privately owned collections of works of art which ante-date the Revolution. The seizures and public sales of movable property were carried through with such thoroughness by the Commissioners during the 1790s that all existing family collections – and not only those belonging to royal personages – were irrevocably broken up. And in addition one must remember that it is virtually impossible to keep any great collection together in France for a number of successive generations because the principle of primogeniture is not legally recognized and whenever the head of the family dies a *partition des biens* occurs among the heirs. That is why it is justifiable to include in this volume the great *ensemble* of the collections at Chantilly (nowadays a museum). These at least contain a number of things which had belonged to the Princes de Condé before 1789 and were bought back, though the greater part was admittedly acquired by the Duc d'Aumale during the nineteenth century.

Since the French Revolution, the pendulum of public opinion has swung away from acceptance of private ownership, more or less all over Europe, in favour of the principle that works of art belong to the community and must be made generally available. We have in this way become aggressively museum-minded and nowadays incline to the belief that the possession of any sort of art collection is a luxury and a privilege which should not be granted to private individuals except on a strictly temporary basis. The state intervenes through taxation, while the scientist and the criminal play additional roles by challenging the owner's ability to guard and conserve that of which he is possessed. And so, through various pressures, which may lead to seizure or abrogation of rights, museums find themselves graciously enriched by the bequest either of entire collections, or at least of the choicest and most famous items they contain. Now in America this system has worked fairly well: the available artistic wealth – all imported – has been widely spread throughout the vast expanse of the country; old-fashioned, half-empty museums have been re-styled and given a new lease of life; while in hundreds of big cities and universities new museums have been created to display the donations accruing to them. But in Europe – except in Germany, where the provincial tradition is still strong and most museums suffered severe war-damage – the situation is quite different. Here, everything is concentrated in the capital city, for prestige reasons, even though this means draining the provinces of their natural resources. But in addition to these accretions to their holdings through bequests and gifts, European museums have felt it their duty, since 1945, to demand a vastly increased state subsidy so that they can emulate the policies of younger American museums and buy more actively than before in the open market. Now it is not only old art that the museums buy today; they also buy new art, the art of the day itself, untried, unjudged, and before it has had a chance to live amongst us.

This has led to a situation where our great central museums are now stocked beyond their rightful capacity, cannot display much of what they own, are making little or no effort to expand their accommodation in order to display their greatly increased series of acquisitions, and at the same time are refusing to share their possessions, even on the basis of temporary loans, with the more and more progressive-minded people of the provincial cities.

Given this new state of affairs, we should be all the more grateful for the continued survival in private hands of hereditary family collections such as those described in the pages that follow. For museums are tomb-houses of art, repositories where works of art, ripped from their functional contexts, have surrendered a part of their living personality in order to assume a new identity as unique specimens of visionary power, manual dexterity, formal perfection, spiritual greatness, or the height of taste. This is all very well in its way. But no thought is given by ninety-nine percent of those who look at things displayed in museums to the inspiration, the daring, or the reason which caused certain individuals to command them to be made. Who bothers to find out through whose hands they have passed down the centuries on their way to their present resting place? How many people are conscious that part of the precious quality attaching to works of art derives from the fact that before they were laid to rest in a museum they had lived – they were, that is to say, objects which served some useful purpose in the life of men?

Unless art is to be deprived of its human significance, it is important for the future of our civilisation that we should preserve and show due appreciation of inherited collections of the type described in this book. Perhaps the study of how they came together appears to be no more than a by-way of art-history, though unquestionably one of the most fascinating. But as one browses among the objects themselves in their natural surroundings, eye and mind alert, one is sure to come across a portrait, a jewel, a set of furniture, a painting, some books or maybe a goblet, whose presence is strange and challenging. Who, what, why, one asks oneself. And how did it get here? Only when one begins to discover the answers to such problems does one really come to appreciate the living and instructive value of all that is to be seen grouped together in these great collections. For they represent a perpetual link between the present and the past and make us aware in many different ways of the curious workings of history. At the same time they are an ever-present reminder both of the vagaries of taste and of the extraordinary vicissitudes of life which have so often been responsible for bringing together these unique assemblages of works of art and curiosity.

May 1965

ROME ITALY

The Princes Colonna

Federico Zeri

The Palazzo Colonna, begun in 1562, is a monument to the later history and artistic interests of a family which can trace its origins back to the tenth century and has always played a vital part in Roman and papal history. Whether by direct patronage, purchase or inheritance, every generation has made its artistic contribution and, surviving more or less intact, the palace and its contents form one of the most sumptuous patrician residences in Rome. Lorenzo Onofrio Colonna (1637–89), who chose Carlo Maratta as his adviser, was the most passionate art-lover and patronized contemporary artists above all. Hence the great richness of the palace lies in a unique ensemble of works by Italian artists such as Guercino, Reni, A. Carracci, Albani, Lanfranco, Testa and Salvator Rosa. But he also acquired works by Rubens, and commissioned a series of works by Claude and Gaspard Dughet, as well as a fascinating series of views of Rome by Vanvitelli. Among his other acquisitions were great works by Tintoretto, Veronese, Bronzino and Ghirlandaio. Subsequent Princes Colonna contributed seventeenth-century French and Flemish tapestries, and classical antiquities, as well as a small but fine group of French eighteenth-century furniture. The nineteenth-century title-holders enriched the collections with great paintings by Central Italian masters of the fourteenth and fifteenth centuries. The rich and varied stucco-work and painted decorations in the palace are unique, and it also contains some perfect examples of eighteenth-century Roman decoration. Many paintings still hang where they were placed in the seventeenth century.

The Princes Colonna

Federico Zeri

The Colonna family has always played an important part in the affairs of Rome, and even the briefest account of their art collections is bound to retell much of the history of Rome itself from the end of the Middle Ages until the present day. Only some of the many treasures in the Palazzo Colonna in the Piazza Santi Apostoli, on the slopes of the Quirinal, can strictly be called the Colonna Collection, namely the series of systematic acquisitions made from the seventeenth century until the present day; but a no less important and numerous accumulation of works of art in the palace illustrates the leading role played by the family for many centuries in the life of the city of Rome, the Papal States, and the Holy See. The Colonna Collections form so close a unity with their surroundings that it is impossible to discuss them in isolation from their setting: the palace whose grandiose eighteenth-century façade conceals a complicated internal structure of different epochs and styles, each of which tells its own part of the history of this ancient family.

The Colonnas were descended from the Counts of Tusculum, who first appear in the history of Rome during the tenth century, and in the later Middle Ages they possessed a series of fortifications in the heart of the ancient Campus Martius. These buildings were frequently constructed on the ruins of imperial Rome. The Colonna property in 1252, for example, included the Mausoleum of Augustus and Monte Citorio, both situated between the Tiber and the Via Lata (now Via del Corso). It was only later that they settled in the place where the present palace was built, and like all the other Roman noble families, they probably lived in a scattered collection of towers and imperial ruins, which were adapted to their new use without any particular plan, but were provided with strong defences.

When Cardinal Oddone Colonna was elected to the papacy as Martin V in 1417, the Colonna houses near the church of the Santi Apostoli became the seat of the Pope, and at least some of them must have been restored and adapted for this use. Unfortunately nothing remains of this or of any other early phase of the Colonna home; everything earlier than the seventeenth and eighteenth century was destroyed, either by violence or by successive modifications and alterations, with the exception of one wing flanking the present church of the Santi Apostoli, built not by a Colonna but the nephew of Pope Sixtus IV, Cardinal Giuliano della Rovere, who later became famous as Pope Julius II. When he was granted the benefice of the church of Santi

GIOVANNI COLONNA BEING PRESENTED TO THE VIRGIN AND CHILD BY ST FRANCIS AND ST JOHN *School of the Cosmati. Mosaic 24½ × 111 ins. Late thirteenth century. The Colonna arms are on the left and the donor, wearing a robe of office, is almost certainly Giovanni Colonna, twice Senator between 1269 and 1291*

Black lacquer and ormolu commode signed by Jacques Dubois (d. 1763). Height 35 ins. c. 1750

Wedding chest carved with scenes from Roman history. Walnut. Dimensions of chest 35 × 74 ins. Rome. Sixteenth century. The base, incorporating a mermaid, the Colonna emblem, is later

Opposite *A ground floor room in the della Rovere wing of the Palazzo Colonna in Rome. The ceiling frescoes are late sixteenth century and include Colonna emblems, grottesche, allegories, and trophies. On the walls are late seventeenth-century frescoes with architectural perspectives, flowers,* putti, *and male figures, among which are seascapes by Pieter Mulier (Il Tempesta) c. 1670. The furniture includes two elaborately carved consoles from the Doná Delle Rose Collection*

Apostoli, he decided to build a large house near the church. It remained unfinished and at the end of the sixteenth century the southern wing came into the possession of the Colonnas, who added it to their own group of houses. It was not substantially altered at the time, and even later, in the course of numerous extensions and conversions, the most important features of its external design and internal decoration were preserved more or less intact. Giuliano della Rovere, who also lived in the Palazzo dei Santi Apostoli after he became Pope, had even then acquired the taste in architecture and the love of painting which he later demonstrated so clearly by commissioning Raphael to decorate the Vatican *Stanze*. To-day his name and coat of arms can still be seen on the architraves of a series of marble windows in the second courtyard of the Palazzo Colonna. Also attributed to Giuliano is the impressive series of travertine arcades (almost certainly the work of the architect Baccio Pontelli) enclosing a magnificent room on the ground floor, once open to form a loggia, with ceiling frescoes by Bernardino di Betto, called Pinturicchio.

Among the works of art in the palace, the only one connected with the Colonna family before the time of Martin V is a mosaic of the second half of the thirteenth century, by one of the Cosmati, probably Giovanni di Cosma, which came from the Church of Santa Maria in Aracoeli on the Campidoglio; on it a Colonna (almost certainly Giovanni, who was twice a Senator between 1269 and 1291) is shown adoring the Virgin and two Saints. This precious relic has survived because, until the seventeenth century, it remained in the church for which it was made; had it been in the palace during the first half of the sixteenth century it would certainly not have escaped the destruction the homes of the Colonna suffered during a series of fierce and bloody struggles against Paul III Farnese and Paul IV Caraffa. It was not until 1561–62, with the accession of Pius IV, that Marcantonio II Colonna was reinstated and his rights and possessions were restored to him. This date marks the beginning of the present palace, apart from the della Rovere wing mentioned earlier.

Marcantonio II, who was appointed commander of the papal forces by Pius V, opens a new chapter in the history of the Colonnas. He played an important part in the great Battle of Lepanto in 1571, which marked the final defeat of Turkish naval power in the Mediterranean. Several sixteenth-century Turkish and Persian works of art in the Palazzo Colonna, including two large carpets and two wooden candelabra of triangular section, covered with gilt and mother-of-pearl, were part of his share of the booty. Marcantonio died in 1584 in Sicily, where he had been appointed Viceroy by Philip II of Spain in recognition of his wide military and administrative experience. From this date, every phase of the history of the Colonnas is documented in the palace. In

Opposite A first floor room with a late fifteenth-century vaulted ceiling. The painted decorations are by a late sixteenth-century artist of the Roman school. The walls are hung with seventeenth-century Flemish tapestries depicting scenes from Roman history. The furniture is seventeenth-century Roman, Venetian or French

Detail from a Flemish tapestry depicting scenes of court life. Height 33 ins. Early sixteenth century

1570 they were given the title of Princes of Paliano by Pius V and were later appointed Princes Assistant to the Papal Throne, a privilege which Gregory XVI in 1834 decreed should remain exclusive to them and to their traditional enemies, the Orsini, in order to mark the final reconciliation of the two families.

Marcantonio II's grandson, Filippo I (1578–1639), swept away all the medieval remains in the palace; he incorporated the della Rovere wing and restored at least a part of its internal decoration. In 1625 Urban VIII Barberini authorized him to destroy the remains of the Temple of Serapis (also called the Temple of the Sun) built by the Emperor Caracalla on part of the Quirinal hill and enclosed in a large garden adjacent to the Palazzo Colonna. With the mass of marble and valuable stone recovered during the demolition of these gigantic ruins Filippo I began to build the large gallery on the south side of the palace, whose size and magnificent decoration is still one of the building's principal attractions.

In the meantime other rooms gradually acquired their present appearance. Their decoration was entrusted to various artists, including the Cavaliere d'Arpino, Bernardo Castello and Giovanni Lanfranco, while the series of paintings and family portraits, acquired towards the end of the sixteenth century as the basis for an art collection, began to take their places on the walls. From 1563 to 1785 the Colonna family were represented at least ten times in the College of Cardinals. Cardinal Girolamo I Colonna (1604–63) was particularly interested in the appearance of the palace, and partly restored the interior of the first floor of the della Rovere wing.

But it is to Lorenzo Onofrio Colonna (1637–89) that the credit belongs for the largest number of acquisitions and for the splendid decoration of so many rooms. He found an escape from his unhappy marriage to Maria Mancini, the famous niece of Cardinal Giulio Mazzarino, in his indefatigable passion for collecting, in which he was helped and advised by some of the greatest connoisseurs and artists of the period, including the painter Carlo Maratta. The collection was further enriched in 1718 by the dowry of Caterina Salviati when she married Fabrizio Colonna (1700–55); this included twenty-nine paintings considered to be among the most important in the whole of Rome. Fabrizio also built the wing which encloses the palace towards the Piazza dei Santi Apostoli and generally re-planned the exterior of the building. He entrusted the principal courtyard, the grand staircase and the so-called Coffee House to several different architects, including Niccolo Michetti (1730) and the Sienese Paolo Posi.

Unfortunately this period when the Colonna treasures were at their most splendid did not last long. The disturbances which spread through the whole of Europe in the wake of the French

Revolution had strong repercussions in Rome, and on the treasures of her princely families. In 1796 Filippo III Colonna, in response to Pius VI's request for help to strengthen the papal army against the French, presented the Pope with a regiment of cavalry, and met the vast expense by selling some precious objects from the collection and melting down the household silver. But the greatest blow fell in 1798, after the proclamation of the republic, when an enforced loan, equivalent to a year's income, was levied from the leading Roman families. Filippo III was taxed at 80,000 scudi and was forced to put himself in the hands of unscrupulous English and Italian speculators, who took advantage of his honesty and the panic provoked by this situation to rob the Colonna Gallery of some of its most famous pieces. Under these circumstances the following paintings left Rome: Raphael's *Madonna* (Berlin Museum), *The Rape of Ganymede*, attributed to Titian (National Gallery, London), Correggio's *Ecce Homo* (National Gallery, London), *Venus and Cupid* by Paolo Veronese, Guido Reni's *Salome* and *The Deposition* by Guercino (Chicago Art Institute) and Salvator Rosa's *Attilius Regulus* (Richmond, Virginia), as well as many groups of minor paintings, by Gaspard Dughet and other Roman landscape painters of the seventeenth and eighteenth centuries. In the same year the gallery lost its most important painting; the great altarpiece painted by Raphael for the convent of St Antonio in Perugia was sold in 1798 to Alexander Day, and passed in 1802 to Cavaliere Domenico Venuti, agent for Ferdinand I, King of the Two Sicilies. After the suppression of the Bourbon Kingdom of Naples in 1860, it eventually passed into the collection of J. Pierpont Morgan and from him, to the Metropolitan Museum, New York.

The Colonna Collections suffered further losses when Filippo III, who had no male heirs, gave as dowry to his three daughters (married respectively to a Lante della Rovere, a Rospigliosi-Pallavicini and a Barberini) numerous paintings not included in the family trust. Exactly half of this group, which includes the famous *Temple of Venus* by Claude Lorraine, painted for Lorenzo Onofrio Colonna, is to-day in the Pallavicini Gallery in the Palazzo Rospigliosi on the Quirinal. Despite these losses, the Colonna Collections were still the most important of any patrician family in Rome, both in number and in quality, and the gaps caused by the French Revolution were filled by an impressive series of new acquisitions made in the course of the nineteenth century by the descendants of Filippo III, particularly by Giovanni Andrea Colonna (1820–90) and by his son Fabrizio (1848–1923). They secured a body of paintings, mainly of the fourteenth and fifteenth centuries, which include the three famous panels by Cosmè Tura: the great wing of the triptych originally in the Church of San Giorgio in Ferrara, showing the Prior Niccolò Roverella kneeling, with St Maurelius and St Paul; the *Virgin of the Annunciation*; and the tiny *Madonna Adoring the Child*. Other fourteenth and fifteenth-century panels by Italian artists, were acquired during the mid-nineteenth century, thus giving balance to the collection of paintings, which until then had contained almost exclusively works of later periods.

More recently, when the social, economic and political changes which followed the unification of Italy led to the dispersal of so many of the private collections in Rome, the Palazzo Colonna found in Marcantonio (1881–1947) and his wife Isabella two impassioned protectors. To-day, thanks to their intelligent work of conservation and restoration, this magnificent building is one of the most complete and sumptuous patrician residences in Rome. Its latest acquisition is the collection of French eighteenth-century furniture which belonged to Dimitri Sursoch, Duke of Cervinara, brother of Princess Isabella.

The best-known part of the Colonna Collections are the paintings in the Colonna Gallery, which is open to visitors. These belong to a trust, founded in 1818 by Filippo III Colonna. But in other parts of the palace there are works of equal importance, not included in the trust, which must be described in their surroundings. Apart from a few minor changes and additions, the interior decoration of the building has remained exactly as it was a hundred and fifty years ago, so that the guide to the palace printed in 1783 remains invaluable, not only for the frescoes, but for the paintings, since most of those described (there are over 1,362 numbers) still hang in the same position.

On the ground floor the antechamber (dominated by the *baldacchino* bearing the Colonna coat of arms together with the papal arms, a privilege reserved to the Roman nobility) is decorated with a series of sixteenth and seventeenth-century portraits, some of them of great artistic value. Scipione Pulzone's portrait of Marcantonio II is one of the most important examples of Roman portrait painting at the end of the sixteenth century. Another room on the ground floor contains an extensive series of seventeenth and eighteenth-century views of Rome and other Italian cities. Almost all of them are by Gaspard Van Wittel, known as Vanvitelli, and include his best work, especially the great canvases of views of Venice, which anticipate to a surprising extent the themes later popularised by Canaletto, Bellotto and other eighteenth-century Venetian landscape painters. There is also a series of *bambocciate* – scenes of low-life by the Dutch painter Dirk Helmbreker, and work by other northern artists, especially paintings by 'Velvet Bruegel', by Jan Mandyn, Paul Brill and a host of sixteenth- and seventeenth-century landscape painters.

The great hall on the west side of the building planned by Cardinal Giuliano della Rovere was completely reconstructed in

THE FUNERAL OF SAINT BENEDICT *Giovanni del Biondo*
(active c. 1356–99) Predella panel 12½ × 14 ins.
Second half of the fourteenth century

NICCOLÒ ROVERELLA WITH ST MAURELIUS AND ST PAUL
Cosmè Tura (before 1431–95) tempera on panel 60 × 29½ ins. c. 1480.
The right wing of a large altarpiece formerly in the church of
San Giorgio, Ferrara

the seventeenth century. Its vaulted ceiling was decorated with frescoes by Giacinto Gemignani, Carlo Cesi and other minor artists, and its walls with landscapes by Crescenzio d'Onofrio, a close follower of Gaspard Dughet. The other great hall, on the north side, is the most important surviving part of the della Rovere building. It was originally open on both sides to form a loggia. The vaulted ceiling is still decorated with delicate frescoes by Pinturicchio, in which figures of pagan divinities alternate with medallions containing mythological and biblical scenes. Contrasting with this oldest part is a central rectangle added in the late sixteenth century, which celebrates the naval victory of Marcantonio II at Lepanto. This is traditionally ascribed to Giuseppe Cesari, called the Cavaliere d'Arpino, though it must be a very early work if it is really by him. The walls are frescoed with views of gardens and buildings by Gaspard Dughet, who was employed for many years by the Colonnas. Cosmè Tura's great tempera, part of the Roverella altarpiece from the Church of San Giorgio in Ferrara, and the two other small paintings by him also hang in this hall. Other paintings include the *Funeral of St Benedict* by Giovanni del Biondo, the *Martyrdom of St Lorenzo* by the Master of the Bambino Vispo, part of the predella of the triptych made in 1423 for the Cathedral at Florence, the *Martyrdom of St Bartholomew* by Neri di Bicci and an unusual *Sacrifice of Isaac* by Alessandro Allori painted in blue monochrome. Among the sculptures in this room, the fountain in the centre dates from the Renaissance and was probably part of Cardinal della Rovere's original arrangement. Another piece of sculpture in the same room, a crocodile in Egyptian granite, comes from the great Temple of Isis on the Campus Martius; its companion piece, also in pink granite, is now in the Capitoline Museum, Rome. Here, too, are the oldest pieces of furniture in the palace – two sixteenth-century wedding chests in walnut carved in high relief with scenes from Roman history.

Another room in this wing of the palazzo is frescoed with seascapes by the Dutch artist Pieter Mulier, called 'il Tempesta', of about 1670. This room is highly typical of Roman Baroque, and contains some of the most important pieces of furniture in the collection, among them the two console tables originally in the house of Donà Delle Rose in Venice, and several pieces of French eighteenth-century furniture from the Sursoch Collection.

The walls of the next room are frescoed with landscapes by Gaspard Dughet, while many fine Italian sixteenth- and seventeenth-century bronze sculptures from the Sursoch Collection are arranged on pieces of French furniture. The last room on the ground floor houses four Greco-Roman herms of philosophers and gods and a large fluted sarcophagus of the third century AD. The beautiful floor comes from an imperial Roman villa. It is made of coloured marble arranged in geometrical patterns, with a

Opposite VIRGIN OF THE ANNUNCIATION *Cosmè Tura*
(before 1431–95) tempera on panel 8 × 5 ins. c. 1475

Opposite THE LEGEND OF ROMULUS AND REMUS *Part of a marble mosaic floor from a Roman villa 24 × 31 ins. First or second century* AD. *The figure on the left represents Rome or Italy*

AENEAS AND THE SIBYL DESCENDING INTO THE UNDERWORLD *Jan ('Velvet') Brueghel (1568–1625) oil on copper 10 × 14 ins. Signed and dated 1604*

centre-piece of *opus sectile*, also polychrome, representing the legend of the finding of Romulus and Remus.

The grand staircase leading to the first floor was designed by Paolo Posi. A number of antique marble sculptures are arranged on it, the most famous of which is a large circular relief in red porphyry, representing a Head of Medusa, which may have been found on the Esquiline Hill, near the ruins of Nero's palace. Stylistically it belongs to the first half of the second century AD and most probably came from the Baths of Trajan, which were built over Nero's palace.

The vast antechamber on the first floor has a ceiling frescoed by the Genoese artist Bernardo Castello, referring to the victory of Lepanto. One wall is taken up by the *baldacchino* and in a niche on the opposite side is a gigantic Roman bust, with other marbles – herms, statues and sarcophagi – below. The walls are covered with large-scale paintings, including two masterpieces of Roman Baroque art: the large *Augustus Closing the Doors of the Temple of Janus* painted by Carlo Maratta for Lorenzo Onofrio Colonna, and the *Raising of Lazarus* by Francesco Trevisani. Two other canvases of unusual proportions are by the Cavaliere d'Arpino and were used as models for the decoration of Michelangelo's dome in St Peter's. Then there is a long series of Colonna portraits, from the sixteenth to the end of the seventeenth century. Another room on this floor has a ceiling with frescoes by

Giovanni Lanfranco representing the Four Cardinal Virtues, and a great marble fireplace, decorated with bas-reliefs of candelabra and with two allegories. This bears the name of Giuliano della Rovere, but its style suggests that it is later than the Pinturicchio frescoes and may in fact belong to the end of the fifteenth or the beginning of the sixteenth century.

This large room is followed by a suite of smaller ones, built in the fifteenth century but redecorated towards the middle of the seventeenth by Cardinal Girolamo I Colonna. The first small room contains an important group of panel paintings, which are some of the earliest in the entire collection. The most striking representative of the Flemish schools is an *Adoration of the Magi* by the Master of the Legend of St Barbara, once part of a triptych whose wings have been identified in the Metropolitan Museum in New York. Among the Italian works is a small altarpiece by Francesco Zaganelli together with three panels in the style of Crivelli and paintings by Bernardino di Mariotto, Jacopo del Sellaio, Cola dell'Amatrice and other lesser Florentine artists of the early sixteenth century. A sixteenth-century Ispahan carpet, almost certainly part of the booty from the Battle of Lepanto, is of such remarkable size and beauty that it quite overshadows the other objects in the room.

The walls of the next two rooms are richly decorated with gilded stucco work, framing two sets of seventeenth-century Flemish

Right *Antechamber on the first floor. The painted ceiling is by Bernardo Castello and the walls are hung with family portraits and other paintings from the sixteenth to the early eighteenth century. The canopy, which bears the Colonna arms, is flanked by two Angels by Giuseppe Cesari (called Cavaliere d'Arpino)*

Below *Astragalus Player. Marble. Height 25 ins. Greco-Roman. The right arm, left hand, and base were restored in the seventeenth century*

tapestries. The cartoons for one of these sets were evidently designed under the influence of Rubens. In the first of these rooms, which also contains a series of landscapes by Jan Frans van Bloemen and a magnificent portrait of Doge Andrea Gritti by Titian, stands a chair turned to the wall, beneath a *baldacchino* overhanging the portrait of Martin V. This chair, according to an ancient custom restricted to the patrician families of Rome whose names appear on the papal roll, is reserved for the use of the Pope if he should ever visit the palace. The rooms along the east side of the first floor, all decorated in the course of the eighteenth century, are remarkable for the rich stucco decorations which alternate with gorgeous silk embroidered panels. By

contrast the large library, which was built towards the end of the eighteenth century in the heyday of classicism, is a model of un-adorned grandeur.

Returning now to the large antechamber on the first floor, we find on the west side the suite of rooms which were intended by Lorenzo Onofrio Colonna to house the choicest of his paintings, and in some of them the arrangement of the pictures, as well as the decoration of the walls, has remained unchanged ever since. The first room is hung with seventeenth-century Flemish tapestries representing the story of Moses. The tapestries in the second room are French, again of the seventeenth century, and the paintings over the doors are by Domenico Maria Muratori and an

unidentified artist of the seventeenth-century Roman School. Both rooms contain many small paintings by the Cavaliere d'Arpino and other artists; Flemish still-lifes hang beside landscapes by Van Bloemen. The room which follows is one of the most perfect and characteristic examples of eighteenth-century Roman art. It is a small room, completely covered with frescoes of landscapes by Giovanni Angeloni, containing figures by the brothers Stefano and Giuseppe Pozzi. Another room, overlooking the garden, is hung with rich seventeenth-century velvets. Alongside family portraits by Jacob Ferdinand Voet hangs Domenico Puligo's *Portrait of a Florentine Courtesan*, one of his finest works.

The first room of the gallery proper contains some of the most precious pieces in the collection: a single fourteenth-century painting, the *Crucifixion* signed by Jacopo Avanzi of Bologna, and the exceptional *Madonna with Angels* by Stefano da Zevio of Verona are the oldest panels, followed by a *Portrait of a Young Man* which has been ascribed to different artists. According to Berenson it is by Melozzo da Forlì, but its execution and the line of the profile suggest an Umbrian artist close to Pinturicchio and Bartolomeo della Gatta. A *St James* from the workshop of Botticelli and a *Madonna* signed in 1471 by Bartolomeo Vivarini, works by Giuliano Bugiardini, Gerolamo Sicciolante, Giovanni Francesco Caroto, Francesco Albani, Simone Cantarini, Francesco Cozza, Pietro da Cortona, Grechetto, Guercino and other

The Turkish Room. The landscape frescoes are by Giovanni Angeloni and the trompe l'oeil *oriental figures by Stefano and Giuseppe Pozzi. Executed c. 1750.* Below *A detail from one of the frescoes*

*A detail from a fresco by Pinturicchio (1454–1513) on the vaulted
ceiling of the great hall, originally the loggia of the palace of Cardinal
Giuliano della Rovere. The medallions show Judith with the head of
Holofernes (centre), Esther before Ahasuerus (left) and Samson (right).
The two lunettes by Francesco Allegrini (1587–1663) show, on the
left,* Horatius Keeping the Bridge *and, on the right,*
The Battle Between Constantine and Maxentius

PORTRAIT OF A YOUNG MAN *Umbrian School, tempera on panel 19½ × 15½ ins. Late fifteenth century. Formerly attributed to Melozzo da Forlì, but probably by one of Pinturicchio's assistants on the frescoes in the Sistine Chapel*

Below THE VIRGIN RESCUING A CHILD FROM THE DEVIL *Niccolò Alunno. Tempera on canvas 56 × 46 ins. Late fifteenth century. The mother's plea for help and the Virgin's reply are written in Umbrian dialect on scrolls*

Italian artists are arranged on the walls in a way which, although no longer acceptable in a modern museum, is the only one possible in a building like the Palazzo Colonna, where the paintings have a contribution to make to the architectural effect of the whole. In the same room, the northern schools are represented by an *Allegory of the Passion of Christ* by Jacob van Amsterdam, a *Lucrezia* by the Master of the Female Half-Lengths and, best of all, by a diptych by Bernard van Orley, depicting *The Seven Joys and the Seven Sorrows of the Virgin*. This painting, which owes something to the influence of Roger van der Weyden, enjoyed great popularity in the sixteenth century to judge from the number of copies, in painting and tapestry, which still exists.

The next room contains some relics of Marcantonio II Colonna: the chart he used during the Battle of Lepanto, and the parchment of thanks given to him by the Roman Senate on his return. A sixteenth-century half-length portrait of Pope Martin V in profile, also in this room, is of great iconographical importance, since it certainly derives from a prototype of the first half of the fifteenth century. The model was very probably the portrait in the frescoes of the Basilica of St John Lateran, which were painted by Gentile da Fabriano and Pisanello at the request of the Pope and then destroyed in the seventeenth century when the building was restored.

MADONNA WITH ANGELS *Stefano da Zevio* (*c. 1375–1451*)
tempera on panel $35\frac{1}{2} \times 19\frac{1}{2}$ *ins. First half of the fifteenth century*

Above right LUCREZIA *Master of the Female Half-Lengths.*
Oil on panel $17 \times 10\frac{1}{2}$ *ins. c. 1520*

The gallery proper begins with the next room, which contains paintings mostly collected by Lorenzo Onofrio Colonna. Apart from the losses which occurred at the time of the French Revolution, this and the adjoining rooms have remained practically unaltered, both in the decoration of the ceilings and the arrangement of the furniture and paintings. The ceiling of the gallery is decorated with, in the centre, a set of canvases of subjects relating to Martin V (by Benedetto Luti) and, in the corners and at the sides, allegories and emblems by Pompeo Batoni and Pietro Bianchi. The paintings include the *Portrait of a Nobleman*, which is recognised as one of the greatest works of Paolo Veronese's maturity. This, together with three portraits by Jacopo Tintoretto (including the *Old Man Playing the Virginal*), a large *Madonna and Child with Saints* by Paris Bordone and a *Dead Christ with Angels* by Leandro Bassano form an important group of Venetian paintings. They are hung beside paintings of equal stature by central Italian artists, including a magnificent *Madonna and Child with St Elizabeth and St John* by Bronzino and the so-called *Portrait of Poggio Bracciolini* by Francesco Salviati, of about 1540. Salviati also painted the *Raising of Lazarus*, once attributed to Parmigianino, while the large *St Jerome*, usually ascribed to Giovanni Spagna, has many similarities with the middle period of Pietro Perugino, as cleaning may well reveal more plainly. Works by Scarsellino, Guido Reni, Guercino and Albani, represented here

THE SEVEN JOYS OF THE VIRGIN *Bernard van Orley (c. 1488–1541)*
oil and gold on panel 13 × 10 ins. c. 1520. Half of a diptych, of which
the second panel, also in the Colonna Collection, depicts
The Seven Sorrows of the Virgin

THE BATTLE OF LEPANTO *Giovanni Coli (1636–81) and Filippo Gherardi (1643–1704). Central part of the ceiling of the great hall. 1675–78*

by his great *Rape of Europa*, culminate in one of the most famous paintings of the seventeenth-century Bolognese School, the *Mangiafagioli*, or the *Bean-eater*, by Annibale Carracci.

It now remains to describe briefly the most magnificent room in the whole palace, the great hall of the gallery; its frescoed ceilings, pictures, painted mirrors and ancient sculptures, and its profusion of rare marbles combine to make it one of the most brilliant examples of the Roman seventeenth century. The great hall forms virtually a single unit, with a square room at either end. It is about two hundred and fifty feet long, and its floor is composed of marbles from the Temple of Serapis. The architect was Antonio del Grande, who worked on it between 1654 and 1663; after his death it was completed by Girolamo Fontana in 1703. The richly decorated ceilings were painted by several different artists over a number of years. The huge frescoes in the central part representing the Battle of Lepanto, the Triumph, and other episodes in the life of Marcantonio II Colonna, were painted by Giovanni Coli and Filippo Gherardi of Lucca, who are known to have been engaged on them between 1675 and 1678. The elaborate monochrome decoration surrounding these scenes with their wonderfully daring perspective, was executed by the German artist Johann Paul Schor with the help of his son Philipp. The frescoes in the two smaller rooms were entrusted to other artists: the room facing the Quirinal, depicting Marcantonio II beside Hercules, was given to Giuseppe Chiari of Rome, who worked on it around 1700, while the *Allegory of the Battle of Lepanto* in the room facing the Piazza Santi Apostoli is the work of Sebastiano Ricci, attributed to the year 1696. In this triple gallery the pictures are so hung that they completely cover the walls, following the 'architectural' principle that Giovanni Paolo Panini represented in an idealised form in his famous *Views of Roman Galleries*. The effect of this arrangement is to fuse the paintings into a single decorative scheme with the frescoes, the polychrome marbles, the large Venetian mirrors painted with garlands of flowers by Mario dei Fiori, the carved and gilded consoles, and the marble statues, of the imperial age, which are said to come from the ruins of the ancient town of Bovillae on the Via Appia near Rome, which stood on land which belonged to the Colonna family in the seventeenth century.

The paintings were collected mainly by Lorenzo Onofrio. They include only a few fifteenth-century works: a pair of panels from wedding chests with scenes from Roman history (the *Rape of the Sabine Women* and the *Peace between Romans and Sabines*) by Bartolomeo di Giovanni and a curious votive painting by Nicolò Alunno. In the latter, following an iconographical type of the Madonna del Soccorso that is typically Umbrian, the Virgin, armed with a stick, appears at the invocation of a woman and rescues a child from the devil. The gallery contains some strikingly

*Looking through to the great hall. The floor is composed of marbles from
the Temple of Serapis while the columns are of yellow marble from Africa*

NARCISSUS *Jacopo Tintoretto* (*1518–94*)
oil on canvas 58 × 75 ins. c. 1550

Opposite PORTRAIT OF A MAN
Paolo Veronese (*1528–88*) *oil on canvas*
48 × 37 ins. 1570–79

beautiful sixteenth-century paintings, notably the *Narcissus* by Jacopo Tintoretto, one of the most lyrical works of the great Venetian Mannerist. Another painting of exceptional quality shows the heads and shoulders of a group adoring the Holy Sacrament; it is usually ascribed to Jacopo Tintoretto, but its colouring and psychological approach suggest the hand of his son Domenico. Various portraits traditionally identified as members of the Colonna family are also the work of Venetian artists. One of them, representing a Cardinal, has often been attributed to Lorenzo Lotto; another, which the critics give to Francesco Beccaruzzi, is said to represent Stefano Colonna di Palestrina (1522–48). In general, however, the identifications are very uncertain and it may well be that the portraits were purchased for the gallery on their merits as works of art. The portrait of Vittoria Colonna, Marchioness of Pescara, is no less open to question. The canvas, attributed to Gerolamo Muziano, is reputed to portray this famous poetess, whose friends included Pietro Bembo, Annibal Caro, Bernardo Tasso and, above all, Michelangelo Buonarroti, but the identification is most uncertain, especially since Vittoria died in 1547 when the artist was only nineteen years old.

There is a magnificent group of sixteenth-century Tuscan paintings; foremost among them is a large panel, signed by Angelo Bronzino, representing Venus with Cupid and a Satyr.

Not even its icy, idealised beauty sufficed to save it from the attentions of a later artist, who was commissioned, probably in the seventeenth century, to cover the goddess's body with a piece of drapery; but the alteration cannot obscure the superbly cold and marmoreal effect of the picture, which is almost certainly the one which Vasari tells us was painted by Bronzino for Alamanno Salviati. The pair of large panels by Michele di Ridolfo del Ghirlandaio representing *Allegories of Night and Dawn* are remarkable as translations into Mannerist language of the famous sculptures of the same name, carved by Michelangelo for the Medici tombs in the new sacristy of St Lorenzo in Florence.

The most remarkable part of the gallery, however, is devoted to the Italian Schools of the seventeenth century. As it is impossible to describe the most important pieces one by one, we must confine ourselves to a brief list. Examples of the Bolognese School include the *Ecce Homo with Two Angels* by Francesco Albani and two paintings by Giovanni Lanfranco, the *Magdalen in Glory* and *St Peter Delivered from Prison*. The various tendencies of the Roman School are represented by *St Sebastian* by Giovanni Domenico Cerrini and by two biblical paintings by Pier Francesco Mola. In contrast to these three, the 'literary' and 'pre-romantic' strains are exemplified in the so-called *Dream of the Shepherd* by Pietro Testa (its real subject has still to be identified) and two paintings by Salvator Rosa *St John the Baptist Preaching* and *St John the*

Opposite THE BEAN-EATER *Annibale Carracci (1560–1609)*
oil on canvas 22½ × 27 ins. c. 1585

PORTRAIT OF A COLONNA *Venetian School, oil on canvas*
43 × 34 ins. c. 1540. Said to represent Stefano Colonna and attributed to
Francesco Beccaruzzi

Below VENUS, CUPID AND A SATYR *Angelo Bronzino (1503–72)*
oil on panel 47 × 98 ins. The drapery appears to have been added
in the seventeenth century

The garden of the Palazzo Colonna on the slopes of the Quirinal. On the terraces on either side of the waterfall are Roman busts and statues

Baptist in the Cave. The splendid collection of landscapes includes gouaches by Gaspard Dughet as well as works by Paul Brill, Herman van Swanevelt, Salvator Rosa and Jan Frans van Bloemen. Among the foreign artists, the influence of Caravaggio is to be seen in the *Wine-Drinker* by Jan van Bylert, while northern Mannerism is represented by a magnificent *Landscape with Noli me Tangere*, one of the earliest works by Lambert Zustris so far discovered. And finally an *Assumption* by Rubens (the Colonna Collection also possesses his sketch for the *Parting of Jacob and Esau*), which shows how close was the connection between the Roman and the Flemish Baroque. Although it was painted after the artist's stay in Italy and was certainly despatched from Antwerp, the Rubens is very close to the work of Bernini, Pietro da Cortona or Baciccia.

The furniture in the gallery includes consoles in carved and gilded wood, made by Roman craftsmen, and a large cabinet, probably Florentine, in ebony and rare woods, inlaid with semi-precious stones and bronzes. Another massive cabinet was designed by the architect Carlo Fontana and made by the brothers Dominicus and Franz Stainhart, between about 1670 and 1680. The cabinet proper rests on a base composed of an elaborate trophy and two kneeling blackamoors carved in ebony; its com-

partments are decorated with twenty-eight ivory reliefs of great delicacy. The central relief is a copy of Michelangelo's *Last Judgement* and the others, scenes from the Old Testament and Greek and Roman mythology, are copied from Raphael's loggias and other famous Italian paintings.

To give an idea of the size of the Colonna Collections, I need only say that the Trust inventory alone includes 762 paintings and that the palace contains hundreds of other paintings and fine pieces of furniture. Some of the treasures in the principal rooms have been described, but there are many others, including spectacular examples of Roman taste in the seventeenth century. Among these are the Gallery of Maps and the so-called Coffee House, a pavilion on the terrace facing the Piazza Santi Apostoli, consisting of a single room, frescoed with mythological subjects by Francesco Mancini, and containing a series of Hellenistic and Roman marble reliefs on the walls framed in elegant stucco designs. No less remarkable than the palace itself is the garden of the Palazzo Colonna, with its Roman statues, reliefs, inscriptions and portraits, arranged on the terraces which run down from the Quirinal towards the lower part of Rome, to make the views which inspired the idealised Roman landscapes of Jan Frans van Bloemen, Andrea Locatelli and Paolo Anesi.

The Princes Doria Pamphili

Luisa Vertova

The Pamphili family is closely connected with three great buildings, the Palazzo Pamphili on the Piazza Navona, the Palazzo Doria Pamphili on the Piazza Collegio Romano, and the castle of Valmontone near Velletri. The Pamphili became eminent patrons of the arts in the seventeenth century, following the election of Giambattista Pamphili to the Papacy as Innocent X in 1644. He and his nephew Camillo commissioned Bernini, Borromini, Pietro da Cortona, Rainaldi and many other architects to design new buildings or to carry out alterations and extensions to existing ones. They employed leading contemporary painters to decorate the two palaces, Valmontone and Camillo's villa, Belrespiro. Camillo Pamphili bought canvases by Caravaggio and Guercino, and the Pamphili love of landscape painting is represented in their collection by a range of works which embraces the brothers Bril, Claude Lorrain, and Salvator Rosa. Camillo's wife was Olimpia Aldobrandini, who brought several fine paintings into the family, notably works by Raphael and Beccafumi. A later connection with the descendants of Andrea Doria contributed masterpieces by Bronzino and Sebastiano del Piombo, in addition to tapestries and the Doria military trophies. The collection consists principally of works by Italian artists, but also contains examples of Brueghel the Elder and Memling, and a group of paintings by Dutch masters. Sculpture by Algardi, antique marbles, and manuscripts are among the other treasures of the Doria Pamphili collection, which is now concentrated mainly in the palace on the Piazza Collegio Romano.

The Princes Doria Pamphili

Luisa Vertova

Following the accession of Cardinal Giambattista Pamphili to the papal throne in 1644, his family emblem, the 'all-loving' doves, spread their wings over Rome; during the next hundred years doves in stucco, stone, marble, and in painting, singly and in pairs, in flight or resting, invaded the cornices, ceilings and balconies of the new Pamphili buildings. The Baroque architect Del Grande decorated all the first-floor windows of the palace facing the Collegio Romano with doves in flight; and since streaming ribbons befit flying doves, ribbons adorn the windows of the floor above. This theme was developed on the façade extending down the Corso by Valvassori, who added lilies and olive branches, thus creating one of the most original and attractive Rococo relief-decorations in Rome. A favourite subject of many artists, the peace-bringing dove is also an appropriate emblem for a family whose fortunes derive, not from military exploits, but from an expert knowledge of law. While other powerful Roman families declined, or even died out completely, the Pamphili were able to survive and keep their art treasures through their juridical skill.

They were a noble family of Gubbio – a town controlled by Urbino – when Pope Sixtus IV (1471–84) summoned Antonio Pamphili to Rome. His grandsons Pamphilio and Giambattista grew up in a small palace on the Piazza Navona, in the shadow of the Sapienza (the University founded by Pope Eugenius IV). Giambattista became a consistorial lawyer, then an apostolic nuncio, and was eventually elected to the office of Cardinal in 1629. In 1630 Pamphilio, himself a competent Capitoline magistrate, acquired a large estate on the slopes of the Janiculum, with a magnificent view of St Peter's. He died young in 1639, and his power-loving wife Olimpia Maidalchini from Viterbo, a widow for the second time, centred her ambitions on her son Camillo and her brother-in-law. Five years later, on the death of Urban VIII, Giambattista succeeded to the papacy as Innocent X, and Camillo was appointed 'Cardinal-Nephew'.

Nepotism pervaded the government of the Roman Church and no Pope of this period was entirely free of it. Even Clement VIII, close friend of St Philip Neri and harsh condemner of Beatrice Cenci, established the fortunes of his own family on becoming Pope. Certainly Innocent X never aspired to sainthood but possibly – to judge from the name he chose – to candour and goodness; he reformed religious orders and prisons, loved justice, encouraged learning and developed the missions. His reign would have passed without incident had not destiny placed at his side the most interfering woman of seventeenth-century Rome, whom Pasquino nicknamed 'the old bawd (Pimpaccia) of the Piazza Navona', or more flatteringly 'the once pious' (Olim Pia). Succeeding Urban VIII, the Pamphili Pope has unfairly passed into history as an ungenerous patron of the arts, but twenty years of extravagance under the Barberini had left a precarious financial position and a legacy of threatened revolt. 'We don't want obelisks or fountains,' Pasquino protested, 'We want bread, bread, bread.' Innocent X bowed to public opinion and started proceedings against the Barberini for embezzlement. However, the Barberini obtained the support of France and the Pope was forced to annul his orders. The splendid portrait of Innocent X by Velasquez (1650) shows a disillusioned man of sanguine disposition, whose penetrating gaze betrays the habit of interpreting lies in the light of human passions. The marble busts by Bernini present a more humorous but no less diffident character. Altogether, one gets the impression of a man subject to outbursts of anger, but essentially cautious. In fact, he did not cherish any ambition to leave his mark on history, but concentrated on avoiding the worst evils.

As far as the arts were concerned, he began by playing for time.

OLIMPIA MAIDALCHINI PAMPHILI *Alessandro Algardi (1598–1654) Marble. The wife of Pamphilio Pamphili and sister-in-law of Innocent X*

INNOCENT X (GIAMBATTISTA PAMPHILI) (1574–1655) *Gian Lorenzo Bernini (1598–1680) Marble. Innocent X created the Piazza Navona as we know it*

But by 1646–7, when circumstances were more favourable, he was employing the best artists, regardless of their associations with the previous régime, and he rewarded them generously. Thus he charged Bernini with the decoration of St Peter's, and entrusted the aged Girolamo Rainaldi with the necessary improvements to the family palace. He also decided to rebuild the little church of St Agnese in the Piazza Navona and to acquire the houses beyond the church in order to build a college and library. The library was to house his own books, notes and manuscripts, as well as literary, historical, scientific and theological texts for the fellows of the college. A competition was organized for a fountain to occupy the centre of the piazza. Bernini was not asked to compete, but when he presented his design for the famous Fontana dei Fiumi, he was commissioned immediately. Thus Innocent X ended by transforming the entire Piazza Navona into a Pamphili '*salone*', bequeathing to Rome one of the most beautiful squares in the world. However, his aim had

not been to advance his family interests, but to glorify the Church and to increase opportunities for education. He died without seeing either S. Agnese or the Collegio Agnesino completed, although these projects were perhaps the dearest to his heart. They were finished by his nephew Camillo, who, although a poor politician, was a real lover of art.

1647 is a crucial year in the history of Pamphili art patronage. It was then that Camillo rebelled against his mother, renounced his cardinalate and married another Olimpia, the attractive and vivacious Princess of Rossano, widow of Paolo Borghese. Innocent X gave the bride a friendly reception and she in her turn gave her patrimony to her husband, reserving only a small personal allowance for herself. She was sole heir to the Aldobrandini fortunes, which Cardinal Ippolito had bequeathed in trust to her second-born. As she was a widow with only one son, the Aldobrandini riches lay waiting for her next male off-spring.

The elder Olimpia reigned supreme in the Palazzo Pamphili,

CAMILLO PAMPHILI (*1622–66*) *Carlo Maratta* (*1625–1713*) *oil on canvas c. 1660. Camillo made substantial additions to the collection, notably landscape paintings*

OLIMPIA ALDOBRANDINI *Giovanni Lazoni* (*1618–88*) *Marble. Signed and dated 1680. Wife of Camillo Pamphili*

and tried to maintain her position at the papal court through a more docile Cardinal-Nephew. Camillo and his wife preferred the hospitality of Caprarola and of the Aldobrandini villa at Frascati. Inevitably the young Olimpia was affected by the competitive spirit which impelled popes and cardinals, especially her Borghese and Aldobrandini relations, to build themselves ever more beautiful villas. The Aldobrandini *regina villarum* at Frascati was known as 'Belvedere', for it commanded a magnificent view of Rome and beyond. Camillo built an equally fine villa for his wife on his father's estate, and owing to the mild climate and constant sea-breezes it was christened Belrespiro. According to Milizia (*Memorie degli architetti*, II, Rome 1781) the planning of the park and gardens, which skilfully exploits the irregularity of the site, the fountains, the ornaments and the small palace itself, called the 'Casino delle Allegrezze', are entirely the work of Algardi. More recent scholars (O. Pollak, R. Wittkower) assume that the Bolognese painter G. F. Grimaldi

The Pamphili coat of arms, incorporating the symbol of the dove. A stucco panel by Alessandro Algardi (1598–1654) in the Sala di Ercole of the Villa del Belrespiro

Stucco panel of Minerva from a frieze by Alessandro Algardi (1598–1654) in the Casino delle Allegrezze at the Villa del Belrespiro

acted as architect and Algardi, a sculptor and restorer of antiquities, as general supervisor. The choice of Algardi, who was still relatively unknown, is a tribute to Camillo's artistic discernment. The estate was very rich in archaeological remains and Algardi understood how to make use of them. The gay exterior of the Casino delle Allegrezze, covered with ancient reliefs in imitation of the Villa Borghese, may have little architectural significance, but is entirely appropriate to a pavilion intended as a country retreat. Inside, Algardi successfully offsets the severity of the antique statuary with delicate stuccoes full of movement and grace. The statues of Roman Emperors, formerly in the forecourt have disappeared, but stone seats with the Pamphili and Aldobrandini devices still bear witness to the first years of a union which was to be so fruitful to the arts. Unfortunately two low wings ending in pavilions, which were to extend on either side of the Casino, were never built. Below the 'secret garden' at the back, a pretty loggia containing a fountain leads into the park. Here the 'teatro delle acque' is backed by an exedra with a covered walk, ornamented with vases, busts, classical and seventeenth-century reliefs, whose decorative effect is enhanced by the contrasts in texture and colour between the blond brick, white marble and grey stalactite (the *Baccanale of Putti* and the *Sacred and Profane Love* by Duquesnoy have recently been moved to the palace on the Corso). Fountains, waterfalls, grottos, statues, wells, sarcophagi, ornamental lakes and fragments of antique sculpture are skilfully placed in the woods and meadows to give a variety of lovely views. Out of this subtle blending of art and nature, so much superior to the obsessive perspectives of eighteenth-century parks, grew the romantic taste of the English landscape garden.

Despite changes in the landscape, even to-day the visitor may well wonder how far the paintings of Poussin (himself a close friend of Algardi and Duquesnoy) may have been influenced by a villa like this, and whether Camillo Pamphili may not have regarded the whole spectacle as one of the most satisfying landscapes in his collection. The existence of a conscious taste for pure landscape is confirmed by Grimaldi's overdoors in the first-floor reception room. Just as Paolo Veronese broke up his Olympian allegories at Maser with landscape interludes, so Grimaldi interpolated his Hercules cycle with naturalistic views of the Roman countryside. Nature was a safe and welcome subject for painters at a time when pagan themes were becoming increasingly suspect to the new order of the Jesuits, and artists were allowed little freedom, even in their treatment of sacred themes. Nature was also a welcome escape for their patrons from the intrigues and stifling atmosphere of the papal court.

It is, of course, not easy to distinguish between the lip-service paid by a prince to the aesthetic canons of his day and the force

Above HERCULES RESTING *G. F. Grimaldi* *(1606–80). A fresco from the Hercules cycle in the Villa del Belrespiro*

Below AENEAS AND DIDO *Detail of a ceiling fresco by Francesco Allegrini c. 1650 in the Palazzo Pamphili on the Piazza Navona*

NEPTUNE CALMS THE WINDS *Detail of a
ceiling fresco by Pietro da Cortona (1596–1669)
in the Long Gallery. 1654*

Opposite *The Saletta degli Specchi. Frescoes and overdoors are by
Stefano Pozzi (c. 1707–68). The central section of the ceiling shows
Venus at the Mirror while in the four corners are nymphs offering her
the gifts of Earth, Air, Fire and Water*

Opposite *A group of objects from the Sala dei Feudi in the private apartments. Left to right: St Sebastian in silver, silver gilt, blue enamel and coral; ivory and amber Madonna and Child standing on a crescent moon; the Child Jesus portrayed as the Good Shepherd (above him are the other figures of the Trinity, at the bottom a penitent Magdalen), seventeenth-century Indo-Portuguese work*

The Galleria degli Specchi built 1731–34 by Gabriele Valvassori and decorated by Aureliano Milani (1675–1749)

Detail of a ceiling fresco by Francesco Cozza (1605–82) in the Biblioteca del Collegio Innocenziano

Opposite top AURORA AND FORTUNE *Detail of a ceiling fresco representing Air by Mattia Preti (1613–99). 1658–61. In the Castello Pamphili at Valmontone*

Opposite bottom *Detail of a ceiling fresco representing Fire by Francesco Cozza (1605–82) in the Castello Valmontone*

of his personal taste. However, the special fondness of the Pamphili for landscape painting is manifest in their collection, which exemplifies all its phases and moods, from the works of Mattheus and Paul Bril and the first 'pure landscapes' by Annibale Carracci and Domenichino, to the opposed trends of Claude Lorraine and Gaspard Dughet; from the romanticism of Salvator Rosa to the tranquil *vedute* of Van der Lint; from a wide selection of lesser-known artists to masterpieces like Brueghel the Elder's magnificent *Bay of Naples*, filled with billowing sails. Although Poussin's style was in accord with Pamphili taste, he is not represented in the collection, probably because he was fully committed to his French patrons. On the other hand, there are various works by his brother-in-law Gaspard Dughet, also known in Rome as 'Pussino', in all the Pamphili residences.

In the palace on the Piazza Navona the reception rooms already had magnificent domed ceilings with polychrome decorations and therefore further ornamentation was limited to friezes. Agostino Tassi had painted a series of seascapes in octagons and medallions in the room at the top of the grand staircase. Giacinto Brandi's delightful *Stories of Bacchus* enlivened the next room. Dughet filled the long friezes of the central hall with coastal and landscape views, using herms and caryatids to soften the transition from the rich, ornate ceiling to his own visions of nature. For the next room Gimignani chose Roman Legends (*Romulus and Remus Reared by the Wolf, Coriolanus, the Rape of the Sabine Women, Fabricius Refusing the Gifts of Pyrrhus*) and just before his death Camassei decorated another hall with *Ovid's Fables* (1648–9). Camillo himself probably inspired all these works, and on their completion Gimignani dedicated to him an etching of his *Rape of the Sabine Women* (1649).

In the same year Olimpia Maidalchini suffered the worst humiliation of her whole political career. Innocent X, tired of her and her protégé, conferred the name Pamphili and the privileges of Cardinal-Nephew on Camillo Astalli. In 1650, a jubilee year, the Pope received over 700,000 pilgrims in Rome. On 9th March one of Algardi's masterpieces, the bronze statue of Innocent X, his hand raised in the gesture of blessing *Urbi et Orbi*, was installed in the Palazzo dei Conservatori. In a new room of the family palace, built at right-angles to the façade, over a massive colonnade dividing the courtyard, the Pope had the following inscription placed beneath a bust of himself: 'Innocentius X pontifex maximus has paternas aedes ampliavit ornavit 1650 sacri principatus sexto.' The new room, reached from the inside through the Dughet room, and from the outside through a loggia, was evidently intended as a music room. A bust of Palestrina faces that of Innocent X, matching it exactly in size and position. The great reviver of sacred music, who had died when Innocent X was only twenty, certainly neither

LANDSCAPE WITH A WATERMILL
*Claude Lorraine (1600–82) oil on canvas
59 × 79 ins. c. 1649. Autograph
replica of a painting commissioned
by Don Camillo in 1646,
while still Cardinal*

FLIGHT INTO EGYPT *Annibale
Carracci (1560–1609) oil on
canvas 52 × 64 ins. c. 1604*

LANDSCAPE *Crescenzio d'Onofrio (1632–98)*
tempera on canvas

The Salone del Pussino in the Palace on the Corso

envisaged such papal homage nor foresaw the way in which music was to develop, thanks partly to Pamphili patronage.

In January 1651 Camillo and Olimpia christened their first male child Giambattista in honour of Innocent X, and the Pope, in a solemn declaration, established the principle of primogeniture in the Pamphili family, investing it in the person of his nephew Camillo. Camillo's eldest son Giambattista was to succeed as the head of the Pamphili line, while second sons were to bear the Aldobrandini name. The pictures and furnishings in the Palazzo Pamphili were entailed on the head of the family, and no more than a usufruct was granted to Donna Olimpia Maidalchini. At this time Camillo and his wife were living in the fine fifteenth-century palace on the Via del Corso which had belonged to the Duke of Urbino, before passing into the possession of Cardinal Pietro Aldobrandini in 1601; but Camillo continued to make improvements in the palace on the Piazza Navona. In the smaller rooms facing the Via dell'Anima, or adjacent to S. Agnese, the vaulted ceilings were decorated by, amongst others, Francesco Allegrini with the story of Dido and Aeneas, and with other cycles devoted to Daniel, Solomon, David, Elijah and heroines from both biblical and Roman history.

In 1651, on Camillo's advice, Pietro da Cortona was commissioned to decorate the long gallery designed by Borromini. This runs right through the palace from Piazza Navona to Via dell'Anima and is lit by large windows that transform the two short ends into loggias. Six doors, surmounted by cornices and niches containing busts, break up each long wall and the task allotted to the painter was to cover the barrel-vaulted ceiling with frescoes illustrating the adventures of Aeneas. Cortona's designs so delighted the Pope that he immediately gave him a much more important commission: the mosaic decoration of the right aisle of St Peter's. Work on the frescoes, therefore, progressed slowly, but the ageing Pope, whose last months were harassed by the Jesuit-Jansenist controversy, by the conflict between France and Spain and by new satirical attacks on his sister-in-law, experienced a moment of great joy when they were completed in the spring of 1654. And we too can still delight in the visual beauty of the windy blue sky; the groups of beguiling girls, roguish children, noble old men and heroes in their prime; the firm bodies glistening in sunshine and water; the contrasts between rosy *putti* and pallid statues, tender jasmine flowers and hard gilded foliage. The Pamphili emblem of the dove, which was associated with the goddess Venus who protected Aeneas and the fortunes of Rome, inspired the theme of the frescoes. This work is strikingly different from the apotheosis of the Barberini family which Pietro da Cortona had painted a few years earlier (1633–9). It is probable that the painter neither could nor would attempt another such *tour-de-force*, and certainly the Pamphili did not wish it. If the sequence of episodes which follow one another across the ceiling of the gallery – *Aeolus releasing the winds*, *Neptune calming the waves*, *The duel between Aeneas and Turnus*, *Evander's welcome*, *Aeneas' descent into the Underworld*, *Aeneas' ascent to Olympus* – have an inner meaning it is to emulate the sailor in knowing how to steer through calm and stormy seas, confidently keeping a steady course. The scales of Justice occupy the place of honour on the ceiling, showing that the greatest virtue is to be able to weigh good against evil – thus there is an evocation of the Divine Justice to be faced after death.

Meanwhile, since Belrespiro had been given to Astalli, the new Cardinal-Nephew, Camillo had commissioned Mattia de'Rossi to restore the castle of Valmontone (1651–61), situated on a volcanic peak not far from Velletri. But in 1654 Astalli fell from favour and the Pope deprived him of the name Pamphili, granting a 'pension' at the same time to Camillo's second son Benedetto, born in the previous year. As a gesture of reconciliation Olimpia Maidalchini also made a present to her grandchild of the magnificent gilt bronze cradle by Bernini. Readmitted to the Vatican, her first thought on realizing the Pope's failing health was to save the treasures she had accumulated by bequeathing them to the new-born child. But such was her passion for managing other people's lives, even from the next world, that she attached to the legacy a clause forbidding the beneficiary to enter the Church, thereby ensuring that her personal estate would pass only to her direct descendants. On 1st January, 1655, Innocent X died. His successor immediately expelled Olimpia Maidalchini from Rome and started proceedings against her. She fled to her native town of Viterbo and thence to her castle of S. Martino, where two years later she died of the plague.

Don Camillo inherited the palace in the Piazza Navona, with the family's collection of books and pictures, and also, on behalf of his four-year-old son Benedetto, his mother's personal possessions at Viterbo and S. Martino. It took a year to draw up the inventories, which list 'various ancient panels with gold' (these

ST JEROME IN THE WILDERNESS *Domenico Beccafumi (1485/6–1531) oil on panel 19½ × 14 ins.*

MADONNA AND CHILD WITH A DOVE *Parmigianino (1503–40) oil on panel 23½ × 13½ ins.*

Opposite top SALOME *Titian (1477–1576) oil on canvas 35 × 28 ins. c. 1515*

Opposite bottom DOUBLE PORTRAIT *Raphael (1483–1520) oil on canvas 30 × 43 ins. c. 1515*

Detail from REST ON THE FLIGHT *Michelangelo da Caravaggio*
(1573–1610) oil on canvas 52 × 64 ins. before 1590

Above *Detail from* ST DOROTHEA *Alessandro Tiarini*
(1577–1668) oil on canvas 62½ × 43 ins.

possibly included the two Giovanni de Paolo), many unimportant paintings, several family portraits and those of other noble sitters, crucifixes, reliquaries, tapestries, embroidered pictures, papier maché figurines, and many other objects. But the substantial part of the legacy was two million gold scudi (see L. Montalto, *Un mecenate in Roma Barocca: il Cardinale Benedetto Pamphili*, 1655). However, the lovely palace in the Piazza Navona was to be deserted.

The arrival in Rome of Queen Christina of Sweden, for Christmas 1655, had created a sensation and the younger Olimpia began to play a leading role at her court. By the time her mother-in-law died, she had become fiercely independent, to the point of shutting herself up in the nearby convent of Tor di Specchi until given (1657) a more generous allowance and the right to entertain her Florentine relations in the palace on the Corso. Pope Alexander VII (Chigi) arranged a reconcilation between husband and wife, and later pardoned Camillo for not having gone to live in the family palace. After Camillo's death the same pardon was sought by his son who, even after his marriage, preferred to remain with his mother. Proud as an Aldobrandini (she wanted to be buried in S. Maria sopra Minerva and not in S. Agnese), Olimpia always got her own way in the end, either through charm or through refusing to settle a quarrel on any terms but her own. Thus the Pamphili never returned to live on the Piazza Navona which is so closely linked with their name. They kept the palace (now an embassy, like the Casino delle Allegrezze) for receptions and all the Pamphili cardinals made gifts to the library of the nearby college. Camillo resumed the work on S. Agnese, which had been halted by the death of Innocent X, and entrusted the task of completing Borromini's project to the young Rainaldi, who was later joined by Antonio Del Grande. His purpose in so doing was to provide a worthy monument to his uncle and to keep his memory from being forgotten. At the same time he decided to improve the little church of S. Maria in Via Lata, thus adding dignity to the palace on the Corso. With a stroke of inspiration Camillo summoned to his aid Pietro da Cortona, and the painter, fired perhaps by the Bramantesque double portico of the palace, designed a façade resembling a double loggia, which is a masterpiece of Baroque illusionism (1658–62).

Meanwhile leading painters of the day had been commissioned to decorate the ceilings at Valmontone (1658–61) with frescoes of the Four Elements. The Room of Water, by G. B. Tassi and Antonio Somigliano, is dominated by such figures as Neptune and Galatea. The Room of Earth, by Courtois, called Borgognone, shows a haughty Cybele in the centre, with the rape of Proserpine and the legend of Pegasus on the two short sides; the two long sides are devoted to an ambitious representation of

Opposite MADONNA AND CHILD IN A LANDSCAPE *Simone Cantarini (1618–48) oil on canvas 19½ × 26 ins.*

Left A SERVANT WITH AN OIL LAMP *Wolfgang Heimbach*
(1610/20–after 1670) 17 × 14 ins.

Above ERMINIA FINDS
THE WOUNDED TANCREDI
Guercino (1591–1666)
oil on canvas 57 × 73 ins.

LANDSCAPE *Giovanni
Momper (c. 1645–c. 1730)*
oil on canvas 49½ × 52½ ins.

Opposite *One of the reliquaries surrounding the altar of the
private chapel of Cardinal Benedetto Pamphili. The skull and tibia
of St Deodata are here arranged with wax flowers and pieces of
embroidered silk*

PORTRAIT OF ANDREA DORIA *Sebastiano del Piombo (1485–1547) oil on panel 55 × 47 ins. 1526*

Opposite *Sarcophagus of the first half of the second century AD representing the Hunt of the Caledonian Boar. Above, three Roman busts set against part of a Brussels tapestry depicting the Battle of Lepanto (1571)*

the arts of Painting, Sculpture, Architecture and, somewhat unexpectedly, Hunting. In the Room of Air, dated 1661, Mattia Preti broke with the Baroque love of massive grouping, and produced a scattered composition more in keeping with the concept of air. By contrast, in the Room of Fire (1658–61), Francesco Cozza executed an elaborate decoration in the manner of Domenichino. Pier Francesco Mola, Christina of Sweden's favourite painter, appears to have worked on the vault of the Sala del Principe at Valmontone before his dispute with the prince in 1661. The walls of this room were probably frescoed by Dughet. A balustrade with figures of men and women is painted round the top of the walls and four slender caryatids reach out from each corner to support a coat of arms in the centre of the vault.

The ceiling of the library in the Collegio Agnesino (1666–73) was frescoed after Camillo's death in a manner resembling Valmontone. Inspired by Mattia Preti's Room of Air, Cozza too arranged his strongly modelled figures in a loose composition depicting the Elements. Next to Earth is the Fall of Manna, the Church, representations of the Liberal Arts and at the apex, Wisdom with her book of knowledge. Here the Pamphili doves fly round enormous Aldobrandini cogged wheels – a justified homage since the younger Olimpia presented the library with books and manuscripts belonging to Clement VIII and to Cardinals Pietro and Ippolito Aldobrandini, as well as the precious texts of St Philip Neri.

Camillo's last enterprise was his greatest. In 1659 Alexander VII ordered the Jesuits to complete the construction of their College with a piazza in front of it worthy of such an imposing building. The Jesuits bought and demolished the Palazzo Salviati, and then put part of the cleared area up for sale. Camillo seized the opportunity of buying land adjacent to his own palace on the Corso, and undertook to erect a building to match the Jesuit College. The wing parallel to the Collegio Romano was finished in 1661, while the wing facing the square on the side of S. Maria in Via Lata was finished under Olimpia's supervision (1666–73) during the minority of her son. As with the S. Agnese decorations, documents reveal the widow's anxiety to adhere to plans which had already been approved.

The dignified façade by Antonio Del Grande is not unlike that of the palace in the Piazza Navona, but the internal arrangement is original. The grand staircase rises from the central entrance hall, towards the extreme right end of the palace, thus allowing for a magnificent sequence of large and small antechambers on the first floor, which ends in one of the loggias of the Bramantesque courtyard. The first reception room overlooking the piazza, known as the *Salone del Pussino*, has a double row of windows and its walls are covered with pictures, their size varying according to the space available. Because of their symmetrical arrangement, the pictures still hang more or less as Camillo intended, and as they are described in the first printed guide to the collection (compiled by S. Tonci, Rome, 1794). Immediately below the cornice, there are twelve huge landscapes with figures such as St Eustace, the Good Samaritan, Cain and Abel. In the second row, and in the paintings below and between the windows, Dughet forgot narrative to render aspects of nature (the *Waterfall*, the *Bridge at Tivoli*) with a powerful simplicity and a boldness which anticipates Courbet.

The *Salone delle Tempere*, on the garden side, is less sumptuous but gayer. The pale blue temperas by Crescenzio Onofri stand out like frescoes on its Pompeian-red walls, conjuring up the sun and wind, and the joys and hardships of life in the country; a contrast to the sombre paintings of Roman ruins, ascribed to Ghisolfi, which frame the windows.

Camillo Pamphili died in 1666 at the age of forty-four. After 1661 his interest shifted from large architectural and decorative projects to the picture gallery and library. Research in the Pamphili archives may one day throw light on his activity and provide more precise information as to which of the pictures in the palace on the Corso were inherited, which commissioned, and which acquired from dealers or other collectors. Meanwhile, the inventory drawn up in 1682 after Olimpia's death, for the division of the Aldobrandini inheritance between her two sons (*vide* P. Della Pergola in *Arte Antica e Moderna* 1962, No. 19) gives a certain amount of information. Part of the Aldobrandini inheritance was later claimed by the Borghese, but the Pamphili kept Raphael's *Double Portrait*, Parmigianino's *Nativity* and small *Madonna*, the *Salome and Herodias* by Solario, the *Angel* attributed to Moretto, various paintings by Mazzolino, the Beccafumi *St Jerome* and the two panels with *Muses* by Bugiardini, which hang in the room now called 'dei Velluti' because of its fine red and gold Genoese hangings, together with the marble busts of Innocent X and his brother Pamphilio, both by Algardi.

Some early seventeenth-century paintings (including works by

BRITANNIA WITH NEWTON AND GRAVESANDE *Giovanni Martino de Bonis (1753–after 1810) oil on canvas*

Opposite Detail of a series of tapestries depicting episodes from the life of Alexander the Great. Tournai. Fifteenth century

Lanfranco, Saraceni, and Albani) came to Camillo through his marriage with an Aldobrandini. But Camillo himself bought four masterpieces by Caravaggio. Three of them (*Rest on the Flight, Mary Magdalen,* and *St John the Baptist*) are still in the collection, while he presented the fourth, *The Fortune-Teller* (now in the Louvre), to Louis XIV a year before his death. Between 1645 and 1665 Claude Lorraine sketched in his 'Liber Veritatis' several landscapes which had been painted for 'il Sig. Principe Pamphili'. Camillo certainly knew how to win an artist's loyalty – Algardi rejected offers from Louis XIV in order to remain with his Roman patron, and Pietro da Cortona so enjoyed acting as his architect that he did little more than supervise the frescoes commissioned from him by the new Pope for Montecavallo. Camillo's predilection for Pietro da Cortona, Mattia Preti, Dughet and Courtois is borne out by the works in the Pamphili picture-gallery, which reveal a similar taste for the naturalistic-encyclopaedic themes developed in the frescoes at Valmontone. Camillo's descendants added series of Philosophers and Continents to those representing the Elements and the Arts. The early seventeenth-century interest in effects of artificial light and in night scenes is particularly well represented in the collection, which includes, besides Guerrier's *Lot and his Daughters* and a pretty *Descent of Aeneas to Hell* by Jacob Isaac Von Swanenburgh, two studies of the bizarre effects of lantern-light by W. Heimbach and a group of half-length figures by the Candlelight Master, now identified as the Provençal painter T. Bigot.

It is surprising that Camillo, surrounded as he was by artists, should never have had his portrait taken. There is only one sketch of him whereas there are a number of pictures of his wife. The full-length portrait in the Salone del Pussino shows Olimpia still young, with an engaging twinkle in her eyes; and even the stiff marble bust done by Lazoni a year before she died, breathes a spirit of irrepressible gaiety. Camillo wrote plays, Olimpia comic verses, and they established a theatre in their palace on the Corso, where performances were given every two days. Their artistic talents were inherited by their favourite son, Benedetto, 'prince of humourists', patron of Scarlatti and Corelli, song writer, author of operatic librettos and carnival plays, which he staged in defiance of Pope Innocent XI. Maybe the canvases by Pietro da Cortona, Guercino and Romanelli in the Pamphili palace illustrating the story of Erminia inspired the pastoral drama *Erminia*, which he wrote at the age of nineteen (1672). Unfortunately his elder brother Giambattista had less interest in the arts and he was probably responsible for a number of statues being badly scarred. An admirer of the antiquities in the Pamphili villa of Belrespiro has left us this account: 'Prince Giambattista was persuaded by the Jesuits to enter their Society and they complained about the nudity of his statues. As a result, the

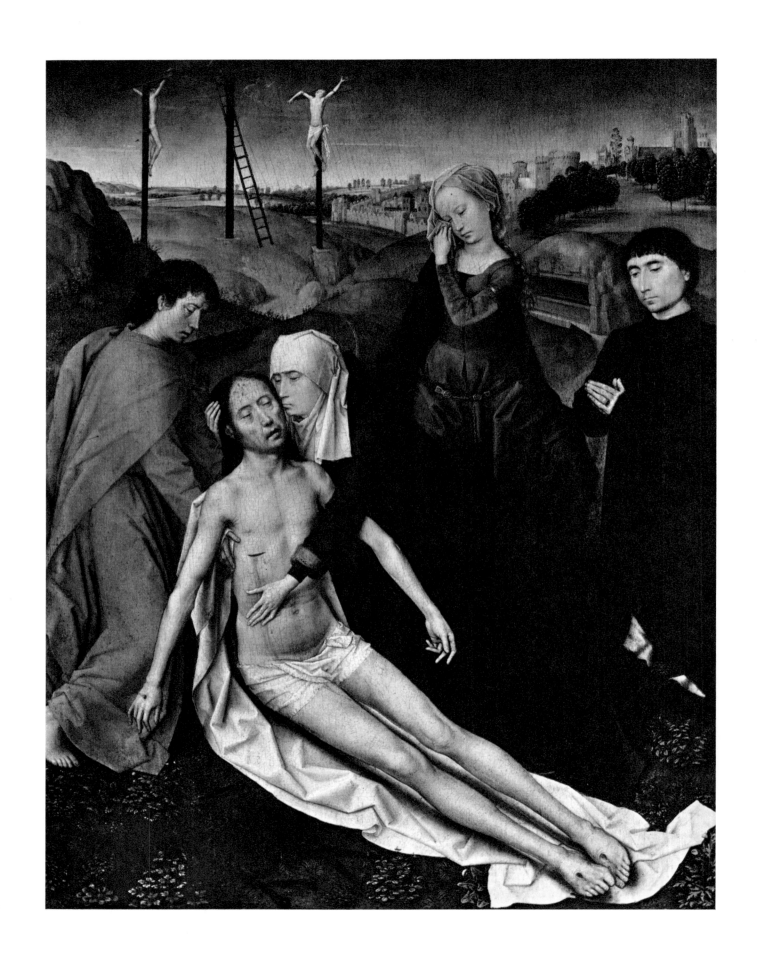

PIETÀ *Hans Memling*
(d. 1494)

young prince ordered his marble subjects – men, women and children – to be clothed with plaster shirts, to the distress of painters, sculptors and scholars. All were mercilessly covered – only one little Bacchus escaped, no-one knows how. . . . Then the prince had a change of heart and coming to prefer the society of a princess to the Society of Jesus . . . ordered the ridiculous plaster to be removed. . . . Unfortunately the masons had hammered holes into the marble to secure the plaster and most of the pieces are much damaged.' (Misson, *Nouveau Voyage d'Italie*, Letter of 11th April, 1688.) Possibly Misson was too pessimistic, for much of the Pamphili collection of antiquities has survived undamaged; the marbles from Belrespiro, now in the former palace theatre, are indeed very fine.

By the time she died, the younger Olimpia had found a wife for Giambattista, married her second daughter Anna to Prince Andrea Doria III of Genoa (1671) and celebrated the election of Benedetto to the office of cardinal. The problems raised by the division of the Pamphili and Aldobrandini inheritances were solved by the settlement of 1684, which gave Benedetto the wing of the palace facing the Collegio Romano, with usufruct of the furniture and paintings for life. Thus the young cardinal was able to take his religious vows despite the provisions of his grandmother's will.

Benedetto increased the collection of paintings from 200 to 1,300, showing a marked preference for flower paintings, landscapes and still-lifes. He commissioned work from Mulier (called il Tempesta), van Bloemen (called l'Orizzonte), the animal painter Philip Roos (Rosa da Tivoli) and the seascape painter A. Manglard. A caricature of Benedetto by P. L. Ghezzi shows him with his faithful architect Carlo Fontana, who until his death in 1714 received a monthly salary for supervising the improvements that were constantly being made to the palace and elsewhere. He was responsible for the façade on via Lata and for Benedetto's private chapel on the first floor, with its secret passage enabling him to look, unseen, into S. Maria (in via Lata). The chapel is a shrine for relics, but cheerful ones – a dashing warrior in uniform, skulls gracefully decked with flowers like fantasies by Arcimboldi. The wax masks of St Leonard and St Philip Neri, on the other hand, are an interesting example of the survival in Catholic Rome of a custom mentioned by Pliny and widely observed in classical times. Next to them, is a large polychrome terra-cotta bust of the Pamphili Pope by Algardi – the most lively effigy we possess of him.

An inventory of 1725 describes room by room Benedetto's possessions in the winter and summer apartments of the palace on the Corso, his Villa at Albano, his Casino at Nettuno, in the Vigna di Porta Pia and in the property at Testa di Lepre. On his death in 1730, his heirs wanted to make the palace conform to new standards of elegance and embarked on a period of feverish activity. Valvassori designed and built a skilful façade on the Corso, as well as enclosing the upper loggia of the Bramantesque courtyard to make four galleries (1731–4). The gallery overlooking the Corso was transformed into a sumptuous Hall of Mirrors with ceiling frescoes by Aureliano Milani of the *Labours of Hercules* and the *Fall of the Giants*. Other galleries were decorated by Ginesio del Barba with chinoiseries and grotesques. In the Braccio Nuovo, to the right of the Hall of Mirrors, Pompeo Aldobrandini, a Bolognese painter of perspectives (died 1739), carried out bold illusionistic architectural fantasies. Stefano Pozzi (1701–68), a pupil of Maratta, transformed a small room of the cardinal's wing with frescoes and overdoors on the theme of the Elements offering their gifts to Venus. Elsewhere are ceiling paintings and ornamental frescoes by Pietro Angeletti, Giovanni Angeloni, Pietro Bernarbò, Domenico Corvi and Giovacchino Agricola.

In 1760 the direct line of the Pamphili family died out and the succession passed to the Doria Pamphili branch, who added a black eagle to the white dove and brought the first military trophies into a house where hitherto only painted battle scenes were familiar. With the personal relics of Andrea Doria, the Condottiere who became the ruler of Genoa and was also a great patron of the arts, two masterpieces of Renaissance portraiture came to Rome: the superb *Andrea Doria* by Sebastiano del Piombo and the *Giannettino Doria* by Bronzino. When Giannettino was assassinated during the Fieschi conspiracy (1547), his uncle transferred his wealth and honours to Giannettino's son, Gian Andrea Prince of Melfi, the leader of the Genoese forces at Lepanto (1571) who was accused of treason by the Venetians and hailed by the Genoese as the hero of the victory over the Turks. Six sixteenth-century Brussels tapestries, showing the positions of the ships during the various phases of the battle, now hang in the Salone Doria and the Salone Aldobrandini.

Soon after the succession had passed to the Doria Pamphili, however, the family became involved once again in religious disputes. During the French Revolution and the Napoleonic Wars, at a time when both the temporal and spiritual power of the Church were severely attacked, there were no fewer than three Doria Pamphili cardinals (Giuseppe 1751–1816, Anton Maria 1749–1821, and Giorgio 1772–1837). After Napoleon's defeat, the ties between the Doria-Pamphili and England, which were long-standing and had been kept alive by the many English noblemen who came to Rome, grew much stronger. Two pictures in the collection illustrate this: an oval portrait by Alexis Simon, dated 1702, of the Old Pretender as a boy, which may have been presented by him or by his son to the Pamphili; and a charming allegorical group of *Britannia between Newton and Gravesande* by the eighteenth-century painter G. Martino de Bonis. In 1837 Filippo Andrea Doria Pamphili went to London with his brother for the coronation of Queen Victoria, and returned there two years later to marry Lady Mary Talbot, daughter of the Earl of Shrewsbury. The portraits of this couple and of their children, painted by Alessandro Capalti, communicate a feeling of domestic happiness and bourgeois respectability which is in striking contrast to the atmosphere of clerical and political formality which pervades the palace in which the finest apartment had been reserved for the celibate member of the family who was a prince of the Church.

Such alterations to the palace as were effected during the nineteenth-century left untouched all that was best from previous centuries. But during the War of Italian Independence the grounds of Belrespiro were the scene of fighting and in 1849 the Casino de'Venti was destroyed.

Several guides to the picture gallery have been published in the last hundred years, culminating in the descriptive catalogue by E. Sestieri (Rome 1942) of those pictures which were once entailed but are now covered by the Italian law of indivisibility and inalienability. On the other hand several outstanding works which were acquired after 1871 such as Pesellino's *Miracles of St Sylvester*, Fra Filippo Lippi's *Annunciation*, Memling's *Pietà* and the *Uomo Malato* by Lorenzo Lotto are not covered by this law. A true friend of the arts, the present Prince Alfonso has purchased (1894) the fine *Salome* by Titian, and performed a service to students, and to his family, by separating the gallery from the private apartments.

Despite two world wars and the far-reaching social and economic changes of the twentieth century, the family has defended its valuable inheritance with a quiet tenacity worthy of the patient Pamphili dove.

MIRACLE OF ST SYLVESTER (*c. 1422–57*) *Francesco Pesellino (1422–69/72) tempera on panel c. 1450. One of three similar scenes, of which the second is also in the Doria Pamphili Collection and the third is in the Worcester Art Museum, Massachusetts*

The Counts Wrangel and Brahe

Erik Andrén · Heribert Seitz · Eva Bergman

Skokloster is unique among European historic houses and enshrines a great amount of Swedish history. It was built by a French architect for the great Swedish commander and statesman, Count Carl Gustaf Wrangel, who decorated and furnished it as a country residence between 1654 and his death in 1676. It is a fascinating example of seventeenth-century domestic arrangements and contains many exceptional and fine works of art. The original collection consists of objets d'art, paintings, tapestries, silver, glass and furniture which were either bought by, or made specially for Wrangel by craftsmen of many nationalities, given to him by royalty, or by towns and countries in which he was stationed during his campaigns, or else acquired by him as war booty. Skokloster also houses the enormous collection of weapons of his period assembled by Wrangel. After his death, the house passed by marriage first to the Brahe family (1676–1930) and subsequently to their descendants the Barons von Essen. The interior decorations have been preserved intact, while additions to the furnishings and artistic contents were made throughout the eighteenth century. The house has thus remained unchanged and is particularly interesting for the historical significance of its contents. During the eighteenth century the weapons collection was increased by the armouries of the Brahe and Bielke families, tapestries and furniture were added and also a vast library. The latest addition was made in 1830 by Count Magnus Brahe, who furnished a room in the Neo-Gothic style as a tribute to his close friend Marshal Bernadotte, who was made King of Sweden in 1818.

The Counts Wrangel and Brahe

now in the possession of Baron Rutger von Essen

Erik Andrén · Heribert Seitz · Eva Bergman

The Skokloster Collection is in many respects unique. It comprises furniture, pictures, tapestries, carpets and other textiles, silver, ornaments and curios, weapons, clothes, books, manuscripts and many other items, all housed in a particularly well preserved baroque setting. The collection dates mainly from the seventeenth century, although some pieces are earlier and there are a good many later additions. One German connoisseur has described Skokloster, probably with reason, as 'das beste Barockmuseum der Welt'. The bulk of it was assembled about the middle of the seventeenth century by the Swedish-born soldier and statesman, Count Carl Gustaf Wrangel, who was born in Stockholm in 1613 and died in 1676 as Swedish Governor-General of Pomerania.

It is not possible to establish in detail just how Count Wrangel acquired each particular item. Some of the things were inherited from his father and some represent war booty from his long campaigns on the continent during the Thirty Years War, when Swedish military victories as leaders of the Protestant forces brought Sweden new power and prestige. Certain of the more splendid pieces are gifts from German princes and towns to the dreaded conqueror, while many works of art, unusual weapons and rare books were bought through agents in various European towns.

Towards the middle of the seventeenth century the fashion for art collecting spread rapidly among the Swedish aristocracy and became one of the expressions of Sweden's newly acquired political eminence. Skokloster is, however, unique among these collections in that the whole setting has been preserved almost unchanged to the present day, and the art treasures have not been scattered by inheritance or sale. This is due to the fact that the

Skokloster Castle, built 1654–68, from the north-west

CARL GUSTAF WRANGEL *David Klöcker Ehrenstrahl (1628–98) oil on canvas 116 × 128 in. 1652. (Detail) The originator of the house and collection*

The Kings' Hall, originally the dining-room, hung with portraits of Swedish kings from Gustaf Vasa (1521–60) to the present day. To the right of the fireplace is a tiled stove installed in 1670

Opposite Another view of the Kings' Hall. The painted stucco ceiling, with a centrepiece representing St George and the Dragon, was executed by Hans Zauch in 1664

palace with all its collections was entailed as early as 1701, and since then the castle has been used as a residence only for brief periods.

Carl Gustaf Wrangel had fifteen children, but at his death in 1676 only three daughters survived. The eldest of these, Margareta Juliana, who inherited Skokloster, married Admiral Count Nils Nilsson Brahe. Skokloster thus passed into the possession of the Brahe family, who continued to inherit it until 1930, when Count Magnus Brahe died and the line ended with him. The entail then passed to his sister's eldest son, Baron Fredrik von Essen who died in 1936. The present owner is his eldest son Baron Rutger von Essen.

During the Brahe period (1676–1930) a great many pieces were added to the collection and each generation made some contribution. The largest addition came in the eighteenth century from Salsta castle. This manor house, situated in the same

Opposite *A second floor guest room hung with Brussels tapestries from the* HISTOIRE D'ALEXANDRE *set. The gilt furniture is of the first half of the eighteenth century*

The Library, consisting of some 20,000 volumes. Portraits of literary personalities of the seventeenth and early eighteenth centuries decorate the ends of the bookcases

province as Skokloster, contained a fine art collection which passed to Count Erik Brahe in 1754 under the will of Count Carl Gustaf Bielke. Some years later, in 1787, the Bielke library and armoury, together with a number of pictures, tapestries and other objets d'art, were transferred from Salsta to Skokloster. These additions greatly increased the value of the Wrangel Collections.

Skokloster Castle lies on a northerly arm of Lake Mälar, about twelve miles south of Uppsala. Captain Herman Wrangel, a Baltic nobleman in Swedish service, was granted the estate as a gift in 1611. His son, Count Carl Gustaf, the founder of the collection, was not satisfied with the simple manor-house built by his father, and in 1654 began the construction of the present castle – a square four-storied stone house built round a courtyard with an octagonal tower at each corner. The building was carried out in stages, the first of which was completed in 1657. The second stage was begun in 1661, but the exterior was not

finally completed until 1668. Work on the interior was carried out independently, but simultaneously. However, when Count Carl Gustaf died in 1676 some of the rooms on the second floor had still not been completed and they have remained unfinished until the present day.

The designs for Skokloster were probably made between 1650 and 1652 by Jean de la Vallée, a French architect who was also employed by the Swedish royal family. Vallée's rival, Nicodemus Tessin the Elder, a North German, also seems to have made drawings for certain details. When Count Wrangel commissioned Vallée to design the castle he probably suggested that it should be modelled on the electoral palace at Aschaffenburg, but in fact the architect more probably looked for inspiration to the Italian renaissance palaces and to French seventeenth-century buildings.

The most interesting features of the interior decoration are the plaster ceilings and wooden fireplaces. The stucco ceilings in the dining-room and the two adjoining ante-rooms are the work of an Italian, Giovanni Antoni, and a German, Hans Zauch. The other fourteen stucco ceilings in the house date from between 1670 and 1677 and are the work of the Swede, Nils Eriksson. Most of them have elaborate stucco work over and between the projecting beams. Others have completely flat ceilings and the decoration is divided into a pattern of panels and borders. There are twenty-one brick fireplaces encased in wood, with carved details and mouldings. The wall paintings on the first and second floors were executed by the Dutch artist, Willem Henrichs in 1661, by Johan Malchow from Stralsund in 1671 and by the German Hans Jurgen Floth in 1673–5. Two ceilings on the second floor painted by Floth are direct copies of engraved designs by Jean Le Pautre of about 1660. All the decorations on the top floor were painted by Christopher Rambergh in 1672.

Wandering through the seventy rooms at Skokloster one is struck more perhaps by the elaborateness of its conception and the variety of its decoration than by superb craftsmanship. The furniture is chiefly from the second half of the seventeenth century, with some eighteenth-century pieces. Some rooms are furnished in the Empire style and some have neo-Gothic pieces from the first half of the nineteenth century. Some of the baroque furniture is in elaborate French-Italian style, with carved acanthus ornament, rich gilding and brocade coverings; other pieces are in the more severe English-Dutch style with dark stained wood, turned chair legs and leather coverings. There are some heavy cabinets of the north German type, their shelves full of glass, porcelain, pottery, silver and pewter. There are also some intricately carved cabinets and reliquaries, their small drawers and secret compartments containing souvenirs, relics and curios of many kinds. One is veneered in ebony and its drawers and doors are decorated with ivory plaques engraved with figures in the renaissance style and stylised scenes. This cabinet, which stands in the great dining-hall, the King's Hall, was made in Augsburg and presented to Carl Gustaf Wrangel by the city.

The bedrooms and some of the guest rooms have state beds with magnificent hangings. These and the beautiful sixteenth- and seventeenth-century Gobelin tapestries are discussed in more detail later.

The eighteenth-century furniture is mainly by Swedish cabinet-makers working in the rococo or Gustavian (Louis XVI) style. It is characteristic of this period that commodes and secretaires are veneered and inlaid and generally follow French models, whereas chairs more often conform to the English style and have openwork wooden backs.

Furniture in the neo-gothic style is rare in Sweden. But the tower room at Skokloster was painted and furnished in this style in 1830 by Count Magnus Brahe, who intended it as a tribute to his friend Jean Bernadotte, Napoleon's Marshal, who had been elected Crown Prince of Sweden in 1810 and became King in 1818.

Where the walls of the rooms are not covered with tapestries, they are hung with portraits from floor to ceiling. There must be nearly 450 portraits at Skokloster, most of them from the second half of the seventeenth and the beginning of the eighteenth centuries. Their quality is uneven – the majority are of interest for the people they represent or for the information they give about the costume of the time – but there are also a number which have an important place in the history of Swedish art.

The artist most in favour in Sweden during the latter half of the seventeenth century was David Klöcker, born in Hamburg in 1628. Wrangel commissioned work from him in Pomerania in 1651 and Klöcker went back with him to Stockholm in the following year. He was presented to Queen Christina shortly after and was appointed court painter. Before very long he became the most fashionable portrait painter among the Swedish military nobility and in 1674 he was himself raised to the nobility and took the high-sounding name of Ehrenstrahl. There are about twenty of his paintings at Skokloster, some of them very early works, including the large equestrian portrait of Carl Gustaf Wrangel.

There are important works by two Dutch painters, David Beck and Abraham Wuchters, who were both active in Sweden towards the middle of the seventeenth century. Beck painted Queen Christina, Gustavus Adolphus' daughter who abdicated in 1654 and became a Roman Catholic, her Chancellor Axel Oxenstierna and Count Per Brahe junior. Wuchters also painted portraits of Queen Christina and of Carl Gustaf Wrangel.

There is a series of officers' portraits set into the permanent fittings of the first-floor corridor. These were commissioned by Field-Marshal Herman Wrangel in 1623–4 from an unknown artist and depict Wrangel himself and nineteen of his brother officers standing feet apart, one hand on their hips and the other grasping their sword hilts. Judging by the names inscribed on the portraits one was French, five were Scots and the rest Swedes and Germans.

This collection contains two of the strangest works in the whole field of portrait painting. These are by the Italian artist Giuseppe Arcimboldo (1533–93), court painter to the Emperor Rudolf II. In one he has arranged a composition of books to form a portrait of Rudolf's librarian and in the other a composition of carrots, parsnips, fruit and flowers to depict the imperial head gardener. Both paintings were part of the war booty taken by the Swedes from Prague in 1648.

In the small dining-room there are two fine ink and wash drawings by Willem van de Velde the elder. They depict the

Ebony cabinet inlaid with ivory scenes of hunting and sports. Height 44 ins. Made in Augsburg and presented by the city to Carl Gustaf Wrangel in the 1640s

Ivory cabinet inlaid with enamels showing scenes from the Passion and Crucifixion. Height 19½ ins. Probably German. Mid-seventeenth century

The first floor corridor set with portraits of Field-Marshal Herman Wrangel, father of Carl Gustaf, and nineteen of his fellow officers. Artist unknown. Executed 1623–24

The Bernadotte Memorial Room in the east tower. Designed (1830) by Count Magnus Brahe in honour of Napoleon's former Marshal who had become Charles XIV John, King of Sweden (1818–44). In the foreground is a marble statue of the king as Mars

Opposite QUEEN CHRISTINA OF SWEDEN *Abraham Wuchters (c. 1610–83) oil on canvas 45 × 31½ ins. 1661*

CATHERINE DE
NEVVILLE.COMTESSE
D'ARMAGNACQ.

naval battle off Fehmarn, a Baltic island off the north coast of Germany, when Carl Gustaf Wrangel commanded the Swedish fleet for the first time and defeated the Danes.

As one would expect there is a fine collection of glass and ceramics, including Venetian and Bohemian glass goblets, German glass beakers with enamel decorations and many other pieces. A lidded goblet with the inscription *Willkomm Ihr Herren* was a gift from the city of Nuremberg to Carl Gustaf Wrangel in 1648. The pottery and porcelain includes Delft, Meissen and Sèvres pieces, export porcelain from China, and Swedish pottery from Rörstrand and Marieberg. Carl Gustaf Wrangel's field service of turned grey-brown serpentine is displayed in a cabinet from Hamburg, and another contains part of an all-white seventeenth-century pottery service manufactured in Frankfurt. Among the ceramics the magnificent tiled stoves supplied and installed in 1670 by a Stockholm stove setter are of particular interest. Five of these are still preserved, two with black-glazed relief tiles and three with a relief pattern in blue and green on a white ground.

The silver, housed in one of the tower rooms, comprises silver plate, ornaments and curios of every description. There is a thirteenth-century bishop's crozier from Limoges made of gilt copper with inlays of enamel, tankards, nautilus goblets, rings, jewellery, miniatures, pocket watches, chessmen, medals and many other small objects. One of the choicest exhibits is a carved ivory tankard mounted in silver gilt and enamel, a mid-seventeenth-century piece from Augsburg.

One of the most remarkable features of Skokloster is undoubtedly the turnery, which is housed in one of the tower rooms, and has remained unchanged since the 1670s. The lathes and countless tools bear witness to the interest in turnery which was one of Wrangel's pastimes later in life. In an adjoining room is a collection of heavier tools for joiners and carpenters that have survived from the period when the palace was being built. These of course have no aesthetic value, but are of great historical interest.

ERIK ANDRÉN

THE ARMOURIES

The weapons preserved at Skokloster were not collected in the modern sense as antiques, but have been inherited with the castle from the days when they were still in use. Skokloster was built by a famous warrior and it could be said with a certain degree of truth that it owes its existence to the Thirty Years War. But Field-Marshal Count Carl Gustaf Wrangel's interest in weapons was by no means restricted to their purely military employment on the field of battle. In the course of his many years of service in central Europe he had excellent opportunities for acquiring a very large collection of weapons in use at the time. This practical interest, which covered the whole range of contemporary small arms, seems to have begun in about 1633 when, at the age of twenty, he first began to distinguish himself in the

Opposite CATHÉRINE DE NEUVILLE, COMTESSE D'ARMAGNAC *Unknown French painter. Oil on canvas 26½ × 22 ins. c. 1670. One of six equestrian portraits of ladies of Louis XIV's court. They were acquired and taken to Sweden in 1682 by Count Nils Bielke, then Swedish ambassador in Paris*

THE BATTLE OF FEHMARN *Willem van de Velde (1611–93) ink and wash 24½ × 57 ins. 1644–50. Carl Gustaf Wrangel, in command of the Swedish fleet, defeated the Danes at this battle in 1644*

Above left *Glass goblet inscribed 'Willkomm Ihr Herren'. Height 8 ins. Made in Nuremberg and presented by the city to Carl Gustaf Wrangel in 1648*

Above right *Carved ivory and silver tankard, the top and base inset with enamels. Stamped BW (probably Baptist Weinet d. 1648). Height 13½ ins. Augsburg. Mid-seventeenth century*

Right *Bishop's gilt crozier inlaid with coloured enamels. Height 9½ ins. Limoges. Thirteenth century*

Far right *Silver tankard engraved with allegorical figures representing the Virtues. Height 8 ins. Probably Swedish. 1683*

campaigns of the Thirty Years War, as Lieutenant-Colonel of Cavalry, and it continued more or less unabated until his death in 1676. Thus of the 1,842 items in this collection – the Wrangel Armoury – none is of later date than 1676. The armoury has always been housed in the western tower room on the third floor and in two adjoining rooms, and the original arrangement of the weapons has been preserved.

There is, however, a second collection of weapons at Skokloster – the Brahe-Bielke Armoury – which was acquired through inheritance and family connections. As the name suggests, it comes from two different sources. Since all Carl Gustaf Wrangel's seven sons predeceased him, Skokloster passed to his eldest daughter, Margareta Juliana, who married Admiral Count Nils Brahe, whose armoury at Rydboholm castle was transferred to Skokloster in 1710. Moreover, as a result of the marriage in 1695 of Major-General Count Abraham Brahe to Countess Eva Bielke, the Bielke family armoury was moved, in about 1780, from Salsta castle to Skokloster, where it is exhibited in the same rooms as the Brahe collection. These are the northern tower room, again on the third floor, and two adjoining rooms, one of which, formerly a guest-room, is known as the Hamburg Room and the other as the Count's Workshop. The two castles of Rydboholm and Salsta are both situated, like Skokloster, in the province of Uppland north of Stockholm. During the course of the nineteenth century further weapons belonging to the Brahe family, who were now the owners of Skokloster, were added to the collection.

In view of the historic nature of the weapons of which the three collections consist, as well as their high quality and the size of the total collection – 3,501 pieces – it is perhaps not unreasonable to describe Skokloster as the finest privately-owned museum of weapons in Europe, and probably in the world. It must be remembered that Carl Gustaf Wrangel and also the members of the Brahe and Bielke families had far-reaching international connections, and their position in society was such as to make the acquisition by them of first-rate weapons a perfectly natural activity. To give a satisfactory account of the contents of these different armouries in a brief survey is hardly possible. The most that can be attempted is to pick out some of the finest pieces.

In the Wrangel Armoury pride of place must go to a Renaissance pageant shield of steel, commonly known as the Skokloster Shield. Even among experts it is hardly less famous than its twin, known as the Emperor Charles V's shield, in Vienna (Waffensammlung, Kunsthistorisches Museum). There is a third stylistically related shield, in the National Museum in Copenhagen. The design of the Skokloster Shield is characterised, like the other two, by a connected outer and inner framework with five mascarons of fauns and one of a woman. The dominating motif is a triumph theme with large figures of bound captives surrounding five medallions with small figure groups. The central and largest of these represents naked barbarians fighting with horses' jaw-bones as weapons. The decorative figures evince skilled workmanship; they are chased in high relief against a dark, pounced ground. The details are damascened with gold, and the borders are damascened in gold and silver against a bluish ground.

In the case of a masterpiece such as this, it is only natural that a number of theories should have arisen as to its origin. One of the most popular during the latter half of the nineteenth century and even later, was that it was executed by Benvenuto Cellini for the Emperor Charles V. It was believed to have been brought to Sweden as war booty during the Thirty Years War. Later research – carried out principally by Professor Karl Erik Steneberg – has established by means of comparative study that the shield is more probably the work of Eliseus Libaerts of Antwerp, based on designs by Etienne Delaune of Paris. The first owner was definitively King Erik XIV of Sweden, who is believed to have commissioned the shield from Master Libaerts in the early 1560s – there is documentary evidence that the king was in communication with him then. Towards the middle of the seventeenth century it was taken from the Royal Armoury in Stockholm and presented to Carl Gustaf Wrangel. Since then it has been preserved in the armoury at Skokloster.

This armoury also contains a large number of swords and guns, the latter mainly for hunting purposes. Among these is a representative collection with locks of the Swedish snaphaunce type, the earliest dating from the end of the sixteenth century. The long, frequently curved, jaws of the cock and the thin, triangular butt are characteristic of this type of gun. Wrangel's personal snaphaunce gun, however, has a silver-mounted butt of the thick German type. There are also Swedish Infantry muskets with the same type of lock – and others with matchlock and wheel lock – used during the Thirty Years War.

Among Wrangel's personal arms are his armour and helmet, which are placed side by side with a contemporary Swedish pikeman's armour, also with the appropriate helmet. His sword is of a type unusual for the period, and has a half hilt, that is to say it lacks a guard on the inside. The silvered iron hilt, therefore, looks as if it had been split vertically. Wrangel's sword is relatively early for this type of hilt and dates from about 1650; later the half hilt became more generally accepted. In Surirey de Saint Rémy's work, *Mémoires d'artillerie*, Paris 1697, the half hilt is referred to in connection with small arms used by the French Navy. Wrangel also commanded the Swedish fleet and his personal loud hailer has been preserved.

The flintlock, an improvement on the Dutch snaphaunce lock,

The Skokloster Shield. Chased steel, borders damascened in gold and silver. Probably made for Erik XIV of Sweden by Eliseus Libaerts. 28 × 19 ins. Antwerp. c. 1560–62

The Skokloster Shield: a detail of the intricate border decorations and the relief motif of bound captives

which was invented in France probably about 1610, began to appear during Wrangel's lifetime. His armoury includes some very early weapons with this mechanism. The earliest would appear to be three French pistols of the period *c.* 1630–40 with butts of chased silver, but almost contemporary are two pairs of pistols from the 1640s, one signed by Jean Dubois of Sedan, the other by Jean Prevot of Metz. There are several pairs of the special type of double-barrelled pistols known in Germany as *Wender*, which have one barrel lying on top of the other (after firing, the barrels twist round so that the loaded one comes uppermost and the one that has been fired drops below); these date from the middle of the seventeenth century and are signed by Claude Roux and Master Cunet, both of Lyons, and by La Pierre of Maastricht. Another pair of double-barrelled flintlock pistols (in this case with the barrels side by side) of the same period is signed by Cornelis Coster of Utrecht. The famous west European pistols with the stock completely of ivory are also represented, one pair being signed by Louroux of Maastricht, *c.* 1660. A pair of English pistols, signed by William Parket of London, are of approximately the same date. These are of a more conventional type and have short barrels. Among a large number of flintlock guns the most notable are those signed by Deverre, Paris *c.* 1670, and David René, Heidelberg *c.* 1660.

The Wrangel Armoury naturally contains a large selection of wheel lock guns and pistols, the most important and interesting bearing the name of Martin Gummi of Kulmbach. He was active about 1620–60, and is represented at Skokloster by some twenty signed guns, the majority of which are dated, some 1648, the year of the Peace of Westphalia. These show Martin Gummi's characteristic arched plate, lying outside the wheel, which is pierced in a pattern of two four-petalled flowers, one on each side above, and a mascaron below. His locks are frequently gilded.

Among many side arms is the sword belonging to Wrangel's wartime comrade, Field-Marshal Count Lennart Torstensson (known as 'Lightning'). The majority of these arms follow the current fashion, but one very distinctive piece is a huge sword of the type known as the Spanish cup-hilted rapier (the guard of which is deep bowl-shaped, while the quillons are straight, long and slender). The total length is 6 ft 4 ins., the length of the slender blade, signed by Meves Berns of Solingen, is 4 ft 10 ins. Its hilt has two grips, one above the other – thus constituting a kind of two-handed rapier. The blade would appear to date from *c.* 1610–20, but the hilt with its extended grips must be about twenty years later. This strange weapon must presumably have been used for some sort of fencing.

As is the case with many old armouries, Wrangel's collection also contains valuable *ethnographica*. A kayak from Greenland, constructed sometime during the first half of the seventeenth century, deserves attention. But in a class by itself is an Indian head ornament which was presented to Wrangel by Johan Printz, Governor of Delaware. This territory was a Swedish colony under the name of New Sweden from 1638 to 1655, and Printz's governorship covered the period from 1643–53. The head ornament is unique both as regards age and type – a wolf's skull with the skin attached.

The combined Brahe-Bielke armoury with its 1,659 pieces is somewhat smaller than Wrangel's. It is also international in character, but the purely Swedish element is more prominent. One of the earliest of the Swedish exhibits is a horse armour from the middle of the sixteenth century, which belonged to Counsellor of State Ture Bielke, whose coat-of-arms is etched on the chanfron – the piece covering the horse's head. Among the guns is a wheel lock gun of German manufacture richly inlaid with silver, which belonged to King Frederick II of Denmark and is dated 1569. Another royal relic is a mid-eighteenth century flintlock gun, which belonged to Louis XV of France and is signed by La Roche of Paris. Another important piece is an air-gun made by Johan Koch of Cologne in 1654. As in the Wrangel Armoury there are Swedish snaphaunce guns, and there is also a good collection of flintlock guns made by the families of gunsmiths, for example, Starbus from Amsterdam, and Bars and Schertiger, both from Germany, who were all active in Sweden during the eighteenth century. That guns with wheel lock were still in use well into the eighteenth century is shown by one of German type, but manufactured in Sweden, and signed by Johan Franz Meidinger in 1751.

The side-arms include an early seventeenth-century sword with a beautifully wrought iron hilt; the blade bears the signature of a well-known Spanish master, DE FRANCISCO RUIZ EN TOLEDO. There is also a rapier of the Spanish, cup-hilted type. Its blade is

Carl Gustaf Wrangel's Turnery in the north tower, with original seventeenth-century lathe and tools

A corner of the Wrangel Armoury. On the left, a Greenland kayak of the early seventeenth century

*Flintlock pistols with
carved ivory stocks.
Maastricht. c. 1660*

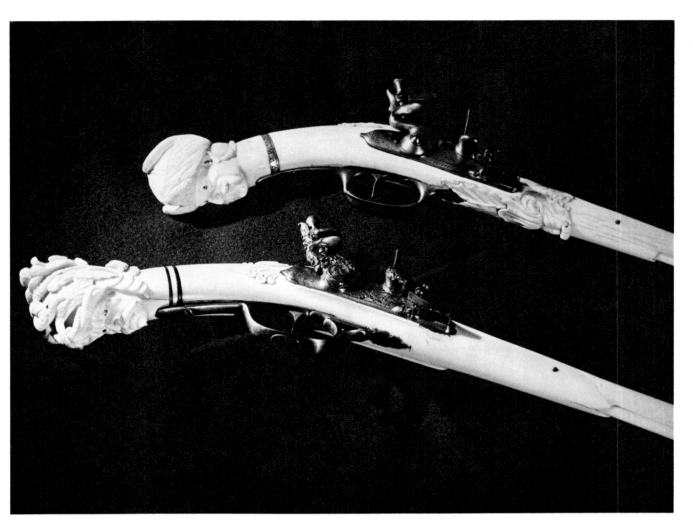

*Flintlock pistol. One of a pair presented by
the Directory to General Bernadotte
on his return from the Italian Campaign in 1797.
Signed Manufacture à Versailles*

4 ft 1 ins. long – even so it is shorter than the one in the Wrangel Armoury. The Bielke family has contributed a fine collection of saddles, including a Hungarian one from the middle of the seventeenth century, which belonged to Field-Marshal Hans Christopher von Königsmarck. Among the saddles from the Brahe Collection there is one, probably dating from the 1640s, which belonged to Queen Christina of Sweden.

The Brahe-Bielke Armoury is particularly rich in pieces with interesting historical associations. There is a small-bladed partisan of the kind used by infantry officers which belonged to Count Nils Nilsson Brahe, Colonel of the Life Guards who was killed at the battle of Lützen in 1632. The uniform – long buff-coat, breastplate – and arms of Colonel Erik Brahe recall an unsuccessful conspiracy in 1756 to strengthen the power of the Swedish crown – young Brahe was afterwards beheaded. There are numerous relics of Swedish participation in the Napoleonic wars, especially of Magnus Brahe, who as a young officer accompanied King Charles XIV John (previously Marshal Bernadotte) on his campaign in Germany in 1813. His horse, Andalouse, which he rode all through the war, has been stuffed and stands in full accoutrements. One of the many testimonies to the close friendship that existed between Magnus Brahe and the king of Sweden is one of a pair of flintlock pistols, presented to the king, then

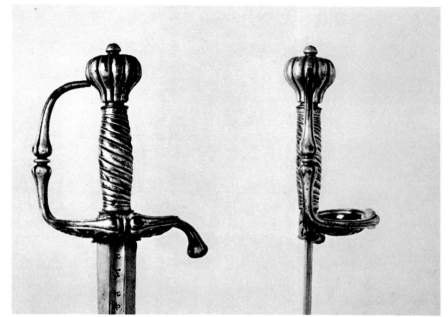

Left *A sword presented by the officers of the Swedish Army to Count Magnus Brahe in 1840*

Below *The hilt of a sword belonging to Carl Gustaf Wrangel. Silvered iron. c. 1650. An early example of the half hilt*

General Bernadotte, by the Directory in Paris on 9th August, 1797, following his great victory during the campaign in Italy. The pistols bear the signature of the famous Manufacture à Versailles, which was directed by Nicolas Boutet. A number of elaborate parade swords of the Empire type, also presented to Magnus Brahe by the king are also included in the collection. These are signed by a well-known Stockholm master, Carl Gustaf Liljedahl.

Finally, we must mention a magnificent sword presented to Magnus Brahe by his fellow officers. It is based on the type which became the regulation sword for the Swedish cavalry in the time of Charles XI and Charles XII. The hilt is of gold, ornamented in relief and set with diamonds, among them, set on the button, a solitaire of impressive purity and size. The grip is bound with silver thread and is decorated in gold and enamel with, on the outside, the Three Crowns of Sweden in a crowned shield, and on the inside the coat-of-arms of the Brahe family. The goldsmith's work is by the Stockholm master, Gustaf Möllenborg, and the etched, blued and gilt decoration of the blade – which includes the monograms of King Charles XIV John and Crown Prince Oscar – is by Liljedahl. The style of the decoration shows the influence of the rococo revival. The sword was presented to Magnus Brahe on Christmas Eve, 1840.   HERIBERT SEITZ

Sword of Field-Marshal Count Lennart Torstensson. Blackened iron inlaid with silver. c. 1675

Countess Wrangel's Bedroom, hung with Brussels tapestries showing Scènes de la Vie du Christ. *Woven in Gouda. c. 1640*

TAPESTRIES AND TEXTILES

There are at Skokloster some fifty tapestries from the sixteenth and seventeenth centuries – the largest privately owned collection in Sweden. The earliest is a verdure woven at Oudenarde in the first half of the sixteenth century; it depicts a wild boar hunt with the quarry half concealed amongst a luxuriant foliage of poppies and mallow plants, curly thistle leaves and large red flowers. The colouring is exquisite and the tapestry is very well preserved.

Two sets of signed Brussels tapestries date from the second half of the sixteenth century. One of them, *Scènes de la Guerre de Troie*, consists of seven tapestries and was executed by Martin Reimbouts. The other, *Scènes de l'histoire de Cyrus et d'Alexandre*, comprises five tapestries, made by three different weavers in Brussels. There is one more sixteenth-century tapestry, *Femmes agenouillées implorant la merci d'Alexandre*. This is unsigned but was probably woven by Jacques de Carmes after a cartoon by Nicholas van Orley. Another set of Brussels tapestries with biblical motifs, *Scènes de la vie du Christ*, comprises eight tapestries. These bear the mark of Gouda, Holland, and were probably woven in about 1640 by T. Schaep. The top border carries the coats-of-arms of the families of Arenfelt and Ulfeldt. These tapestries are made of wool, unlike the others which are of wool and silk (in some cases also with metal thread). A beautiful set of seven unsigned tapestries known as *La chasse anglaise* is of the same date, or a few years later. It was ordered (in Delft?) by Carl Gustaf Wrangel

and carries his and his wife's coats-of-arms in the upper border.

The most magnificent set of tapestries at Skokloster is *L'histoire d'Alexandre*. It consists of six large tapestries, which hang in the three main guest rooms on the second floor. The set was woven in Brussels during the second half of the seventeenth century after cartoons by Charles Le Brun. These tapestries are signed at the bottom by Johannes Franciscus van den Hecke. Charles Le Brun's tapestry designs were published in the form of engravings and the most popular of all was this Alexander set, of which many versions, some better than others, were executed in Brussels, Oudenarde, Antwerp, Aubusson and Felletin. Louis XIV particularly favoured this series, of which he presented sets on various occasions to royal and other personages. The Skokloster set was in fact a gift from the French king to the Swedish Ambassador in Paris, Count Nils Bielke.

Tapestries being a rich form of wall-covering were reserved for the most important living and guest rooms. In other rooms the walls were covered with gilt leather or with so-called French woven wool hangings, while the lesser rooms were painted with whitewash applied directly onto the plaster. The embossed leather wall-hangings are preserved in a few rooms. The ground colour is silver or gold and the ornamentation is picked out in one or more bright, clear colours. The 'French hangings' are woven in a striped pattern, for example a grey or brown ground colour with red, white and blue, or blue, white, green and yellow stripes. Most of these were woven after French originals at Carl Gustaf Wrangel's Pomeranian residence, Wrangelsburg. Some of a simpler type were made in Sweden, for example the so-called Västgöta tapestries (the province of Västergötland in south-west Sweden had long been a textile centre). None of the rooms at Skokloster still have their complete wall-hangings, but here and there – underneath a tapestry, or behind a bed – one may come upon fragments of either the French originals, or of the copies woven at Wrangelsburg. In the Textile Room fragments of woven carpets, furnishing materials, and oriental textiles have been specially preserved. Naturally changes have been made in the furniture, textiles and tapestries at Skokloster over the centuries and they have been moved many times. Some of the seventeenth-century furnishings were removed during the eighteenth century and replaced by more up-to-date articles. But thanks to some inventories of the late seventeenth and early eighteenth centuries which have survived, we know more or less what the furnishings looked like at that time.

It is possible to form a pretty clear idea of the furnishings at Skokloster during Wrangel's lifetime from an inventory dated 1672. There were then, for example, about 250 chairs in the whole palace – an average of five to each living room. The finest chairs were covered in gilt leather, decorated with flowers in brilliant colours against a black background, or green vine-trails against a silver ground. There were two dozen such chairs, and most of them are still there today. There were also the same number of chairs covered in the striped tapestry cloth that was woven at Wrangelsburg, but these also had a protective covering of flowered material.

A tent captured in Poland by Field-Marshal Herman Wrangel during the Thirty Years War. White linen with appliqué borders. Dated 1633

At the beginning of the eighteenth century the fashion was to cover sofas and chairs in petit-point in Bérain designs with flower or vase motifs, sometimes inspired by the popular East Indian porcelain. One set of sofa and chairs at Skokloster is covered in Chinese-style embroideries in many-coloured silk and red wool, executed in Hungarian stitch. And in the Kings' Hall (the Wrangel dining-room), there is now a group of chairs with seats and backs covered in petit-point. These embroideries were probably the work of Countess Eva Catharina Sack (died 1753), wife of the second tenant in tail of Skokloster, Colonel Erik Brahe.

The Skokloster Collection contains sixteen old oriental rugs, twelve of which are mentioned in the 1672 inventory. In this they are referred to as 'Turkish table coverings', for here as elsewhere these rugs were used in the seventeenth century as table coverings. It was only towards the end of the eighteenth century that Skokloster eventually adopted the new fashion of laying these rugs on the floor. The most remarkable of the oriental rugs at Skokloster are two so-called 'Polish rugs'. As Fredrik Martin has shown, these 'Polish rugs' are, so far as can be judged, a group of central Persian rugs which were made in the province of Feraghan in the first half of the seventeenth century. They were intended for the Persian court at Isfahan and were also used as ambassadorial gifts to foreign princes. In 1604 Shah Abbas I sent one of these rugs to the Doge of Venice, and the so-called Coronation Carpet and four smaller rugs at Rosenborg Palace in Copenhagen were a gift from Shah Safi I in 1639 to Count Fredrik of Holstein-Gottorp. These rugs are justifiably regarded as among the finest products of the Persian textile art. They are knotted in silk on a background run with gold and silver threads, which gives the rugs their special lustre. The misleading term 'Polish rugs' arose after the Paris Exhibition of 1878, when a Polish nobleman, Prince Czartoryski, exhibited some of these rugs, onto which his own coat-of-arms had been embroidered.

On the top floor of the palace there is a special costume room, in which nineteen suits of men's clothing and uniforms belonging to members of the families which owned Skokloster are preserved in glass cases. Here may be seen a jacket worn by Count Nils Brahe when he was mortally wounded at the Battle of Lützen on 6th November, 1632. In the large hall on the second floor there are also four seventeenth-century officers' tents decorated with elaborate appliqué work.

The collection at Skokloster presents a unique history of the development of the textile arts during the seventeenth and eighteenth centuries.

EVA BERGMAN

The Counts Harrach

Robert Keysselitz

Of the great Austrian collections of the past, only the Harrach Collection still remains in the possession of the family. It was chiefly assembled between 1670 and 1780 and consists, in great part, of paintings (often by contemporary artists) brought back by four successive generations of Counts Harrach from Spain, Italy and the Netherlands, countries in which they carried out official missions on behalf of the Emperor. The first collector, Count Ferdinand Bonaventura (1636–1706), spent many years between 1667 and 1700 in Madrid, where he was a friend and patron of both Juan Carreño and Luca Giordano. His taste also extended, however, beyond artists of the contemporary Spanish School to Ambrosius Benson, Van Dyck, Rubens, Tintoretto and Ribera. His son, Count Aloys Thomas (1669–1742), was Viceroy of the Kingdom of Naples (1728–34), where he acquired works by Solimena, Cavallino, Preti, Stanzione and Salvator Rosa. Count Friedrich August (1696–1749), son of Count Aloys, served the Stadtholder of the Netherlands, and he returned with works by seventeenth-century masters like Ruysdael and Terbruggen. Then came Count Ernst Guido (1723–83) who, in line with the classicising taste of his day, added to the collection works by contemporary artists working in Rome such as Pannini, Batoni, Mengs, Vernet and Carlo Bonaria. Later Counts Harrach have added paintings by early German masters and Italian painters of the Renaissance, as well as further works by Flemish and Dutch artists of the seventeenth century.

The Counts Harrach

Robert Keysselitz

On 14th September, 1697 Ferdinand Bonaventura, Count von Harrach, bought at an auction in Madrid a picture 'of unknown authorship' of 'three women, one playing the flute, and two singing'. This is now one of the pearls of the Harrach picture collection and is called *The Concert* by the Master of the Half-Lengths, a name invented by Scheibler in 1887 for this anonymous master. We know that he must have been active *c.* 1540 and after much art historical debate it seems probable that he was the Bruges painter Hans Veryecke (active 1530–60).

An aura of mystery hangs over this picture of the three porcelain-like ladies making music and singing a sad song about youth by Clement Marot. Can they be Camilla, Lucretia and Diana, daughters of Jean Morel, in whose house the earliest of the Parisian literary salons met in the first half of the sixteenth century? Morel's daughters were celebrated by all the poets of the time as the 'three pearls', and compared with the Muses for their

skill in singing. But whatever significance beyond its high artistic quality the painting may have had for Count Ferdinand Bonaventura, he surely never anticipated that two hundred and fifty years later, this and the innumerable other paintings and objets d'art which he acquired would be the only surviving evidence of his activities.

The picture gallery of the Counts Harrach is the last of the great Austrian private collections to remain in family ownership and is a living reminder of the magnificent tradition of collecting under the Austro-Hungarian monarchy. It has been open to the public since the middle of the nineteenth century, although the contents of the private rooms, both in Vienna and at Schloss Prugg (at Bruck on the Leitha) have remained little known and for the most part unpublished.

The history of the collection is the history of the family, which in its turn is reflected in the history of the Habsburg Empire. The

Schloss Prugg at Bruck on the Leitha. Owned by the Harrach family since 1564, rebuilt by Hildebrandt in the eighteenth century, and altered in 1845. The tower on the left is all that remains of the medieval castle

The picture gallery in the Palais Harrach, Vienna

PORTRAIT OF COUNT FERDINAND BONAVENTURA HARRACH
Hyacinthe Rigaud (1659–1743) oil on canvas 36 × 28¾ ins. 1698.
The originator of the family collection

ERNST ADALBERT BARON VON HARRACH, ARCHBISHOP OF
PRAGUE, AND LATER CARDINAL, BEING RECEIVED BY
POPE PAUL VI *Pietro da Cortona (1596–1669) oil on canvas*
67 × 67½ ins. 1620

story of the family begins in 1165 with Thomas Harrach, who is recorded as taking part in a tournament that year in Zürich. The line has remained unbroken since 1338. The title-page of a fourteenth-century Missal, which belonged to Hans Harracher shows a genealogical tree with miniatures of his ancestors.

The Harrach family is said to have come from Bavaria to Upper Austria, where it is mentioned in documents of about 1300. Later, in 1524, Leonhard III acquired the castle and demesne of Rohrau near Bruck on the Leitha; and in the same year the Archduke Maximilian conferred on him the right to style himself 'von Rohrau', to create knights 'as if he was born a Prince of the House of Austria', and to seal with red wax. In 1552 Leonhard IV and all his heirs, were raised to the rank of Barons of the Empire, and in 1560 he became high-steward and high-chamberlain to the Emperor Maximilian. On July 15th of the same year Muso, the Papal Nuncio, preaching in the church of the Augustinians in Vienna, urged the Emperor to re-open the Council of Trent. The painting of this historic scene, by Jacob Seisenegger (1506–67) was acquired by the Harrachs and became the cornerstone of a collection which was only seriously begun a hundred years later.

The great period of the family began with Karl Harrach, who, on 25th August, 1625, was raised to the rank of hereditary Count of the Palatinate. In 1623 his daughter Isabella Katherina had married Wallenstein, then a forty-year-old widower, in the presence of the Emperor Ferdinand II. Karl's son, Ernst Adalbert, Archbishop of Prague, crowned Ferdinand II, Ferdinand IV and Leopold I as Kings of Bohemia. The painting by Pietro da Cortona, which shows the Austrian ambassador presenting Cardinal Ernst Adalbert Harrach, before his ordination, to Pope Paul V and the College of Cardinals in 1620, came into the collection in the nineteenth century, and is said to have belonged to the Duke of Gesso in Naples.

On July 25th, 1636, Cardinal Ernst Adalbert baptised his nephew Ferdinand Bonaventura, the son of Count Otto Harrach and Countess Lavinia Gonzaga, in St Wenzel's chapel on the Hradschin in Prague. The Emperor Ferdinand II was the godfather. The tradition of art patronage and collecting of the Counts Harrach began with Ferdinand Bonaventura, and his descendants have lived up to their responsibilities generation after generation, though it has sometimes been impossible for them to do more than preserve what was already there.

Opposite THE PAPAL NUNCIO CORNELIUS MUSSO
PREACHING AT THE CHURCH OF THE AUGUSTINIANS, VIENNA
Jacob Seisenegger (1505–67) panel 28 × 19 ins. Signed and dated 1561.
The first great acquisition by the Harrach family

PORTRAIT OF CHARLES II OF SPAIN IN
THE REGALIA OF THE GOLDEN FLEECE
*Juan Carreño de Miranda (1614–85) oil on
canvas 85½ × 55½ ins. 1677. Given to Count
Ferdinand Bonaventura while he was Imperial
Ambassador in Madrid by the King of Spain*

Opposite THE CONCERT
*Master of the Half-Lengths (active c. 1530)
panel 23½ × 20¾ ins. c. 1530*

Count Ferdinand Bonaventura was an eminent seventeenth-century statesman. In 1661 he married in Madrid Johanna Theresia, Countess of Lamberg, maid-of-honour to Queen Anna. Four years later, at the age of 29, he was back in Madrid as Imperial envoy charged with presenting gifts from her suitor, Leopold I, to the Infanta Margarita. From 1667 to 1675 he was ambassador in Madrid and two years later was sent back there charged with a special mission to persuade the Spanish king to raise an army of twenty-five thousand men in Belgium and to give financial aid against the French invasion of the Rhineland. In 1697 we find the Count in Madrid for the last time, his third son, Aloys Thomas Raimund, being by then ambassador. On this last occasion, his mission was to persuade the weak and childless Charles II to make a will in favour of the Austrian branch of the Habsburgs; but owing to French intrigues he achieved nothing and returned to Vienna empty-handed. The War of the Spanish Succession was imminent.

So much for the historical position and political activity of Count Ferdinand Bonaventura, who died on 17th June, 1706. While he was in Spain he kept a detailed diary, which is not only the chief source of our knowledge about his political mission, but also records the artistic taste and collecting activities of the court, as well as minute details of court life. Like most collections made before the nineteenth century, or like the Guggenheim Collection and the various museums of modern art to-day, the collection of late Baroque art which he made was, in its time, a modern one. The idea of escaping from the present into the past through works of art of earlier periods was an idea that nineteenth-century collectors derived from the Romantics.

While Count Ferdinand Bonaventura's sons and grandsons were influenced primarily by what was in fashion at court, he himself, apart from falling in with the taste current in his period, followed no specific line in his collecting activities. He acquired whatever appealed to him, that is to say not only valuable paintings, but things written by saints, including a prayer by St Theresa, and he is even said to have owned a magic girdle. However, only the paintings have survived. Unlike his successors, the Count did not employ an agent to build up a more comprehensive collection for him. He went to see the painters of his day in person, and frequently visited dealers and auctions, as many collectors do to-day. But of course he did not regard his collecting as a financially profitable activity and certainly never thought of building up his collection systematically.

Among the paintings which the Count bought at auctions, besides the major work by the Master of the Half-Lengths, are the diptych of the *Annunciation* and *Visitation* by Ambrosius Benson (active 1519–50), the *Head of a Boy* by Anthony van Dyck (1599–1641) (Ein Kopf Schizo Original von van Deik), and *Soldiers in a*

Farmhouse by Willem van Herp (1614–77), one of the rare fully signed pictures by this master. The fact that the Count was able to attend public auctions in person and make such purchases throws an interesting side-light on the social life of the time. A generation later it would hardly have been possible for an Imperial ambassador to be seen at such a gathering.

What primarily interested the Count was the artistic life of his own day, and he was delighted to be shown round the Spanish royal palaces by Juan Carreño de Miranda (1614–85) who had succeeded Velasquez as Court Painter. He was fascinated to see, in 1674, works by 'del Bosco' (Hieronymus Bosch), who had been such a favourite of Philip IV's and had 'painted so many marvellous caprices'. And he followed up this discovery by acquiring for three doubloons a *Christ in Limbo* by a follower of Bosch.

Knowing the passionate collecting instincts of the Emperor's special envoy, the Spanish King and Queen presented him with portraits of themselves by Carreño as a parting gift in 1677. However, the pictures were not finished in time, and the painter himself had to follow the ambassador to the village of Mandes near Madrid, in order to hand them over. The Count showed his gratitude by presenting him with a golden chain, imperial medals, and a filigree bowl. The two portraits are not only technically speaking among the finest of the artist's works, but in particular the *Portrait of Charles II in the Regalia of the Golden Fleece* is by far the best likeness of the king.

The ambassador's taste is characterized by his unqualified preference (as shown in this collection) for works by van Dyck, Rubens, Tintoretto, Breughel and Ribera, over those by such painters as Titian, Raphael and Parmigianino. The people of Lorraine, aware of his particular love of Ribera, bought an *Immaculate Conception* (signed and dated 1637) by this artist in 1676, and presented it to the Count in gratitude for his protection. The picture once hung in the chapel of his palace in Vienna, but to-day it is in the Gallery. In 1676 the Count also acquired Ribera's *St Joseph with the Flowering Staff* (signed and dated 1644).

In 1692 the leading Neapolitan painter, Luca Giordano (1632–1705) was summoned by Charles II to Spain. We cannot be quite certain which of the twelve pictures by this master now in the Harrach Collection were originally acquired by Count Ferdinand. But there is an important entry in his diary for 18th August, 1697, where he recorded that he found the pictures the artist had painted in Naples superior to those he was doing in Spain. Giordano had apparently discovered that in Spain 'the art of painting is very little understood' and they only appreciated bright colours. Consequently, he painted very rapidly and never really finished a picture. The Giordanos on view in the Harrach gallery in Vienna illustrate the extraordinary diversity

IMMACULATE CONCEPTION *José Ribera (1591–1652) oil on canvas 98 × 65¾ ins. Signed and dated 1637. A gift to Count Ferdinand Bonaventura from the people of Lorraine*

Opposite PORTRAIT OF COUNT ALOYS THOMAS RAIMUND HARRACH, VICEROY OF NAPLES *Francesco Solimena (1657–1747) oil on canvas 13¾ × 10⅝ ins. c. 1726. A sketch for a lost work*

ISAAC BLESSING JACOB *Luca Giordano*
(1632–1705) oil on canvas 55¼ × 73¼ ins.
c. 1650

STILL LIFE WITH LOAVES *Francisco de*
Palacios (1640–76) oil on canvas 23¾ × 31½ ins.
Signed and dated 1648

and adaptability of the master, qualities which his father had not been slow to exploit when he was a young man. Giordano had a natural talent for making deceptively good imitations of other famous painters, and many of his youthful efforts were sold by his father as genuine works by Ribera and others.

The ambassador's diary is of major importance not only for the history of the Harrach Collection but also as an art-historical source document because it gives the names of the artists who painted certain pictures, thus providing us with a sure guide for identifying further works by these same artists. Examples of this are the *Christ in the Tomb worshipped by Angels*, by José de Ledesma (1630?–70), an important but very little known pupil of Carreño, and *St Catherine of Cordoba*, by Juan de Alfaros (1640–80). Then there are two outstanding still lifes dated 1648, by the almost unknown Francisco de Palacios (active 1640–76), to whom very few other works can be attributed. They have something of the magic of Chardin – although painted a hundred years earlier – and may be considered among the finest of all Spanish still-life paintings.

It is known from literary sources that the Spanish court-painters produced numerous miniatures. Fortunately several of these are preserved in the Harrach Collection, having been included among the many gifts the ambassador received from the royal family. They are all painted on copper, but have unfortunately lost their original frames. The most important are the portrait of Philip IV's daughter, Margarita Teresa, very probably by Claudio Coello (died 1693), and the portrait of Maria Anna of Austria as a girl, by Velasquez's son-in-law, Juan Baptista Martinez Mazo.

Beginning with occasional purchases, Count Ferdinand Bonaventura developed in time a real passion for art collecting. He took as his ideal and example the collection of the Archduke Leopold Wilhelm, the appearance of whose gallery he knew through a copy of the picture by Teniers which he either bought or perhaps commissioned specially.

From 1689 until 1703 Domenico Martinelli was supervising, on the Count's orders, the building of a palace on the Freyung in Vienna, which has remained in the family's possession until today, though it was considerably altered between 1845 and 1859. The roof was raised and a skylight added to make room for the gallery, and what was to all intents and purposes a second façade was added over the original, with columns and balconies in contemporary taste. Most of these modifications were removed in the rebuilding which followed the severe bomb damage the building suffered in 1944, so that the palace has been restored more or less to its original appearance. Of the original interior decoration little survives except the staircase and the private chapel, both noteworthy in their way, as well as a frescoed ceiling in one salon with an allegory on the Harrach crest, which consists of a golden ball and three ostrich feathers. In this fresco, Minerva is plucking the ostrich feathers from the plume of her helmet; Hercules is offering one of the golden apples of the Hesperides while Jupiter proffers the Count's coronet. This central panel is flanked by two other allegories; one representing the arts and sciences, the other military glory.

In 1728 the Ambassador's third son, Count Aloys Thomas Raimund (1669–1742), was appointed Viceroy of the Kingdom of Naples which had been annexed to the Empire by the Treaty of Utrecht (1713). During the five years in which he served in this important post, Count Aloys reorganized the chaotic finances of Naples and raised trade and industry to new levels of prosperity. We can discover all we want to know about the Viceroy's style of living from three colossal paintings by Nicolo Maria Rossi, a pupil of Solimena, which now hang on the staircase wall of the Harrach palace in Vienna. They represent *Funzioni Pubbliche* of the Viceroy: his departure from the Royal Palace, a solemn procession over the Chiaia to the pilgrimage church at Piedigrotta, and his benediction at the altar on Corpus Christi Day. The Viceroy appears to have lived in a manner befitting a great lord, and the splendours of his court almost equalled those of the Emperor himself. There was no longer any question of continuing his father's custom of visiting auction rooms and dealers to buy pictures, most of which, for obvious reasons, had had to be rather small. The Viceroy needed enormous canvases to give the right sort of atmosphere in his numerous palaces. The best painters in the kingdom worked for him, at their head being Francesco Solimena (1657–1747), who had taken Giordano's place as leader of the Neapolitan School.

This School is better represented in the Harrach Gallery than anywhere else outside Naples, for it contains two masterpieces by Bernardo Cavallino (1616–56), *Solomon and the Queen of Sheba*, and the *Murder of Amnon* – fine examples of his late style – and, among many pictures by Solimena, a *St Januarius* which is one of his most outstanding works. The Viceroy commissioned this picture soon after his arrival, when he visited Solimena to thank him on behalf of Prince Eugene for the *Deposition* now in the Kunsthistorisches Museum in Vienna. The *St Januarius* was probably intended for the chapel of the Count's Summer Palace in the Ungargasse in Vienna. In fact a curious exchange of saints took place, for while the Neapolitan patron Saint was brought to Vienna, the Viceroy's wife, Ernestine, Princess Dietrichstein, erected a statue to St John Nepomuk, patron Saint of Bohemia, in the middle of the Ponte della Maddalena in Naples.

Like his father, the Viceroy also received many pictures as presents, and an interesting light is cast on the customs of the day by the story connected with the *Solomon and the Queen of*

MARGARITA THERESA, DAUGHTER OF PHILIP·IV OF SPAIN
*Claudio Coello (d. 1693)
oil on copper 2¼ × 2 ins. c. 1650*

ST JANUARIUS VISITED IN PRISON BY ST PROCULUS AND ST SOSIUS *Francesco Solimena (1657–1747) oil on canvas 50 × 40 ins. 1728. Commissioned by Count Aloys Thomas for the Chapel of St Januarius in his summer palace in Vienna*

Sheba by Mattia Preti (1613–99). This picture belonged to a man called Giordano – whether or not he was related to the painter is unknown – who through his ability and his good connections had been made Duca di Monte Accolici. When the Viceroy called on the new Duke in his splendid palace he admired the picture, and the Duke immediately made him a present of it, together with another and now untraceable painting by Vaccaro. Overcome by the munificence of this gift, the Viceroy hastened to repay it with a purse containing a hundred gold doubloons, whereupon the Duke felt himself obliged to send yet another picture – a *St Jerome*.

Unfortunately, nothing is now known about the history of the five pictures by the mysterious Monsù Desiderio which figure in the collection. This painter's real name was François Nomé; he was born in 1593, and his last known works are dated 1644. He has only recently been rediscovered, and is now highly prized for his surrealist qualities. It would be foolish to believe that the Viceroy bought these works because he foresaw the future fame of their fantastic and dreamlike visions, particularly since they had nothing in common with the taste of his own times. It is much more likely that they were presents, or were bought, together with other pictures, for small sums. One very interesting point that came to light during their restoration is that the ones dated 1622, containing extraordinary architecture against a lowering, cloud-filled sky, were completely falsified early in the eighteenth century by being skilfully overpainted. In every case, the stormy sky was transformed into a pale blue cloudy one, so that they became much less sinister. This may have been done to make them more attractive to buyers, in exactly the same way that in pictures of Salome the head of St John the Baptist on a charger was often transformed into a dish of fruit.

At the end of the Viceroy's term of office his pictures were sent back to Vienna, and a long inventory made at that time shows that Count Aloys Thomas had acquired in Naples alone a greater number than were collected by the Ambassador Count Bonaventura during his entire lifetime. Among the pictures mentioned in the inventory are Stanzione's dramatic *Massacre of the Innocents*, and an early *Lucretia* by Vaccaro. The large animal pieces by Domenico Brandi (1684–1736), one of Giordano's little-known pupils who is well represented only in the Harrach Gallery, are all furniture pieces, but of much higher quality than is usual in such works, and, in fact, in their subtlety and accomplishment they not only recall the better known Rosa da Tivoli, but actually surpass him. The enormous *Martyrdom of St Bartholomew* by Salvator Rosa (1615–73), who was principally regarded as a landscape painter during the seventeenth century, is a masterpiece done at the time when he was strongly influenced by Ribera. The inventory lists numerous works by Giordano and

ARCHITECTURAL FANTASY WITH THE
HEALING OF THE MAN SICK OF THE PALSY
*Monsù Desiderio (1593–1644) oil on canvas 35 × 27¾ ins.
1622*

THE MURDER OF AMNON
Bernardo Cavallino
(1616–56) oil on canvas
40½ × 52⅜ ins. c. 1650

SOLOMON AND THE
QUEEN OF SHEBA
Mattia Preti (1613–99)
oil on canvas 114 × 128 ins.
c. 1650

ST SEBASTIAN *Jan van Bylert* (*1603–71*) *oil
on canvas* 44½ × 39½ *ins. Signed and dated 1624*

Solimena, including one great rarity in the latter's small sketch portrait of the Viceroy, made for a lost large-scale work. The sitter's elegance of bearing is heightened by the daring colour scheme in which blue, red, and a brilliant yellow predominate, and the inimitable bravura of handling gives this little portrait, although it is only a sketch, as much impact as a large-scale ceremonial work.

Count Aloys Thomas not only continued the collecting tradition of his father, he was also the greatest builder in the family, for he commissioned Lucas von Hildebrandt, the most outstanding architect of the day, to build his numerous country houses. Only the drawings by Salomon Kleiner survive to give an idea of the splendour of the former Summer Palace in the Ungargasse in Vienna. Schloss Aschach on the Danube, the Hunting Lodge at Halbthurn, rebuilt after the Turks destroyed it in 1701, and the church at Georgswalde in Northern Bohemia no longer belong to the family. Apart from Rohrau, only Schloss Prugg at Bruck on the Leitha is still owned by the Harrach family, who have lived there since 1564. The old Schloss was rebuilt and enlarged by Hildebrandt, but unfortunately it was again much enlarged and altered in 1845, though the interior still retains many of the Baroque furnishings.

The Viceroy's eldest son was Count Friedrich August Gervas (1696–1749), high-steward to the Archduchess and Stadtholder Maria Elizabeth in Brussels and, after her death, Stadtholder until the arrival of the new Regent, Marianne. As a collector, his additions to the family treasures are less unified than those of his father or grandfather, although like them he collected the work of artists of the countries where his diplomatic career took him. Thus the gallery owes to him a small but carefully chosen collection of Dutch and Flemish masters, some of whose works Count Bonaventura had already begun to acquire when he was in Spain, and others were added in the course of the nineteenth century.

Van Dyck's *Lamentation*, Jan Breughel's studies of negro heads, a *Portrait of a Lady* by Cornelis Vos (1585–1651) were the Flemish pictures, and the Dutch ones included a *Rocky Landscape* by Everdingen (1621–75) and the *River Landscape* by Jacob Ruisdael (1628/9–82). But by far the most interesting is a group of Dutch works showing strong Italian influence, of which the *St Sebastian* by Jan van Bylert (1603–71), and the *Mater Dolorosa* by Terbruggen (1588–1629) are the most typical. He also acquired a series of battle scenes by Pieter Snyers (1592–1667) which are very important for the history of warfare because of their topographical accuracy; these pictures, which included a *Relief of Pressburg* and *Bethlen Gabor's Troops Marching on Vienna in October 1619*, had belonged to General Karl Emanuel, Count Bouguoy-Longueval, who married the Viceroy's sister in 1700.

ROMAN RUINS *Gian Paolo Panini (1691/92–1765) oil on canvas 40 × 53 ins. 1751*

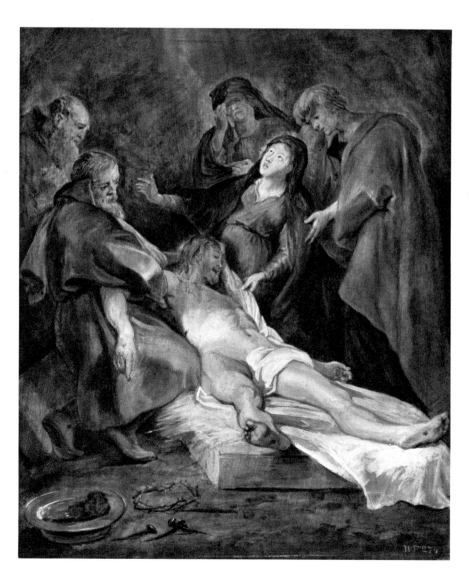

THE DESCENT FROM THE CROSS *Van Dyck panel 24½ × 19 ins. c. 1620*

GREAT ARCHED ROCK
Carlo Bonaria (1730–80)
oil on canvas 21 × 33½ ins.
c. 1755

SEAPORT AT SUNSET
Claude Joseph Vernet (1714–89)
oil on canvas 38¼ × 53½ ins.
Signed and dated 1751

Count Friedrich August brought not only pictures from Brussels but also a valuable series of tapestries woven by Jan van der Borcht from designs by Ludwig van Schoor. These are mythological scenes such as the *Triumph of Bacchus and Ariadne, Flora crowned by Amor and Zephyr*, and *Venus and Adonis*, and their exceptional condition and unimpaired luminosity make them the outstanding feature of the saloon at Prugg. A similar series, formerly in the Imperial collection, now hangs in the Kunsthistorisches Museum in Vienna. This interest in the Netherlandish masters was, however, only an interlude in the development of the Harrach Collection, for later generations once again turned to the art of the south. The era of the systematic study of art was beginning; classical ruins were being re-discovered, Pompeii and Herculaneum excavated. Winckelmann (1717–68), whose theories were derived from the study of ancient art, and who demanded that modern art should be based on classical prototypes, dominated for many years the history of creative art.

Count Ernst Guido (1723–83), grandson of the Viceroy, was a contemporary of Winckelmann. By now, the period of independent collecting and of personal contact with artists was over, to be replaced by the age of agents and dealers, at first mainly members of the lower clergy, who guided aristocratic travellers round Rome, and gave learned lectures on the antiquities. It was they, too, who got in touch with artists and advised collectors on their purchases. Count Ernst Guido's agent was the Abbé Dionigio Crivelli, who wrote him pious and often confidential letters in which he rarely omitted to ask some favour, such as, for example, the revenues of some Hungarian bishoprics that came under the jurisdiction of Harrach bishops. But, despite his eye for personal advantage, Crivelli took his activities seriously, and advised his patron with considerable taste and knowledge. In 1751, he ordered for 120 scudi two pictures of Roman ruins from Gian Paolo Pannini (1691–1755); these were not the usual topographical views, but were *capricci* composed, according to the taste of the day, from various classical buildings scattered over the city, such as the Pantheon and the Arch of Constantine. Crivelli reported despairingly about progress on the pictures he had ordered from Claude Joseph Vernet (1714–89), during one of the painter's visits to Italy. The *Seaport at Sunset* had been begun, and, what was even more important, paid for, when the painter suddenly left for Avignon. He might die there, the unfortunate Abbé complained, but in fact Vernet completed the picture there, and painted several more for the Count on his return to Rome. Later, however, Vernet excused himself from undertaking any more commissions, as he was overburdened with work for his King, Louis XV, and recommended as a substitute his pupil Carlo Bonaria (1730–80), who asked for a visit to the coast to be arranged, so that he could make studies from

nature for the sea-pieces that had been ordered. The Austrian envoy, Count Firmian, invited him to stay at his seaside villa, which is probably the one that appears in the *Villa by the Sea*. Another of Bonaria's works, the *Great Arched Rock*, so delighted the Countess when it arrived in Vienna that she immediately had it hung in her own apartment. Where Vernet sought to combine fantasy with topographical details, his pupil, like a kind of Neapolitan Bellotto, took infinite pains to achieve a precise representation of nature. From correspondence, as well as from the signature on the *Villa by the Sea*, it is clear that the painter's name was Bonaria, and not Bonavia, as Italian art-historians have generally assumed. An affection for Naples which dated from the Viceroy's residence there probably accounted for two views ordered from Adrien Manglard (1695–1760) in 1750, and the tradition was continued into the nineteenth century with Giacinto Giganti's charming views of Naples and the Temple at Paestum.

Presumably, the Abbé Crivelli was dissatisfied with the composition of the first version of *Susanna and the Elders* by Pompeo Girolamo Batoni (1708–87), since he obliged the painter to modify it, and to repaint it almost entirely, before it was despatched to Vienna on 4th December, 1752. The Count, however, was delighted with it, and willingly paid 160 scudi for the picture, which is one of the best things the painter ever did.

Vernet was not the busy agent's only worry; Anton Raphael Mengs (1728–79), the most important and admired artist of the day, seems to have caused him particular anxiety. Crivelli had been able to take advantage of the painter's temporary financial embarrassment to commission a *Nativity* for a mere 70 scudi, but progress on the work slowed down when Mengs was commissioned to copy Raphael's *School of Athens* for no less a sum than 2,050 scudi. Crivelli lamented over the size of the fee, comparing it with the 800 scudi which was all that Annibale Carracci himself had received for the decoration of the whole of the Farnese Gallery, and when he complained to Mengs over the delay in completing the work, the painter very nearly threw the earnest money of 50 scudi back at him, declaring that he was only painting the picture out of friendship, since he could easily have had far more for it even in its unfinished state. But when at last it was completed, the Abbé's room was crowded with people who came to see it as if on an artistic pilgrimage – 'una processione esigente per vederlo'. Cardinal Albani came twice, and Batoni, who was by no means a friend of Mengs, praised the picture to the skies. Eventually the picture travelled to Vienna, with precise instructions as to how the packing-case was to be opened; for weeks the unhappy agent remained in suspense, until at last he received from his client an expression of 'piena soddisfazione'.

Count Ernst Guido's purchases were the last involving work

by contemporary artists. Admittedly, as members of numerous commissions and societies for the encouragement of art, the Counts Harrach have occasionally acquired individual works by living artists, but these are no longer incorporated into the permanent collection.

Count Johann Nepomuk Ernst, Ernst Guido's son, increased the collection by the purchase of some two hundred pictures. Though Crivelli had always taken great pains to give his client the best possible advice, his successors were much less reliable. The art-market now became the chief source for acquisitions, and the trade in antiquities was just beginning. The great masters of the Quattrocento were rediscovered, and collecting on an historical basis became the fashion. Certainly in Vienna, centre of the Nazarene movement, a gallery without a Raphael, a Perugino, or a Ghirlandaio was unthinkable, and with the desire for paintings of this kind opened the era of hopes and disappointments that have been the collector's lot until our own day.

The dealer Goldmann offered the Count a Correggio, authenticated by the great experts of the time, and he bought it for 3,000 gulden. This treasure was carefully preserved, but a later cleaning has revealed it as one of the many copies of the *Ecce Homo* in the National Gallery in London.

But the disappointments were not always so bitter, and discoveries and strokes of good fortune were not uncommon. The *St Jerome*, bought in 1826 as a Francesco Caroto is, in fact, a magnificent Bernardino Luini (1480–1532) in exceptionally fine condition; the *Nativity*, by Ghirlandaio's brother-in-law Sebastiano Mainardi (1460–1513), a composition which is repeated in a fresco at Brozzi, near Florence, has all the charm of Ghirlandaio's immediate following. The *Nativity with St Paul and St John the Baptist*, bought as a Palma Vecchio and then given to Niccolo dell'Abbate, is now attributed to a Neapolitan master, possibly Giovanni Filippo Criscuolo (*c.* 1500–84), so that a work of the first half of the sixteenth century was inadvertently added to the group of High Baroque pictures.

Not only were early Italian pictures acquired, but the collection of Netherlandish works was also extended and developed. These additions included the great hunting scene by Frans Snyders (1592–1667), and the *Sack* by David Ryckaert III (1612–61). Some pictures were acquired by exchange, and others paid for in linen and yarn, since the family owned a linen mill at the time. For example, the *Madonna and Child with SS Rosalia and Catherine*, by a follower of Perugino and a variant of the picture in the Louvre, was acquired in this way. The Count sought to

Left PORTRAIT OF GEORG HÖRMANN *Christoph Amberger (1500–61/62) panel 39 × 30¼ ins. 1530*

NATIVITY *Anton Raphael Mengs (1728–79)*
oil on copper 26¼ × 19 ins. 1774

Opposite *Faience plate decorated with the Harrach
arms, one of a service ordered by Count Ferdinand
Bonaventura. Marked APK (Adrianus Pieter Kocks).
Delft 1701–03*

extend and balance his collection according to the new art-historical ideas by also buying early German pictures, of which the most important is the *Portrait of Georg Hörmann* by Amberger (1500–61/2), which came with others from the Thurn-Hoffer Collection.

About the middle of the nineteenth century the present galleries were laid out in the palace on the Freyung, as part of the rebuilding mentioned earlier, and the top lighting is still adequate for all the needs of a gallery. The Harrach Collection of pictures was then brought together as the Harrach Picture Gallery, and opened to the public. The first Director was the painter Anton Gruss, author of the first printed catalogue issued in 1856, and the collection was first treated critically in Waagen's *Die vornehmsten Kunstdenkmäler in Wien, I, 1866*. The gallery has been rearranged and enlarged several times, chiefly in 1903, when many pictures from the Harrach castles were added to it. At that time the walls were covered with pictures right up to the ceiling; frame jostled against frame and quality was swamped in quantity, so that the general impression was one of a giant stamp-collection.

Then came the chaos of two world wars. The fall of the monarchy ended the political importance of the Austrian nobility, who retired to their castles and estates to live as wealthy private citizens, dreaming dreams of past greatness, until the Second World War ended even this. The material losses were on a huge scale; the greater part of the Harrach fortune in Bohemia was lost, and the works of art that remained in Schloss Hradek near Hradec Kralove (Koniggrätz) could not be recovered. The contents of this castle consisted of a unique collection of very valuable Renaissance furniture, and rare examples of early craftsmanship. The severe bomb damage to the Vienna palace in 1944 fortunately did not involve the picture collection which was in a place of safety.

Count Ferdinand Bonaventura, the Viceroy Aloys Thomas and Count Ernst Guido were not only responsible for accumulating the greater part of the collection: they were at the same time the greatest personalities the Harrach family produced. To-day, Countess Stéphanie Harrach ranks beside them, for it is due to her that the Harrach Gallery still exists. In spite of the enormous losses caused by the war, and in spite of many personal griefs, she has accomplished the seemingly impossible. At a time of social upheaval, when many families have dispersed their ancestral collections, and when wealth has been replaced by poverty, Countess Stéphanie rebuilt the bombed palace, and fifteen years after the end of the war reopened the gallery. Now only the best works are hung, and this new arrangement is a permanent memorial to the former director of the Kunsthistorisches Museum, Ernst Buschbeck, who died in 1963. He recreated the charm of a Baroque private gallery with great sympathy and understanding.

To the Counts Harrach, only the pictures counted as a proper collection, and only this part of the collection has remained unchanged. Furniture and furnishings were valued chiefly for their usefulness, and thus were often replaced by more 'modern' pieces in prevailing fashions. Nevertheless, many rare and precious pieces of furniture have been discovered relegated to back-rooms. Typically, and this is true of almost all the residences of the Austrian nobility dating from the beginning of the eighteenth century, the furniture, especially for the State Rooms, was ordered from the leading European centres, and only after the mid-century was the quality of local work high enough to satisfy their exacting demands. Among the earliest pieces is a Boulle writing table with two guéridon tables, probably South German work of the late seventeenth century, given by the Emperor to Count Bonaventura. Similar pieces, inlaid in *contre-partie*, from the Imperial collection, are now in the Austrian President's office. A magnificent grandfather clock by Daniel Quare (1649–1724), inventor of the repeater movement, is of the same period. Its richly decorated Boulle case may have been

made in Augsburg, which would be an example of collaboration between two leading international centres. A commode in ebony, inlaid with pewter, was presumably brought by Count Bonaventura from Spain with other pieces whose style and technique were uncommon in Central Europe. The most valuable and characteristic pieces of state furniture are the four richly carved and gilded ornamental tables with marble mosaic tops. These came from the Viceroy's Italian house, together with several console tables which have tops supported on richly carved tendril and leaf forms in the manner of Andrea Brustolon, and with them are small glass display cases which are particularly rare and interesting.

These, and some of the other surviving pieces, give a rough idea of the furnishing of the Harrach Palace in the first half of the eighteenth century, with all the show and the lack of comfort common in a period 'when the highest orders of society had to forgo amenities and comforts which no servant of our own day would go without'. But from about 1750 onwards, in Vienna as in the rest of Europe, there was an increasing concern for comfort and convenience. Ceremonial receptions were replaced by an easier and more intimate kind of life; furniture by local craftsmen

Boulle style writing table. South German. Height 34½ ins. c. 1700. Probably a gift from the Emperor to Count Ferdinand Bonaventura

Opposite SUSANNA AND THE ELDERS
Pompeo Batoni (1708–87) oil on canvas 39 × 53½ ins. 1751

now stood alongside expensive pieces imported from abroad; beauty of form, achieved by fine craftsmanship, and marquetry work, was a primary consideration; the more exuberant types of carving and gilding disappeared.

The interior of Schloss Prugg is very important, as it is a typical example of an Austrian aristocratic house towards the middle of the eighteenth century. France was the great model, then as always, but despite this international tendency something of a national character can be detected. The furniture is simpler, more homely, and reflects a less formal atmosphere. At a time when the French tended to prefer small pieces of furniture, the saloon at Prugg was still dominated by enormous and richly inlaid cupboards and chests, typical products of South Germany and Austria. Instead of the open fireplaces usual in France, the rooms were heated by magnificent tiled stoves, a type of local ceramic work of which there are veritable masterpieces at Prugg and in the palace in Vienna.

Two beds and their matching chests, given to the family by the Empress Maria Theresa, are specially characteristic of Austrian furniture, and their elegant, undulating lines and use of fine wood is typical. The beds turn the room into a bedroom in the modern sense – that is, a room into which strangers did not penetrate, whereas the contemporary French bedroom with the bed hung with costly brocade, was also a reception room where friends gathered and the *levée* remained a public function.

Besides the furniture, many other objets d'art, equally closely connected with family history, establish the atmosphere of the living-rooms at Vienna and Prugg. During the Napoleonic Wars, the Counts Harrach followed the patriotic example of other great Austrian families and helped the State by melting down their family silver. A china service, many pieces of which survive, is of particular importance. It came from the Delft factory known as 'The Greek A' ('de grieksche A'), and carries the mark of Adrianus Pieter Kocks – APK – (1701–03). All the plates are decorated with the Harrach arms painted in blue, and the service was probably made to the order of Count Bonaventura, who had many commercial contacts with the Netherlands when he was negotiating the purchase of numerous tapestries for the Emperor.

In 1719, soon after the discovery of porcelain, the Vienna factory was founded by Claud Innocentius du Paquier. His products rapidly rivalled those of Meissen, and became the treasured collectors' pieces of the ladies of the Harrach family. The preference for unpainted porcelain figures and groups is typical of the Austrian nobility. A small collection, which includes numerous early pieces, is still preserved with particular affection and is added to whenever possible. The most important piece is the only known example of the *Bird Nesting* group, of a size which

Bird Nesting Group. White Vienna porcelain. Height 11 ins. c. 1745

A bedroom at Schloss Prugg. The beds were a gift to the Harrach family from the Empress Maria Theresa. Austrian c. 1750

Opposite *A richly carved and gilded Italian table with a top inlaid in different coloured marbles. Height 31½ ins. Early eighteenth century*

shows remarkable boldness at a time when mastery of the material, and the production of a quantity of really white paste, was fraught with considerable difficulty. This group has the family coat of arms impressed on it, and dates from about 1744, when du Paquier's private factory passed under State control.

Another rarity is the painted figure of a kneeling man, holding up in his right hand a scroll bearing an Italian poem. In his *Histoire de la Porcelaine*, Jacquemart records that before one of her confinements Maria Theresa wagered Count Dietrichstein that the child would be a girl, while the Count bet on its being a boy. The Count lost, for the child was Marie-Antoinette, and he is said to have commissioned from Meissen a group of the Empress and her new-born infant, with himself kneeling before her presenting a poem by Metastasio. The group went to Paris and disappeared, but presumably either the whole, or at least the kneeling figure, was copied in Vienna, for the Harrach piece, though it bears no mark, is certainly Viennese, and the careful workmanship and painting show that it was a single, specially commissioned piece. In 1848, certainly with Count Harrach's permission, the Vienna factory made several replicas of this figure. The collection of white porcelain figures also includes several pieces from other factories, chief among them being the

horse modelled by Dominikus Auliczek in Nymphenburg in 1764.

To list all the rare and often curious pieces left by the members of the Harrach family to their descendants as tokens of affection, or souvenirs of special occasions, is quite impossible. But there is one group which must be mentioned: the Harrach glassware. The Counts were not simply collectors and patrons; they themselves established a factory where the craft could flourish under their direct control and according to their wishes. About 1700, the Viceroy founded a glass-works in the north-eastern corner of his Bohemian estate and called it the 'New World'. Well-known painters and engravers like Biemann and Pohl worked for the factory; its products became world-famous, and courts and noble households obtained choice pieces of Harrach glass. It was chiefly in the Harrach factory that such special glasses as milk-glass, heliolite-glass, and portraits in fused pastes, which were specialities of the Bohemian glass-blowers at the beginning of the nineteenth century, were developed, and show-rooms were opened in Karlsbad and St Petersburg. Several magnificently cut and richly engraved goblets and glasses still belong to the family, but the main collection remained in Czechoslovakia. Harrach glass is no longer produced, but Harrach Street in Leningrad is still a reminder of this once world-wide aristocratic enterprise.

Vienna porcelain figure of Count Dietrichstein.
Height 6¼ ins. c. 1770. Copied from a lost
Meissen group known to have been presented by
Count Dietrichstein to the Empress Maria Theresa

Engraved glass goblets from the Harrach factory
in Bohemia. c. 1700

The Princes Pallavicini

Franco Russoli

The Pallavicini family came originally from Genoa and the first member to show an interest in the arts was Marchese Nicolò, a friend and patron of Rubens, from whom he commissioned two great paintings for Genoese churches. His son, Cardinal Lazzaro Pallavicini (1602–80) formed a great collection of seventeenth-century paintings, including works by Rubens, Van Dyck, the Carracci, Strozzi, Reni, Caravaggio, Vouet and others, which he settled on his niece Maria Camilla and her descendants shortly before his death. Thus the collection was transferred to Rome, because Maria Camilla had married Prince Giovanni Rospigliosi. The Prince and Princess Rospigliosi-Pallavicini added works by other seventeenth-century artists, such as Domenichino and Giordano, as well as a remarkable group of contemporary still-life paintings, while the Prince's uncle, Pope Clement IX, further enriched the collection with a bequest of drawings and paintings by Bernini, Claude and Maratta. No additions of consequence were made during the eighteenth century. But in the nineteenth century Prince Giuseppi was responsible for the acquisition of a major group of Renaissance paintings, while other seventeenth and eighteenth-century works by artists who had worked in Rome were added as a result of marriages and bequests. The collection is housed in a great seventeenth-century palace, richly frescoed by Reni, Tempesta and Bril, and containing several outstanding pieces of furniture.

The Princes Pallavicini

Franco Russoli

At the beginning of the seventeenth century Cardinal Scipione Borghese Caffarelli, nephew of Pope Paul V, began the construction of the great palace which has borne the name, and housed the treasures, of the Rospigliosi-Pallavicini family since 1704. The history of this building, which stands on the slopes of the Quirinal on the site of the Baths of Constantine, like that of the collection it contains, is deeply involved both with the history of the great Roman patrician families, and of famous artists who worked for them. The palace and the collections may have been added to, re-organized, and transferred from one owner to another, but as a result they reflect the rise and decline in the fortunes of great families, and the changes in artistic taste of the Roman aristocracy from the seventeenth century to the present day. Above all, they give a picture of several centuries of continuous, informed patronage of the arts, and record the Pallavicini family's devotion to its artistic heritage. Among the outstanding names associated with the collection were Marchese Nicolò, friend of Rubens, Cardinal Lazzaro who created the nucleus of the collection of paintings, and Don Giuseppe Rospigliosi-Pallavicini who at the beginning of the last century was still making valuable additions. The present Princess, Donna Elvina, has done much towards the conservation of the collection, and has instituted research into its history, one result being the superb *Catalogue of Paintings in the Pallavicini Gallery*, compiled by Federico Zeri between 1949 and 1956 (Sansoni, Florence 1959). In his introduction to the catalogue, Zeri notes that this magnificent gallery, containing about 550 works of art, is the only one of the great collections formed in Rome during the seventeenth century which has not only escaped any serious depredations in the last three hundred years, but has also continued to grow up to the present day.

The Pallavicini Collection is the result of a complex series of legacies through which great treasures from the Borghese and Bentivoglio families (who, during their tenure of the Palazzo, commissioned the frescoes in the main rooms), were united with others from the Borromeo, Colonna and Medici del Vascello families. The major works of the Rospigliosi Collection, intimately linked with the Pallavicini name and history, had to be sold in 1931 and 1932, so that only a few lesser pieces now remain in the Rospigliosi apartments on the second floor of the palace. But the Pallavicini apartments, with their frescoed halls and exquisitely furnished salons leading out to gardens and terraces, are themselves a work of art of the greatest fascination and historical importance.

Some knowledge of the history of the family and the palace is essential before one can understand and appreciate what this great collection represents in the way of artistic activities at various times by popes, princes, cardinals and great ladies.

It was Cardinal Lazzaro Pallavicini (1602–80), the son of Marchese Nicolò, for whom Rubens painted the *Circumcision* and the *Miracles of St Ignatius* for the church of Saints Ambrose and Andrew in Genoa, who first established a branch of this ancient Genoese family in Rome, through the marriage in 1670 of his niece Maria Camilla (1645–1710) to Giovanni Battista Rospigliosi, nephew of Pope Clement IX. Their descendants, for whom the family estates and fortunes were held in trust, had however to retain the name Pallavicini, and at the same time became heirs to the titles of Duke of Zagarolo and Prince of Gallicano, both going together if they had only one son, or being divided at the discretion of either family if there was a second son, who could establish a branch of the Pallavicini family in Rome. When Cardinal Lazzaro Pallavicini set up a family trust in 1679, he included a group of paintings from his own collection and from that of his brother Stefano, the father of Maria Camilla, which

was to be the nucleus of a Pallavicini Collection in Rome. Over the centuries this collection has been enlarged by virtually half of everything inherited or acquired by the various Rospigliosi-Pallavicini descendants, since the second sons who should have created the Pallavicini line of the family either died young, or without heirs. The division of their possessions was thus only nominal and the successive Princes Rospigliosi-Pallavicini had control of the entire Collection until eventually it had to be divided in the nineteenth century, by Don Francesco. Whereas the Rospigliosi inheritance was dispersed in 1931–32, the Pallavicini part of the collection has survived and has recently been enriched by the addition of works by Piedmontese artists added by Donna Elvina Medici del Vascello, wife of Guglielmo de Pierre de Bernis de Courtavel, the nephew and adopted son of Don Giulio Pallavicini, who has inherited the family's name and possessions.

Cardinal Lazzaro Pallavicini owned a representative collection of pictures, made up both of his 'Genoese' inheritance (Rubens, Van Dyck, Strozzi), and of works bought in Bologna (Carracci, Reni, Cantarini, Mastelletta, Albani), where he was Papal Legate, and in Rome (the inventories record works by Caravaggio, Cerquozzi, Pietro da Cortona, Dughet and Sacchi). The Cardinal's taste was mainly for the lively and cultivated style of the Bolognese 'reform' movement, but he had a keen eye for new developments in Rome, the international centre for artists, where naturalism and scenes of everyday life were the fashion. To these, Maria Camilla Pallavicini (1645–1710) added works by Domenichino, Luca Giordano, von Tamm, van Bloemen, Vogelaer, and others, while further additions came through a legacy from Pope Clement IX which included drawings and paintings by Bernini and Claude Lorraine – artists who had enjoyed his personal patronage.

As Federico Zeri records in the introduction to his catalogue, none of the additions to the collection during the eighteenth century were of great importance, although a large number of pictures were either bought, commissioned or inherited by various members of the family, particularly portraits. Early in the nineteenth century Don Giuseppe Rospigliosi-Pallavicini bought an

Far left PORTRAIT OF MARIA CAMILLA
PALLAVICINI ROSPIGLIOSI (*1645–1710*)
*Benedetto Luti (1666–1724) oil on canvas
34 × 26½ ins. c. 1700/05. Maria Camilla added
substantially to the collection inherited from
Cardinal Lazzaro Pallavicini*

Left PORTRAIT OF GIULIO ROSPIGLIOSI,
POPE CLEMENT IX *Giovanni Battista Gaulli
called Baciccia (1639–1709) oil on canvas
29 × 23½ ins. 1667/69. Clement IX
bequeathed to the collection numerous works
by Claude Lorraine and Bernini*

Right PORTRAIT OF CARDINAL GIACOMO
ROSPIGLIOSI *Carlo Maratta (1625–1713)
oil on canvas 29½ × 24 ins. 1668*

outstanding group of paintings by Botticelli, Lotto, Lorenzo Monaco and Zanobi Macchiavelli. These are certainly among the most valuable and famous works in the collection, and they gave a twist to its character, for Don Giuseppe was a connoisseur whose taste was in advance of his times. Until then, the paintings chosen by his predecessors had borne witness to a sense of enlightened patronage and a desire to adorn and enrich the palace, but although their judgement had been good, their taste had not ranged beyond the work of fashionable painters of the time.

The remarkable collection which Margherita Gioemi Colonna brought to the palace when she married Giulio Cesare Rospigliosi-Pallavicini was again different, as was that which came from her sister, Maria Colonna Lante della Rovere, in 1841. These works had not been individually acquired from dealers or private owners by one man, as were Don Giuseppe's additions, but were the artistic patrimony of one of the great Roman houses. That is to say, their significance lay more in the historical associations than in their artistic merit. The Pallavicini share consisted of about seventy outstanding paintings, mainly works

of the Emilian and Roman schools, or of French and Flemish painters working in Rome during the seventeenth and eighteenth centuries, and these form an admirable complement to the paintings in the original collection because they give more meaning to the whole as a record of Roman culture and civilization. Finally, in 1952, Donna Elvina brought into the collection works by two Piedmontese artists of the Renaissance, Defendente Ferrari and Gandolfino d'Asti. The main rooms of the Pallavicini palace with their famous frescoes make a splendid setting for these works.

Cardinal Scipione Borghese engaged Flaminio Ponzio, Onorio Lunghi, Giovanni Vasanzio and Carlo Maderno to design the palace and to lay out the gardens which rise in three terraces to the level of the Via dei Serpenti. Before 1616, the date when the Cardinal handed the palace over to the Duke of Altemps, the three galleries opening on to the terraces had been completed and decorated with murals, sculptures, stucco work, and with architectural fantasies like the so-called 'Theatre' fountain on the second terrace. The enlargements and re-organizations

that followed considerably altered the garden front. Some parts of it were demolished, for example the loggia on the third terrace; additions were made to other parts and new decorations and frescoes were commissioned. But the first floor, and the gallery built by Vasanzio on the first garden terrace, which still houses the Pallavicini Collection, have not been greatly altered, although the frescoes in the first-floor rooms date from a few years after the palace was built. These were commissioned some time after 1621 by Cardinal Guido Bentivoglio, into whose possession the palace had recently passed, from Giovanni di San Giovanni, who painted *The Burning of Troy* and *The Death of Cleopatra* and, in collaboration with Francesco Furini, an *Allegory of Night*. Other decorations were added on the ground floor in the time of the Bentivoglios, while their successors the Lantes, followed by Cardinal Giulio Mazzarini and his heirs the Mancinis, and finally the Rospigliosi-Pallavicinis have each made important additions to the building itself.

Cardinal Scipione Borghese was responsible for adding the superb Casino on whose central vault, in 1613 and 1614, Giudo Reni painted his *Aurora*, one of the glories of early seventeenth-century Italian painting. The gracious façade of this little building extends towards a wooded garden in a series of arches, ornamented with antique marble sculptures. Inside, below the *Aurora*, which is like an opening to the skies, are frescoes by Paul Bril (*The Four Seasons*), Antonio Tempesta (two *Triumphs*) and Cherubino Alberti, who painted the putti carrying the Borghese arms. Architecture and decoration balance and complement each other here, while the flowing lines and luminous colours of Guido Reni's masterpiece dominate the whole room.

This classic masterpiece sets a very high standard for the rest of the Pallavicini collection of seventeenth-century Roman paintings, which include, among others, landscapes by Tempesta, Tassi, Bril, Gaspard Poussin, Claude, as well as Domenichino's *The Fall*, busy domestic scenes by the *bamboccianti*, and works by followers of Caravaggio. Another gem of the Pallavicini Collection are the frescoes in the Casino of the Nine Muses on the second garden terrace, where an elaborate décor by Agostino Tassi surrounds groups of figures making or listening to music painted by Orazio Gentileschi above representations of Apollo and the Muses which decorate the pendentives of the vault. It is impossible to think of the movable paintings in this Palazzo apart from such harmonious ensembles, or as not belonging with the series of wall frescoes by Giovanni Baglione, Domenico Passignano and Giovanni di San Giovanni. The continuous and interwoven histories of the great families who have lived in the Palazzo Pallavicini are reflected not only in the general harmony but also in the way the settings and the works of art there assembled seem made for each other.

Opposite DISTRIBUTION OF SOUP TO THE POOR *Viviano Codazzi (c. 1603–72) oil on canvas 39 × 29 ins. c. 1650. The result of collaboration between Codazzi and Michelangelo Cerquozzi, who executed the figures*

It is difficult to select from such an extensive collection those specific pictures which best represent the unique relationship which existed between the various collectors and the civilisation of their time. However, I shall here attempt briefly to trace the various stages of the collection's growth and to draw attention to those paintings within each group whose artistic and historical qualities most fully represent the taste and personalities of the men who acquired them.

The nucleus of the collection is formed by paintings which were acquired by Cardinal Lazzaro Pallavicini. A set of thirteen pictures of Christ and the Apostles, is almost certainly identical with those mentioned by Rubens in a letter of 28th April, 1618 to the British Ambassador as having been painted by himself and his pupils. These paintings are in fact replicas of a series which formerly belonged to the Duke of Lerma, and is now divided between the Prado and the National Gallery of Ottawa. In 1665 these panels, painted in about 1608, were hanging in the chapel of Giovanni Battista Pallavicini's palace in Antwerp, but on his death they seem to have passed to Stefano and Lazzaro Pallavicini and to have been sent to Genoa. Compared with the Lerma set which is wholly from the hand of Rubens, the Pallavicini set is seen to be largely his pupils' work. Nevertheless they are works of very high quality, and are an eloquent testimony to the bonds of friendship between Rubens and the Pallavicini family. Artistically more important, and wholly by Rubens, is the *Portrait of Hélène Fourment in her Wedding Dress*, a half-length figure, as in the preparatory study in the Rijksmuseum, Amsterdam, for the great full-length portrait in the Alte Pinakothek in Munich. This is a late work, painted shortly after 1630, and probably came to Maria Camilla Pallavicini from the collection of her father Stefano in Genoa. It is mentioned in the 1713 inventory. Another important example of the interest of the Pallavicinis of Genoa in Flemish painting is Van Dyck's *Portrait of a Gentleman*, mentioned in Cardinal Lazzaro's will of 1679, and identified by a family tradition as Nicolò Pallavicini, the father of Lazzaro and the friend of Rubens. This must once have been the central figure in a much larger painting executed by Van Dyck during his time in Genoa. The general tone of the picture is dark, but with strong contrasts of light and shade. The other Van Dyck in the collection, the *Portrait of a Lady*, is more mannered, but still a very assured work, and dates from the end of the artist's time in England. This painting did not enter the collection until 1952, coming in with other pictures from the Casa Medici del Vascello. Another work which was in the Pallavicini family collection at Genoa is the magnificent painting by Bernardo Strozzi which is now in the Hermitage at Leningrad. The tiny *Adoration of the Shepherds*, one of the most delightful works of Valerio Castello (1624–59), with its vivid light and contrapuntal

LANDSCAPE WITH A SHEPHERD *Claude Lorraine
(1600–82) oil on canvas 19½ × 15 ins. c. 1636*

Opposite LANDSCAPE WITH MERCURY,
AGLAUROS AND HERSÉ *Claude Lorraine (1600–82)
oil on canvas 38 × 48 ins. 1643. There are seven works
by Claude in the collection*

use of movement, was probably also one of Cardinal Lazzaro's
acquisitions.

Among the works by contemporary Emilian painters which
Cardinal Lazzaro bought in Bologna were the finely characterized *Portrait of a Lady with a Little Dog* by Annibale Carracci and
Christ Healing the Blind by Lodovico Carracci, in which the classical 'Roman' style is softened by the tenderness of the emotions
portrayed. The magnificent *Bean-eater* by Annibale Carracci,
which once hung beside them, later passed to the Colonnas, and
is illustrated on page 44. Many other paintings of the Emilian
school, by Badalocchio, Canuti, Scarfaglia, Garbieri and Massari, interpret in their own way the tradition established by the

Carracci, Reni, Guercino and Albani. Of particular interest is an *Andromeda Rescued by Perseus* attributed in the will of 1679 to 'Elizabetta Sirani with the help of Master Guido Reni', but fine enough in quality to be considered the work of Reni himself, like the great *Crucifixion*, referred to in the same will as a copy. The Pallavicini Collection contains also three fine examples by Simone Cantarini of Pesaro (two others came into the collection as part of the Colonna bequest in 1841), as well as works by Cignani (*The Five Seasons*) and Flaminio Torre, whose style, with its echoes of Reni and Cantarini, recalls Guercino in its use of chiaroscuro.

Culturally speaking, there were many similarities between Rome and Bologna in the seventeenth century, and the works bought in Rome by Cardinal Lazzaro to decorate the Palazzo Barberini, the first Roman residence of the Pallavicini family, were in the Bolognese artistic tradition in so far as they represented a blend of the classical and the baroque. The Cardinal's collection included works with an 'antique' flavour such as the *St Jerome* then attributed to Mantegna, but now believed to be a sixteenth-century Flemish (or perhaps Venetian) painting, or the *St Peter* painted in 1563 by Antonio Moro of Utrecht, which was attributed in those days to Moretto da Brescia. However, the majority of the paintings bought by the Cardinal in these years were fine examples of work by contemporary Roman artists. The

AURORA CARRYING OFF CEPHALUS
*Pietro da Cortona (1596–1669) pen and bistre
wash heightened with white* $10\frac{1}{2} \times 14\frac{1}{2}$ *ins.
c. 1650*

THE HOLY FAMILY *Gian Lorenzo Bernini
(1598–1680) pen and watercolour* $6\frac{1}{2} \times 6\frac{1}{2}$ *ins.
c. 1670*

Cardinal's will refers to two works by Caravaggio which can no longer be identified, and several works in the manner of Caravaggio. The beautiful, stylized *St Cecilia*, now known to be by Calvaert, was believed to be by Artemisia Gentileschi, while the *Portrait of a Young Man* attributed in the will to a 'Monsù Guetti' is undoubtedly by Simon Vouet. It is known that the Cardinal also owned works by Maratta, Pietro da Cortona and Sacchi, although these are no longer in the collection. There are, however, numerous examples of the new types of landscapes, genre scenes and 'views' then current, including Venetian scenes by Joseph Heintz the younger, and luminous *Imaginary Roman Landscapes* by Alessandro Saluzzi, with figures by Michelangelo Cerquozzi. The finest genre paintings are examples by the *bamboccianti*, that is to say they are lyrical records of everyday life, in which Flemish realism is combined with the romantic landscapes of classical Roman painting. One may cite as typical the two landscapes with figures and ruins by Viviano Codazzi, again with the figures painted by Cerquozzi: *Distribution of Soup to the Poor* and *Farm in Latium at Sunset*.

While actively buying works with sacred or profane subjects by 'classical' and 'reforming' artists, Cardinal Lazzaro Pallavicini did not hesitate to add also examples of a more revolutionary poetic type. However, the pictures which Giulio Rospigliosi, who became Pope Clement IX, bequeathed to the collection, are in a more solemn, elevated style. These included Baciccia's portrait of Pope Clement and a portrait of Cardinal Giacomo Rospigliosi by Carlo Maratta, as well as several magnificent paintings and drawings which had been acquired by the Pope directly from Claude, to whom he was both a friend and an enlightened patron. Giulio Rospigliosi was also a patron of Bernini and Poussin long before he became Pope (a copy of Poussin's *Self Portrait* [Louvre] is still in the collection). He owned the early painting by Claude, *Landscape with a Shepherd*, one of the artist's most poetic pastoral scenes and the *Landscape with Mercury, Aglauros and Hersé*, executed as a commission for Giulio Rospigliosi in 1667 or 1668.

Besides these masterpieces, which are duly recorded in the *Liber Veritatis*, the collection contains four other drawings by Claude, one of which is a preparatory study for the above-mentioned landscape. The group of Bernini drawings were probably given to Clement IX by the artist – whom he commissioned to do sculptures on the Ponte Sant'Angelo – and are datable to the same period, 1660–70. These consist of a *Holy Family*, and of five *Angels with the Symbols of the Passion* which clearly relate to the figures on the Ponte Sant' Angelo, carved by Bernini with the help of assistants.

Giovanni Battista Rospigliosi and his wife Maria Camilla Pallavicini thus inherited from their forbears Cardinal Lazzaro

FLOWERS IN A CRYSTAL VASE
Christian Berentz (1658–1722)
oil on canvas 18 × 12½ ins. c. 1695

and Clement IX, a remarkable collection and to this they added considerably. Various inventories made for the Duke and Duchess between 1708 and 1713 allow us to follow the growth of the collection which, in 1713, consisted of about 740 pictures. This Duke and Duchess, who took up residence in the Palazzo di Montecavallo in 1704, favoured works by contemporary artists and by famous masters of the Counter-Reformation. They had a great liking for still life, a genre which was in fashion at the end of the seventeenth century, and they acquired several examples in which on the whole the subject was decoratively elaborated rather than treated realistically. The finest of these are four huge flower compositions, some with fruit, animals and architectural elements, two by 'Monsù Francesco da Pret', the Italian name for the German artist Franz Werner von Tamm, who worked in Rome between 1685 and 1695, and two more by 'Monsù Carlo Olandese', alias Karel van Vogelaer, who worked with Maratta and Baciccia. Rich in colour, somewhat fantastic, and yet with many realistic details, these canvases deserve a place of honour in the history of still life painting in Italy. Giovanni Battista and Maria Camilla also assembled an important collection of works

by Paolo Porpora, Mario Muzzi, known as Maria de' Fiori, Christian Berentz, Pietro Navarra, Brugnoli, Monsù Otto van Schrieck Marseus, Giovanni Stanchi, Zenone Varelli and other painters of the Roman school, that is to say painters whose work shows the influence either of Caravaggio and the Neapolitan school, or of Flemish artists. As a matter of fact the 1708 inventory lists several Flemish still lifes, among them a *Kitchen Scene* by David Teniers the Younger, possibly painted in collaboration with Pieter Boel. Among the important later acquisitions are small works by Jan van Kessel and Spadino's *Eggs with Melons and Other Fruit*.

After still life, landscape was the other fashionable genre in the eighteenth century, and both types of subject lent themselves to decorative treatment. Maria Camilla added to her group of superb works by Claude and Codazzi others by Van Bloemen (*The Horizon*), Jan Both, Grechetto, Swanevelt, Antonio Tempesta, Paul Bril, Bartolomeo Torrigiani, and others. This uniquely representative collection of seventeenth-century landscape painting was augmented in the nineteenth century by others from the Colonna and Lante Collections. Other paintings

PORTRAIT OF AN UNKNOWN MAN *Corneille de Lyon (c. 1534–74) oil on canvas 6½ × 5½ ins. Mid-sixteenth century. Attributed in the 1713 inventory to Giorgione. An inscription on the back of the frame, dating from the seventeenth century, claims that the subject is Martin Luther*

Opposite ANDROMEDA RESCUED BY PERSEUS *Guido Reni (1575–1642) oil on canvas 107 × 85 ins. c. 1635. Attributed in the will of Cardinal Lazzaro Pallavicini to Elisabetta Sirani and Guido Reni*

PORTRAIT OF LILLINA PALLAVICINI *Eighteenth-century Roman school. Crayon heightened with white lead. 11½ × 8 ins. c. 1730*

TRANSFIGURATION *Botticelli (c. 1445–1510) tempera on panel 10½ × 7½ ins. c. 1500. The left wing of a triptych of which* St Jerome and St Augustine *forms the centre*

Above right ST JEROME AND ST AUGUSTINE *Botticelli (c. 1445–1510) tempera on panel 10½ × 3 ins. and 10½ × 3¼ ins. c. 1500*

Opposite LA DERELITTA *Attributed to Botticelli (c. 1445–1510) tempera on panel 18½ × 16½ ins. c. 1475. One of a series of panels of the Story of Esther that originally decorated two marriage chests. The subject is probably Mordecai in despair before the gate of the king*

Overleaf left VIRGIN AND CHILD WITH TWO ANGELS *Zanobi Machiavelli (1418–79) tempera on panel 32 × 22 ins. 1450–55*

Overleaf right VIRGIN AND CHILD WITH ST JOHN THE BAPTIST AND ANOTHER SAINT *Luca Signorelli (c. 1450–1523) oil on panel 30 × 20 ins. c. 1480–84*

which came into the collection at this time and deserve special mention are the *Battle Scenes* by Jacques Courtois, known as Jacques de Bourgogne, and Christian Reder, known as 'Monsù Leandre', and works by *bamboccianti* like Jan Miel and Michelangelo Cerquozzi, who are particularly well represented. There is also a *Seascape* by an unknown Dutch painter, believed by Federico Zeri to be a follower of Agostino Tassi, a large painting of good quality which throws new light on the relations between northern and Italian artists working in Rome in the early seventeenth century. Another picture to reach the Pallavicini palace at this time, brought possibly from the estate at Zagarolo, was *The Fall of Man*, one of a series of huge paintings executed for Cardinal Ludovico Ludovisi by Domenichino and his assistants. This painting, together with Massari's *Victory of David* and *Samson Destroying the Temple* from the studio of Ludovico Carracci, form a homogeneous group representing various aspects of the Bolognese school.

Maria Camilla and her husband made a less felicitous choice of altar-pieces and religious paintings, but they were fortunate enough to acquire from the estate of Simone Giogalli in 1693 two major works by Luca Giordano, *The Death of Julian the Apostate* and *The Conversion of Saul*. These are both violent scenes, with writhing bodies, luridly lit by shafts of lightning, yet as compositions they are beautifully balanced and reveal the influence both of Venetian painting and of Pietro da Cortona. It is not known when the other two important works by Giordano, *The Death of Lucretia* and *The Judgement of Paris* entered the collection, but they were probably painted a few years later than the others, that is to say about 1685 during Giordano's time in Florence. Two later works by Giordano which formed part of the Colonna bequest are interesting, but not of the same quality.

Among the pictures inherited by the Pallavicini from Giovanni Battista Rospigliosi in 1722 are numerous works by Roman Baroque painters such as Gemignani, Romanelli and

Opposite top AURORA *Guido Reni (1575–1642) fresco on the central vault of the Casino Rospigliosi-Pallavicini. 1613–14. The fresco depicts Apollo driving his chariot, preceded by the figure of Aurora.* Bottom *The Casino Rospigliosi-Pallavicini also contains wall frescoes by Paul Bril, Antonio Tempesta and Cherubino Alberti*

TRIUMPH OF CHASTITY *Lorenzo Lotto (c. 1480–1556) oil on canvas 30 × 46 ins. c. 1530*

Brandi, that is to say painters influenced by Poussin, Pietro da Cortona, Gaulli and Maratta. There are also many Caravaggesque paintings by Caroselli, as well as a masterpiece by Mattia Preti, *Sophonisba Taking the Cup of Poison from Massinissa*, in which the Caravaggesque chiaroscuro is softened by a Venetian sense of colour. Venetian sixteenth- and seventeenth-century painting is represented by Titianesque portraits, works by Padovanino and Palma the Younger, and a typical genre scene *The Schoolmaster*, by Pasquale Rossi of Vicenza. Other artists well represented are Barocci, Schedoni, Toschi the Florentine mannerist, and foreign painters like Keil and Koeninck. Two very important works of the French School were wrongly described in the 1713 inventory as being of the Italian School: a superb *Portrait of a Man* by Corneille de Lyon, then attributed to Giorgione, and a *Poppea Sabina* (a variant on the famous painting in the Geneva Museum) by a painter of the school of Fontainebleau which was described as 'Anne Boleyn, School of Raphael'. From Giovanni Battista Rospigliosi the collection also gained a Titianesque painting by Poussin, *Genius Bearing the Horn of Plenty*, and two magnificent drawings by Pietro da Cortona.

Other paintings added to the collection during the eighteenth century, such as those by Batoni and Subleyras, represented the new academic style of Roman painting. Most of these were portraits, but special mention should be made of a delightful series of small drawings of Pallavicini ladies and children, drawn with an affection and irony that suggest the authorship of Amorosi or Ghezzi. At the beginning of the nineteenth century the collection received an addition of far greater significance through the acquisition by Don Giuseppe Rospigliosi Pallavicini of some great Primitives, as well as of a group of masterpieces by Tuscan and Venetian painters of the Renaissance.

In 1816 the Prince acquired from the Amigoli family in Florence the small picture – probably the most famous of the whole collection and certainly one of the most beautiful of all fifteenth-century Italian paintings – Botticelli's *La Derelitta*. In those days it was believed to be a *Rea Silvia* by Masaccio, and the correct attribution was only made in 1896 by Adolfo Venturi, although he thought that a biblical scene was represented, perhaps that of the Levite's wife. This strange and fascinating work, which appealed so strongly to the Romantic and pre-Raphaelite

PORTRAIT OF PRIAMO LECHI,
PROCURATOR OF ST MARK'S *Tintoretto*
(*1518–94*) *oil on canvas* 38½ × 31 *ins.*

Opposite THE QUARREL *Attributed to Velasquez*
(*1599–1660*) *oil on panel* 11 × 15½ *ins. 1630*

Below YOUNG MAN HOLDING A FLOWER
Eberhard Keil called Monsù Bernardo
(*1624–87*) *oil on panel 13 × 13 ins. c. 1675*

imagination, has been variously interpreted by art historians and critics, many of them seeing it simply as a perfect symbol of a frequently encountered human condition. The best modern scholarship has identified the picture as one of a series of panels (the others are now distributed among several museums and collections) which originally decorated two marriage chests. They represented the story of Esther, and were painted in about 1475 in Botticelli's studio by the young Filippino Lippi. But whereas Horne, Gamba, and later Wind, to whom we owe the correct interpretation, maintain that the style and quality of the Pallavicini picture clearly justify the attribution to Botticelli, Zeri believes that, like the others, this must be the work of Filippino, although heavily influenced by his master. At all events, the painting has the feeling of a Botticelli, and is certainly worthy of him, so he may well have conceived and executed this panel himself, leaving the others to his pupils. Only a genius like Botticelli could have achieved the inspired relationship between the architectural setting and the figure, crushed and closed in on itself, as well as the apparently casual arrangement of the garments strewn across the steps. The subject of the scene is almost

FUNERAL OF ST FRANCIS OF ASSISI *Lorenzo Monaco*
(*c. 1370–c. 1425*) *panel 29 × 10½ ins. c. 1420. Part of the*
same series of works as St Francis Receiving the Stigmata,
now in the Rijksmuseum, Amsterdam

certainly not that of an 'Outcast' (nor can it be Rea Silvia, the Levite's wife, Lucrezia Romana, Thamar, or Queen Vashti, as critics have suggested, nor even an Allegory of Truth or Honesty) but Mordecai in despair before the gate of the King (Esther IV, 1).

It was probably Prince Giuseppe Pallavicini who also bought the two other Botticellis in the collection: a small triptych with *The Transfiguration, St Jerome and St Augustine* and a circular *Madonna and Child with St John the Baptist and Two Angels.* The triptych is a typical late work, painted about 1500, its delicacy being enhanced with gold tracery in an 'archaic' style, and its dramatic impact heightened by the elaborate arabesques of the design. The tondo, datable about ten years earlier, is a studio work with traces of the hand of the master, and was attributed in the nineteenth century to Ghirlandaio or Cosimo Rosselli. There is also something of Botticelli in the *Communion of St Jerome,* which was bequeathed to Prince Giuseppe by Angelo Mezzeri in 1817; this painting derives from an original work by the master, now in the Metropolitan Museum of New York. Zeri has attributed it to Bartolomeo di Giovanni, a follower of Ghirlandaio. A beautiful *Madonna with Angels,* one of the best works of the Florentine painter Zanobi Macchiavelli shows unmistakably the influence of Filippo Lippi and Domenico Veneziano. The feeling of light and movement in this picture, and the aristocratic grace and formal clarity of the design entitle it to rank in the first flight of Florentine Renaissance paintings.

In 1817 the collection was enriched with the *Funeral of St Francis of Assisi,* part of a polyptych (the remaining portions are now in the Rijksmuseum, Amsterdam) painted by Lorenzo Monaco and his pupils in about 1420. The handling of the subject here is more austere than in the comparable painting by Giotto; nevertheless there is some lively characterization in the figures. Another fifteenth-century masterpiece is a *Virgin and Child with Saints,* an early work (*c* 1482) by Luca Signorelli, which shows extraordinary intensity in the handling of line and mass.

In addition to these works by Tuscan painters, the collection was enlarged during the eighteenth century with other fine examples of Renaissance and Mannerist painting, including a *Madonna* by Antonello de Saliba, a *St James* by Garofalo, a tiny *Crucifixion* by Strada, a *Calvary* by Fenzone and *Landscape with St Jerome* by Niccolò dell' Abbate. Another important acquisition, attributed at the time to Luca Cambiaso, was Lorenzo Lotto's *Triumph of Chastity,* one of the finest sixteenth-century Venetian paintings and datable *c* 1530. The icy splendour of the colours and the hard light suggest a purely intellectual type of sensuality. It is always fascinating to look for the symbols which Lotto liked to include in his pictures, here for example the ermine on Chastity's breast, the shells on Venus's arm, and also her necklace.

Above THE HOLY FAMILY *Giovanni Battista Benvenuti*
called L'Ortolano (1488–c. 1525) oil on panel 17 × 12½ ins.
c. 1515–20

But these symbols, like the classical references, are introduced unobtrusively to add to the enchantment.

Apart from these fifteenth and sixteenth-century paintings, which were chosen with discernment and are of exceptional quality, the additions made to the collection during the nineteenth century were designed to strengthen the character prevailing when Prince Giuseppe inherited it. The landscapes by Breenbergh and Paul Bril, the hunting scenes by Vinkboons and Verdussen, the still lifes, portraits and other works by Manfredi and Vouet, as well as the Caravaggesque series of *Angels with Symbols of the Passion* were all probably acquisitions by Prince Giuseppe. This part of the collection was greatly enriched in 1841 by the Lante bequest. Apart from a *Holy Family* by the sixteenth-century Ferrarese artist Giovan Battista Benvenuti, known as L'Ortolano, and two biblical scenes by Scarsellino, the most important paintings which came to the Pallavicini from the Lante-Colonna collection were all by seventeenth and eighteenth-century artists of the Roman school. The majority were landscapes, including Claude's masterpiece, *Temple of Venus*, painted for Lorenzo Onofrio Colonna in 1672.

Other important pieces were landscapes by Gaspard Dughet, Swanevelt, van Bloemen and Andrea Locatelli, views of Rome by Vanvitelli, and a similar but later series by Henrick Frans van Lint, all of them paintings of historical interest for what they tell us about the changes in the city's appearance. Among the works by foreign artists living in Italy are paintings by Leonard Bramer, Ribera, and a fascinating little portrait of a *Young Man Holding a Flower* attributed to Eberhard Keil, known as 'Monsù Bernardo'. But the finest and unquestionably the most interesting work in this group is a small canvas *The Quarrel*, attributed

A detail from ST NICHOLAS OF TOLENTINO *by Defendente Ferrari*

Left ST NICHOLAS OF TOLENTINO *Defendente Ferrari (active 1500–35) oil over gold ground on panel 49 × 16 ins. c. 1510–15*

by Roberto Longhi to Velasquez. It is a typical scene that could be witnessed in any Roman countryside inn and is treated in a style related both to that of the Flemish anecdotal painters and to the *bamboccianti*. Originally, when in the possession of the Colonnas, it had a companion of exactly the same size showing *Soldiers Playing at Dice*. This, however, is by a considerably less talented artist, possibly a minor follower of Elsheimer. Surprising as it may seem that Velasquez should have agreed to carry out such an important commission, which meant fitting in with a minor genre painter, the possibility must be considered that he met *bamboccianti* and artists from Northern Europe in Rome in the 1630s and was tempted to try his hand at a realistic theme of this sort. There are certainly echoes in the painting of other famous works by Velasquez (Longhi, for example, has pointed out that the same model recurs here as a soldier and as a secondary figure in the *Forge of Vulcan* which was painted in Rome *c* 1630). Also it is so greatly superior in conception and execution to other genre paintings of the time that it is difficult to avoid attributing it to a major master. The characterization, the colouring, and above all the easy, naturalistic gestures of the figures anticipate the *Treaty of Breda*.

Through the Colonna bequest the Pallavicini collection also acquired some fine examples of religious and classical painting of the Bolognese and Roman schools by Mattia Preti, Sebastiano Conca, Gramatica, Trevisani, Simone Cantarini and Giacinto Brandi. There are however a number of other important pictures, which do not figure in any of the inventories or catalogues and about whose provenance nothing is known for certain. Among these are a *Beggar* by Pedro Nunez in the style of Murillo, a *Madonna* by Giampetrino, a *Sermon of John the Baptist* by Bartolemeo Schedoni, a powerful though somewhat damaged portrait by Tintoretto, and two genre pieces by Schoenfeld, vivid and elegant examples of the Neapolitan style.

The latest and most significant addition to the Pallavicini collection is a group of Piedmontese paintings which came as part of the dowry of the Princess Elvina Medici del Vascello from the family palace in Genoa. The *St Nicholas of Tolentino* and six panels from a predella by Defendente Ferrari are fine examples of the work of a painter who combined Flemish elements with a more severe Lombard style. An even rarer example of this same tradition is the *Presentation of Jesus in the Temple*, formerly attributed to the Ligurian painter Luca Baudo, but now identified by Longhi as a work by Gandolfino di Roreto. These works were acquired during the present century by the Medici del Vascello, whose tradition of art collecting rivals that of the Pallavicini, and has been continued by Princess Elvina.

The magnificence of the Palazzo Pallavicini as a whole is incomparable, and it contains a splendid array of furniture, brocades and silver. Nevertheless its greatest glory is the collection of paintings. Not only are they great works of art, but also a great testimony to the enlightened patronage shown by successive generations of a great family.

THE PRESENTATION IN THE TEMPLE *by Gandolfino di Roreto (active 1493–1510) tempera on panel 49 × 75½ ins. c. 1510*

CHATSWORTH ENGLAND

The Dukes of Devonshire

Michael Jaffé

The heart of the Devonshire Collections, now gathered at Chatsworth, lies in the great library created by the sixth Duke (1790–1858) from the first Duke's Picture Gallery. Amongst the treasures to be found there are the books chosen by Thomas Hobbes for his pupils, the second and third Earls, and many incunabula, as well as the collection of drawings by Northern and Italian artists formed by the second Duke (1673–1729), the real founder of the family collection. The vast range of drawings and prints brought together by the second and third Dukes, and increased by the inheritance of the fourth Duke's wife, heiress to Lord Burlington (1695–1753), is unrivalled by any other private collection in the world. Fine books also came from Georgiana, the beautiful fifth Duchess (1757–1806), and from the library of Henry Cavendish, the chemist and physicist. The last major contribution was by Georgiana's son, the sixth Duke. He added little to the wealth of paintings, graphic work and jewels, but concentrated on enriching the comparatively meagre inheritance of sculpture by patronage of contemporaries such as Canova and Thorwaldsen, as well as by some brilliant purchases of antiquities.

The Dukes of Devonshire

Michael Jaffé

'The valley through which we pass on the way to Chatsworth House is uncommonly beautiful; and the building itself (an immense mass of stone) has a very striking appearance at a distance. It is built of yellow stone, has a square form, and is three stories high. The architecture is similar to that of Hampton Court, near London. It is a hunting-seat of the Duke of Devonshire, who, as we were informed, usually visits it in harvest time for the purpose of having large hunting parties in its very extensive park, which abounds in game.' The writer, the account of whose post-Waterloo tour of Great Britain was thus translated, is the Librarian of the King of Prussia. He goes on, 'We did not view the interior of the house, which is said to contain nothing remarkable.'

When Dr Spiker passed through Derbyshire in 1816 the mansion built by the first Duke of Devonshire and William Talman happened to have as few treasures on show as at any time since its completion just over a century beforehand. The owner, William Spencer Cavendish, was barely twenty-six. He had only been Duke for the five years since the death of his father, the fifth Duke. But he was already deep in the task of converting the house, improved by the fourth Duke, and of enlarging it by a whole wing in order to accommodate more splendidly the library and art collections to which he was to add so substantially. All the good paintings were in London, at Devonshire House or at Chiswick. Indeed at Chatsworth itself, apart from walls and ceilings decorated by Laguerre and Verrio in the Painted Hall, Grand Staircase, and the State Bedroom on the first floor, there

The west front at Chatsworth, built 1700–03, and probably designed by the first Duke, assisted by John Fitch and Thomas Archer

Above left WILLIAM CAVENDISH, SECOND DUKE OF DEVONSHIRE *(1672–1729) Charles Jervas (c. 1675–1739) oil on canvas 49 × 39 ins. Originator of the collection of drawings and prints. The Boulle coin cabinet on his right is still at Chatsworth*

Above RICHARD BOYLE, THIRD EARL OF BURLINGTON *(1695–1753) George Knapton (1698–1778) oil on canvas 49 × 39½ ins. 1743. The creator of Chiswick House. In the background, Rysbrack's white marble bust of Inigo Jones which remains at Chatsworth*

Left WILLIAM SPENCER CAVENDISH, SIXTH DUKE OF DEVONSHIRE *(1790–1858) Giuseppe Carelli. Watercolour 11¼ × 7⅝ ins. 1833. The Duke is throwing away his crutches after recovering from a mishap during an Italian tour*

The Blue Drawing Room. Right, Georgiana, Fifth Duchess of Devonshire playing with her Daughter *1784, by* Sir Joshua Reynolds. *The circular library-table on the left contains a selection of Georgiana's books*

CONTES DES FÉES *Charles Perrault (Lamy, Paris 1781) 12mo. Specially printed on vellum for Madame Royale and with the artist's original drawings. On the binding are the arms of Madame Royale*

were no more than a dozen or so pictures of any kind. Also still in London, probably, were the best of the young Duke's newly-acquired books and manuscripts, since the Library which he was to make out of the first Duke's Gallery was not completed until after 1827.

Nevertheless few travellers during the past century and a half can have been so misinformed as Spiker about the contents of Chatsworth. He missed the astonishing wealth of drawings and prints inherited from the second Duke of Devonshire and from the creator of Chiswick, the third Earl of Burlington. The books bearing the stamp of Henry Cavendish, the chemist and physicist – roughly a third of the total of about 35,000 now at Chatsworth – may not have been transferred from London since his death in 1811. But fine incunabula from the second Duke's collection could have been brought out for such a visitor. Spiker could have investigated the *Benedictional of St Aethelwold*; or Henry VII's illuminated *Missal*, with prayers inscribed by that King himself, a manuscript which had been bought by General Wade a hundred years before and later given to Lord Burlington; or the *Roman de Gillion de Trasignies* and other manuscripts quite 'remarkable' enough. There were other Devonshire treasures awaiting their place in the library: for example, the *Hypnerotomachia Poliphili* of 1499, one of only three copies printed on vellum, or 'a Petrarch printed by Aldus later than the edition of 1514, and most beautifully illuminated for a Princess of the House of Medicis'.

Not the least deprivation for a man officially concerned with what noble houses had collected was to miss the chance of meeting the author of these last words, the sixth Duke himself. The sixth Duke was the first Cavendish regnant with the interest as well as the freedom of a rich bachelor out of politics really to attend to the enormous artistic patrimony of his family. In 1844, most of his endeavours in this direction realized, his *Handbook of Chatsworth and Hardwick* – the other great house of his family in Derbyshire – was privately printed in the form of two highly discursive letters addressed to 'Dearest Harriet', his sister, Lady Granville. Every subsequent writer on Chatsworth is happily indebted to this man who, as a collector and as a builder, transformed the place indoors and out.

The sixth Duke's mother, the beautiful Duchess Georgiana, was painted at play on a sofa with her other child, Lady Carlisle to be. This famous masterpiece of 1784 by Reynolds, the most lively and enchanting invention of any eighteenth-century English portraitist, hangs still in the Blue Drawing Room at Chatsworth, close to the circular book-table which was Georgiana's; and that is still filled with small octavos from her exquisitely chosen library of gifts and purchases. In the portrait she wears mourning for her father, the first Earl Spencer. With her brother, the second Earl, she exchanged various Devonshire books; but mystery surrounds the absence from Chatsworth of Van Dyck's Italian Sketch-book, which had been noted by Vertue and by Walpole as being in the Library of the fourth Duke. It probably

Opposite *Top: Tournament page from the* ROMAN DE GILLION DE TRASIGNIES. *Text by David Aubert. From the atelier of Van Lathem.* $14\frac{1}{2} \times 9\frac{7}{8}$ *ins. Bruges, 1464. Bottom:* LE COSE VOLGARI *Petrarch.*

Printed on vellum by the Aldine Press, reputedly for the Medici. Illustrations attributed to Raymond of Lodève, miniaturist to the Sistine Chapel and Sacristy (1535–49). $5\frac{3}{4} \times 3\frac{1}{2}$ *ins. 1514*

disappeared during the late eighteenth century, only to return a few years after Lady Louisa Egerton, daughter of the seventh Duke, remarked its absence in 1895. Otherwise, apart from the transfer on long loan by the eighth Duke of the purely architectural drawings from the Burlington collection to the Royal Institute of British Architects, there were few significant separations from the collection before the sales and transfers occasioned by enormous duties on the death of the tenth Duke in 1950. The so-called *Kemble Plays*, a celebrated collection of dramatic material printed in English, including many items of Shakespearian interest, in addition to the four folios and forty-four quartos of Shakespeare's own works, which had been bought by the sixth Duke, were sold to the Huntington Library in 1912. And, on the sixth Duke's own admission, Sir Thomas Lawrence, who had copied for Windsor the Reynolds of *Georgiana, Duchess of Devonshire Playing with her Daughter*, and who had provided for Chatsworth a painting of *Cardinal Consalvi* on which Thorwaldsen's posthumous bust was partly based, was allowed to enrich his own collection of drawings with no less than three of the five magnificent studies for the then recognised as Raphael's *Transfiguration*.

The sixth Duke does not remark the fact that the first house at Chatsworth of which any record survives was begun by Sir William Cavendish and his wife Elizabeth Hardwick in 1552, three years after they had bought the estate. Of her four husbands, Cavendish was the only one by whom Bess of Hardwick had a family; her second son was created Baron Cavendish, and, in 1618, Earl of Devonshire. She herself, outliving the last and grandest of her husbands, the Earl of Shrewsbury, began immediately on his death in 1590 to build a second great house, Hardwick. The second and third Earls of Devonshire had Thomas Hobbes for their tutor and the extant manuscripts of the political philosopher, together with the books acquired by him for his pupils, are amongst the most illustrious items in the Chatsworth Library. But the collection in the Library began effectively with the fourth Earl, who was rewarded for his part in the Glorious Revolution with the Dukedom.

From 1680, when he first came to carve for the mansion which replaced the mid-sixteenth-century house at Chatsworth, until his death in 1715, Samuel Watson of Heanor kept a notebook of observations. 'In the Duke's Bed Chamber' he sketched the *Conclusion of Peace with Navarre and the Marriage of Louis XIII with Anne of Austria*, now an overdoor on the first landing of the West Stairs. Nobody knows how this French Royal picture, one of a series painted by Simon Vouet for St Germain, came to the first Duke. However, at the Lely Sale of 18 April, 1682 he paid £31 for 'Brouwer. A man singing. 10 in. × 1 ft. 11 ins.', easily identifiable with *A Tavern Scene*, a panel of those dimensions, which also remains in the house.

The magnificent chandelier of Dutch workmanship, possibly a present from William III himself, testifies to the first Duke's fine taste in silver. The light and the chief ornament of the State Dressing Room, it is precisely datable to 1694, since the smaller cherubs each hold a shield with the Cavendish cypher surmounted by an Earl's coronet, whilst the large one at the top has his coronet as a Duke. Certainly deriving from his adherence to William and Mary is the superb toilet service of twenty-three pieces made by Pierre Prevost, most likely for their royal marriage. The first Duke patronised the leading Huguenot silver-smiths, Pierre Harache, David Willaume, and Pierre Platel. By the last there are no less than six pieces of plate at Chatsworth, besides a cake-basket of 1732-33 by one of his apprentices, Paul de Lamerie. Platel himself in 1701 made of gold the exquisite helmet-shaped ewer with its oval platter, quartering the bearings of Cavendish, Smyth, Hardwick, and Scudamore.

Nevertheless most of the money and energy which the first Duke could spare from party politics went on building. It was the second Duke, his family fortunes at their zenith, who was able from his succession in 1707 to concentrate on acquiring what he could of the famous collections then being dispersed. 'Si l'*Italie* est le principal Apartement de la grande Collection du Monde, l'*Angleterre* est le Cabinet des Desseins,' pronounced Jonathan Richardson senior and junior in the 1728 Amsterdam edition of their *Account of Some of the Statues, Bas-reliefs, Drawings and Pictures in Italy*. This hyperbole, an addition to the earlier 1722 London edition, was almost certainly inspired by the second Duke's having made in 1723 his greatest single purchase to date, the bulk of the collection of about 500 drawings formed by Nicholaes Anthoni Flinck (1646-1723), son of Rembrandt's pupil Govaert Flinck. Flinck's mark is on 225 drawings in the Chatsworth collection, accompanied with fitting pride in 105 cases by the coroneted D of the second Duke, to whom, not long after this acquisition, one of the most eminent collectors of drawings, Pierre Crozat, wrote from Paris, 'I take the liberty of complimenting you on the drawings of the late Mr Flinck of Rotterdam, which you have just acquired. It is in my opinion the finest and best chosen collection I have ever seen and will materially enrich yours and make you the richest nobleman in Europe.'

The second Duke had bought 288 amongst the drawings at the second sale of Sir Peter Lely's collection in November 1694, and others from the collection formed by Lely's assistant in landscape, P. H. Lankrink. Some drawings with Flinck's mark also bear Lely's. These include one long celebrated as a Raphael, but no longer so accepted, *Constantine Haranguing his Troops*, for which the Seigneur de Ravestyn had paid the unheard of price of £100 at Lely's first sale. The second Duke's *coups* were resounding. Van

The Library, created for the sixth Duke by Wyatville. The ceiling, with painted medallions by Verrio, is all that survives from the late seventeenth-century decorations of the first Duke's Long Gallery

One of the two Boulle cabinets acquired by the second Duke, opened to display a group of cameos. Height with stand 32 ins. c. 1700

Twenty-three piece toilet service in silver gilt by Pierre Prévost (active Paris 1672–1715). Probably made in 1677 for the marriage of William of Orange and Mary Stuart, and acquired by the first Duke

Dyck's Italian Sketch-book is stamped P.L. for Lely; and the Sketch-book kept earlier in Antwerp is stamped PHL for Lankrink. Both books had in all likelihood been together, since Van Dyck died in London, and were purchased at one go by the second Duke. Some time between 1720 and 1728 he bought the *Liber Veritatis* of Claude, a volume containing 200 drawings made by the artist to record his paintings, which Louis XIV himself had tried to acquire through the French Ambassador in Rome. It is pleasingly ironic that the only piece of modern sculpture obtained by the second Duke was a very handsome gilded bronze bust, with draperies of onyx, *Le Roi Soleil* by Coysevox.

Since less than half the Flinck drawings bear the second Duke's mark, the remaining 120, including thirty-five pen and ink views sketched by Rembrandt in the neighbourhood of Amsterdam, may only have been acquired in 1754 and by the third Duke. These Rembrandt landscapes, together with sixteen other Flinck drawings not marked by the second Duke, which were formerly bound in the Rembrandt–Rubens–Van Dyck volume, are for many the unmatched glory of the whole collection. But even if we count them to his successor's credit, the second Duke's collecting activity remains outstanding. He amassed for Chatsworth at the same time as the drawings a stock of prints, some indeed of Lely, Lankrink, and so – likely enough – of Rubens provenance. The print collection, which comprises such luxuries as Rembrandt's *Ecce Homo* on silk paper, is surpassed in England only by that in the British Museum.

The second Duke also acquired the lion's share of paintings by Old Masters, although modern scholarship does not accept all his attributions. In the list of present owners at the end of the *Liber Veritatis*, against number 159, the pastoral landscape of *Mercury and Battus*, is written 'mine'; that is, probably his acquisition. In 1722 he paid Crozat 1800 livres for a small painting on copper by Domenichino, the *Expulsion from Eden*. The seller wrote that he would have asked anyone else three times the money. An account of 20 November, 1725 presented by John Vandervaart for the restoration of Gaspard Dughet's *Cephalus and Procris*, suggests that the second Duke had been the buyer. Certainly he paid £20 for Lot 74 at the Duke of Portland's Sale in February 1725/1726, 'Quintus Cincinnatus' by Pietro da Cortona, now identified as *Curius Dentatus Rejecting the Bribes of the Samnites*; and at the same sale £367 10s. od. for Lot 75, *The Adoration of the Magi*, as the work of Paolo Veronese, which looks to be an excellent copy by Jacopo Bassano. For the author of his Titian of *St John Preaching in the Wilderness* the names of Schiavone, Lambert Sustris, and Paolo Fiammingo have been suggested with varying degrees of plausibility. However, the second painting of his connected with Titian, the copy of *Philip II in Armour*, is now attributed decisively to Rubens, 'Le pourtrait du Roy Philippe Second, figure

TREE TRUNK AND BRAMBLES *Rubens (1577–1640) red and black chalk, pen and brown ink and some colour on white paper 13¼ × 11¾ ins. c. 1615–20. Annotated in the artist's own hand*

STUDY FOR THE HEAD AND LEFT HAND OF THE APOSTLE POINTING UP AT CHRIST IN 'THE TRANSFIGURATION' *Raphael (1483–1520) black chalk on paper 14⅜ × 13⅝ ins. c. 1520. One of two studies for Raphael's last altarpiece still remaining at Chatsworth*

A FARM BY A STREAM *Rembrandt (1606–69) pen, brown ink and brown wash on paper 4¼ × 8¹¹⁄₁₆ ins. c. 1652–53*

Right LANDSCAPE WITH
MERCURY AND BATTUS
*Claude Lorraine (1600–82) brown
ink and wash 7½ × 10 ins. 1663.
From the* Liber Veritatis
*(1636–75) and now in the
British Museum*

Opposite top A GARTER
KNIGHT BOWING *Sir Peter Lely
(1618–80) black chalk on grey-
blue paper 18⅞ × 14¹¹⁄₁₆ ins.
c. 1663–71. One of the few
drawings added to the collection
since the eighteenth century. It was
purchased after the Warwick Sale
of 1896*

Opposite bottom NATIVITY
*Parmigianino (1503–40) pen and
brown ink with brown wash
10 × 8½ ins. c. 1527–30*

entière', listed in 1640 among the copies by that master after his admired predecessor. This one was painted evidently in 1603, during Rubens' first diplomatic mission to the Spanish Court; the original Titian being recorded three years earlier at Madrid, in the Wardrobe of the Alcazar. One of the most haunting of the directly Venetian pictures bought by the second Duke hangs to the left of his so-called Veronese in the Yellow Drawing-Room; a three-quarter-length of a man, in recent years convincingly attributed to Cariani. No doubt except about the identification of the sitter surrounds the 'Portrait, Frans Hals' recorded in Dodsley's *London* (1761) as at Devonshire House. This, dated 1622, hangs now at Chatsworth as pendant to another 'Portrait, Frans Hals', similarly recorded at Chiswick: the three-quarter length portrait of an unknown lady, which came with the Burlington heirlooms. From that same source came 'A man half-length by Rembrandt', signed and dated 1651. This portrait of an *Old Man Seated in an Armchair*, wearing a dull purple cape and a furred robe, joined the magnificent *King Uzziah Struck with Leprosy*, bought at the de Piles' Sale by the second Duke as 'Lott 36 A Man's head with a Turban. Rembrandt. £78 15s. od.' This early masterpiece, signed and dated 1635, was recorded by Vertue in 1743 'at the Duke of Devonshires new-built house [*Devonshire House*] the Turks head a most excellent picture by Rembrandt'.

Besides collecting European Masters of the sixteenth and seventeenth centuries, the second Duke patronised at least one eminent contemporary, Sebastiano Ricci. It is the odder therefore that such a typical Sebastiano as the little canvas of *Susannah and the Elders* should have been accepted by Mrs Strong, when cataloguing the paintings earlier this century, as by Annibale Carracci. This bizarre attribution had been current since Vertue made his Notes in 1741, despite its requiring no more than the removal of surface dirt in 1947 to reveal the inscription, 'Riccius fecit 1713'.

In addition to paintings, drawings, and prints the second Duke formed yet another distinguished collection: coins and classical and renaissance gems. The coins, which came partly from the collection at Smyrna of Consul Sherard, are long gone from Chatsworth, although the cabinet made by Boulle to house them remains, with the matching one for the gems. About 1724 the Duke employed Gosmond to draw the gem collection as a prelude to engraving, and ninety-nine prints were made from his drawings before he fled to France. Sets of these were circulated without more formal publication. One of the Nuremberg Preislers was similarly employed. He took liberties such as introducing a wreath round the bull's neck in the antique amethyst intaglio of *Nike Sacrificing*. Cataloguing, however, awaited the fourth Duke's obtaining the services of Lorenz Nattier, the writer on, and engraver of, gems, some time after his arrival in England in the mid-seventeen fifties. This Duke furthered the enterprise of his grandfather by buying jewels from the most famous private collection in Europe at the death in 1757 of its owner, Baron Philip von Stosch.

After the fourth Duke's time no change of importance was made in the collection of gems until the sixth Duke had the extravagant fancy to have eighty-eight, including the finest, mounted by Hancock in an elaborate parure. The settings of gold and enamel were modelled on the supposedly contemporary frame in which had been fixed, at some time beyond the sixth Duke's memory, a miniature portrait, attributed to Hilliard, of Queen Elizabeth and Essex *ad vivum*. This finery, tiara, bandeau, necklace, and stomacher was to enable the Duke's niece by marriage, Lady Granville, to astonish the Court of St Petersburg at the coronation celebrations of the Czar. Unfortunately the light reflected from the broad and brilliant enamel borders must have eclipsed the delicate translucency of the gems themselves. Yet the parure has never been dismantled. The superb red sard intaglio signed by Dioscorides, *Diomed Stealing the Palladium from the Temple of Minerva at Troy*, still adorns the centre of the bandeau, flanked by an emerald head of *Medusa*, Roman work, and by a Greek head of *Silenus*, a jacinth worked in high relief. The Greek *Nike Adorning a Trophy* still hangs from the stomacher. These classical antiquities are oddly assorted with portrait gems of the English royal house, *Henry VIII and his Children*, *Edward VI* and *Charles I*. Miniatures on vellum of Elizabeth and Essex, once fitted to a book-cover, are set in a locket which has a cameo head of Elizabeth.

In the grand total of 500 items, there are, as in most collections largely formed in the eighteenth century, things good, bad and indifferent. The antique intaglios, numbering signed works by Dioscorides and Gnaios, are by far the most important. There are a few Renaissance crystal intaglios of excellent quality: a signed Valerio Belli; a signed Giovanni Bernardi del Castel Bolognese; and an interesting group of crystal backed with gold leaf to simulate the solid metal. Most of the cameos are sixteenth century; the *Rape of Europa*, set in the stomacher, balances one of the few antiques, thought to be the work of a Greek in Rome; and one of the finest *cinquecento* pieces is a lapis lazuli cameo of a lady, nearby in the same ornament.

When he came to commission his own portrait the second Duke chose his countryman Charles Jervas, rather than the more fashionable Dahl. Jervas shows the collector seated with his treasures, the *Benedictional of St Aethelwold*, and one of his Boulle cabinets from which he handles a coin. Such presentation is no less appropriate to the sitter, and more natural seeming, despite mediocrity of execution, than the state attitude rendered by

Kneller of the first Duke, standing full-length in Garter Robes and with his Wand of Office. The first Duke's portrait hangs as he would have wished. It keeps company with that of his father, the *Third Earl of Devonshire*, and with two other full-lengths also by Van Dyck, *Arthur Goodwin MP* and *Jeanne de Blois*, lining the great gilded trunk of a Dining Room with which the sixth Duke extended his forebears' house. The second Duke's portrait hangs upstairs in the little Theatre, which has been recently and skilfully adapted as a Gallery to display selections from the drawing collection. Suitably, he looks across to the portrait of his grandson's father-in-law, *Richard Boyle, Third Earl of Burlington* by Knapton. Burlington, like the second Duke, wears Garter insignia in sign of his quality; and to denote his enthusiasms he holds a red morocco volume lettered 'Inigo Jones'. Behind him is placed the marble bust of Jones by Rysbrack, who took for his model the Van Dyck portrait. Knapton shows Burlington in middle-age, the 'positive' man of whom Pope warned Swift.

The Rysbrack bust of Jones remains at Chatsworth. So does a portrait in black chalk, from the Flinck collection, which bears on the mount, 'Van Dyck's original drawing, from which the print by Voerst was taken in the book of Van Dyck's Heads. Given me by the Duke of Devonshire. *Burlington*'. This *modello* for Van Dyck's Iconography returned to Devonshire possession following the marriage in 1748 of Burlington's daughter, Char-

lotte Boyle, to the fourth Duke. The Boyle connection was of the greatest consequence to the Devonshires. It brought to them the villa at Chiswick with all its contents of painting and furniture, including scenery and costume designs by Jones for the masques and plays at court. One costume design illustrated here can only suggest the fascination of the rest, being one of four surviving at Chatsworth for 'The Lords Maske presented in the Banquetinghouse on the Mariage night of the High and Mightie Count Palatine, and the Royally descended the ladie Elizabeth' by Thomas Campion on 14 February, 1613. 'The eight Maskers appeared in their habits, which were infinitely rich, befitting States (such as indeed they all were) as also a time so farre heightened the day before with all the richest show of solemnite that could be invented. The ground of their attires was massie Cloth of Silver, embossed with flames of Embroidery; on their heads, they had Crownes, Flames made all of Gold-plate Enameled, and on the top a Feather of Silke, representing a cloude of smoake.' Even the scene on which these moving visions irrupted was all silver and fire.

The Masque drawings at Chatsworth were bought at a sale by G. Yales in 1722. Two years earlier Burlington had paid 'To Mr Jnº Talman for a Book of Designs and Drawings by Palladio . . . £170.' The latter were a portion of the haul brought back by Jones from his second Italian tour of 1613–15. These, with his own drawings and books, had passed to his assistant Webb; and

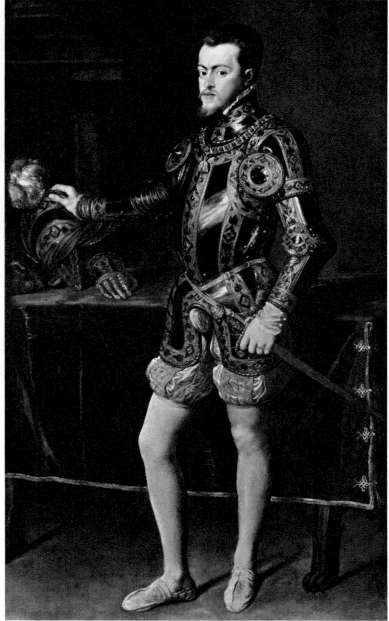

Above PHILIP II OF SPAIN IN ARMOUR *Rubens (1577–1640) oil on canvas 70 × 41 ins. 1603. After a portrait by Titian executed at Augsburg in 1551*

Left HENRY VII AND HENRY VIII *Hans Holbein (1497/8–1543) ink and wash on paper 101 × 54 ins. 1537. Full-scale drawing for the left half of a wall painting of the family of Henry VIII in the Privy Chamber at Whitehall Palace, destroyed by fire in 1697/8. Now in the National Portrait Gallery, London*

thereafter, despite Webb's testamentary injunction, had been divided. The Burlington-Devonshire Collection includes architectural drawings both by Jones and by Webb, as well as those by Palladio, forming together the material of the Jones-Palladian revival in which Burlington himself took such a resolutely active lead. His own designs for his villa at Chiswick are the most personal expression of his dominating taste. Algarotti, a finger on the pulse as always, wrote to him in 1751, after a dinner at Berlin with Frederick the Great, 'The name of My lord Burlington came to be mentioned together with those of Jones and Palladio. I mentioned to His Majesty Burlington House, Chiswick, the Egyptian Hall at York, the Thermae which you my Lord have had engraved and the Palladian façade which you have executed for General Wade's House.' Burlington, in great measure through his activity as a collector of books and drawings, had indeed made himself, as the antiquarian Scipione Maffei called him, 'il Palladio e il Jones de' nostri Tempi'.

Burlington was 'converted' to serious architectural aims by the publication in 1715 of the first volume of Colen Campbell's *Vitruvius Britannicus*, followed shortly by Leoni's edition of *I Quattro Libri*. In Spring 1714 he had set out, as a carefree English *milord* of twenty, on the Grand Tour, with Charles Jervas as his companion. During the following winter he made a few important acquisitions in Rome. Amongst them possibly was a panel about eighteen inches square, on the back of which is penned on a label, in an eighteenth-century hand which may well be his, 'Storietta della chiavetta' and 'wrote on the old frame Pierino del Vaga'; in fact it is one of the Biccherna tablets from Siena, with the coat of arms and most of the inscription removed by the vendor as some sort of concealment of its origin. Painted by Domenico Beccafumi in celebration of the town militia's unexpected victory over the papal army at Camollia, it represents *The Offering by the Consistory of the Keys of the City to the Blessed Virgin, in Siena Cathedral, July 22, 1506.* Other purchases documented on his first visit to Rome were more conventional. He began discreetly with a *Temptation of St Anthony* after Annibale Carracci, at 300 crowns. A few months later he spent 210 crowns on a *Madonna* by Carlo Maratta and 75 on another by Pascolini. After that he got a second Maratta, *Noah Sacrificing*, and a painting by Viviani. But by far his biggest purchase, even taking account of his payment of 1,350 crowns for a diamond ring, was on 13 January, 1715, when he 'Paid to Mr. Giovenale Superior of the Convent of Sta. Maria Victoria for a Picture of a Madonna by Domenicana 1500 [crowns].' Outlay of such a prodigious sum may be taken as a decisive mark of the *gusto* for a Grand Tourist of his generation to acquire such an incontestably genuine Domenichino as the *Madonna della Rosa*.

Burlington's architectural preoccupations did not put an end

ALLEGORY OF THE CONCLUSION OF PEACE WITH NAVARRE
AND THE MARRIAGE OF LOUIS XIII WITH ANNE OF AUSTRIA
Simon Vouet (1590–1649) oil on canvas 61½ × 62½ ins. c. 1648

to his collecting. He needed pictures for Chiswick, besides the Hals and the Rembrandt. At Lord Oxford's Sale in March 1741/42 he paid 8½ guineas for Lot 53 *The Marriage of St Catherine* by Pietro da Cortona. And £1,000 were spent in Paris on two large canvases to hang as pendants in a sumptuous pair of carved gilt frames, first at Chiswick, and now at Chatsworth; one, the *Acis and Galatea*, has always been recognised as a Luca Giordano; the other, noted by Dodsley in 1761 as 'Belisarius, Vandyck', was presumably bought as such because it came from some palace in Genoa. It seems to be by that rare Genoese master, Gioacchino Assereto. Chiswick had also to be furnished in the grandest style. Chatsworth has gained thereby mahogany chairs, gilt-wood tables, and looking glasses designed by William Kent for Burlington. The vast oval wine cistern in silver-gilt by David Tanqueray, now at Chatsworth, came from Burlington's marriage to Dorothy, elder daughter and co-heir of William Savile, Marquis of Halifax; it makes an accompaniment fitting in wealth, politics, and personalities to the pair of silver-gilt bottles by Adam Loots, unique in Dutch silver, which were presented by the Prince of Orange to the fourth Earl of Devonshire, as one of the seven signatories to the Invitation of 1688.

Two collectors noticeably enriched the inheritance from the first two Dukes and from Lord Burlington: Georgiana, with her

Drawing of the South and East fronts of Chiswick Villa by William Kent (1684–1748) pen and ink with brown wash 9½ × 12¾ ins.

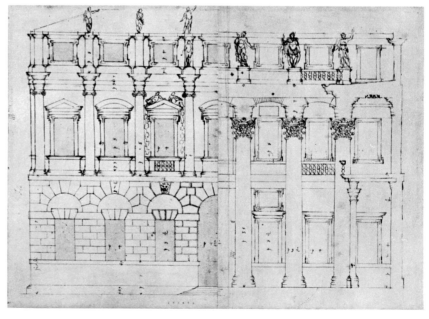

Design for the Palazzo Iseppo de' Porti by Andrea Palladio (1508–80) pen and ink 11¼ × 14¾ ins. 1552

Above left *Page from Van Dyck's Italian Sketchbook showing characters of the Commedia dell'Arte. 1621–27. Brown ink on paper 8¼ × 6 ins. Now in the British Museum*

Above INIGO JONES *Van Dyck (1599–1641) black chalk on paper 9½ × 7¾ ins. c. 1630. Inscribed in Lord Burlington's hand 'Van Dyke's original Drawing, from which the Print by Van Voerst was taken, in the book of Van Dyke's Heads. Given me by the Duke of Devonshire'*

Left *Scene for the Masque* Luminalia *or* The Festival of Light *performed 6th February, 1638. Inigo Jones (1573–1652) pen and black ink washed with grey and splashed with the scene-painter's distemper. 6⅜ × 8¾ ins. Inscribed 'The first scene of night'*

Opposite *Costume design for a Gentleman Masquer for the* Lordes' Masque *by Thomas Campion performed 14th February, 1613. Watercolours heightened with gold and silver 12⅜ × 6⅞ ins.*

MADONNA DELLA ROSA *Domenichino (1581–1641) oil on canvas 43½ × 33 ins. c. 1620*

THE CEREMONY OF THE KEYS IN SIENA CATHEDRAL, JULY 22ND 1526 *Domenico Beccafumi (1486–?1550) panel 18¼ × 18 ins. Bought by Lord Burlington in Rome in 1713*

books, and – supremely – her son, the bachelor sixth Duke. His insatiable zest for *rariora*, hard stones to be polished for his grandiose new East Wing, and exotic plants to fill his colossal conservatory, marks him as the most idiosyncratic in taste amongst the heads of his house. His raving over two vases of *occhio di paone*, or over a specimen of the *Amberstia nobilis* from India might have verged on the ridiculous in any man less amusingly self-aware.

The sixth Duke inherited almost no sculpture except the Coysevox and Rysbrack busts and another, unidentified, from Devonshire House. He starts his Chatsworth tour for 'Dearest Harriet' with the antiques which he placed in the Sub-Hall. 'On the steps are two colossal busts; one magnificent of Alexander,

found at Burlington House; the other, an acquisition of mine at Smyrna, to which Campbell the sculptor, has supplied a nose'. In the Sub-Hall also is a marble group, just over life-size, of a *Woman Seated Beside her Daughter*, a rare type in Roman portraiture. The high mass of artificial curls, as on coins showing Julia Titi and Domitia, implies a date not long after Trajan, even if the group is provincial. Presumably the sculptor was Greek influenced – seated portraits are frequent in Greece – and worked in southern Gaul. This astonishingly well preserved statue and the considerably more damaged portrait of a partially draped man from early Imperial times which stands opposite, both purchases by the sixth Duke at the Wanstead Sale, were discovered 'dans le territoire d'Apt en Provence', according to the 1724

Opposite ET IN ARCADIO EGO *Nicolas Poussin (1594–1665) oil on canvas 39¾ × 32¼ ins. c. 1630*

Supplément to *Antiquité Expliquée* by Montfauçon, who received drawings from the Marquis de Caumont at Avignon immediately after the find.

The bust restored by Thomas Campbell, to provide a balance for the idealised head of *Alexander the Great* now regarded as an early copy after a lost masterpiece by Leochares, was not the sole antique from Smyrna. The first noted 'of seven objects of antiquity' bought there in March 1839, was 'A large bronze head of Apollo found amongst the ruins of Salamis in Cyprus'. This laconic entry records an original of about 460 BC, which was for almost 120 years the most, apparently, priceless rarity at Chatsworth. However in 1957, a valuation having been agreed, it was handed over, with other treasures of longer standing in Devonshire houses, to the custody of the British Museum.

Primarily the sixth Duke wanted work from living sculptors. 'My Gallery was intended for modern sculpture, and I have almost entirely abstained from mixing with it any fragments of antiquity.' Of this beloved Sculpture Gallery which he planned with Wyatville, he wrote, 'A place that was to receive three of Canova's works excited grand ideas.' He tracked down specimens of every rare coloured marble to make pedestals. Canova's *Hebe* and the colossal bust of *Napoleon*, which had been in the great sculptor's bedroom until his death, were mounted on drums of oriental porphyry, thrown in by Chantrey with the purchase of the giant monolithic columns for the South End of the Gallery. Chantrey had negotiated the sale of *Hebe* by the heir of Lord Cawdor who had been Canova's earliest patron. The *Napoleon* came to Chatsworth under the will of Lady Abercorn, the 'Acqua Infelice', who had wept so profusely over her friend the sculptor. The sixth Duke had bought on his own account, through the Paris bookseller Renouard, *Napoleon's Mother, Seated*, of which Canova made no replica. This portrait, sculpted in the city of purchase, was for the buyer 'First acquired treasure, next to *Endymion* the most valued'. In earnest of this he accepted very high charges for marble white and fine enough 'to stand beside the high finishings of Canova'. Such Campbell demanded for a seated *Pauline Borghese* to balance *Madame Mère*, a task which only after fourteen years could he bring himself to complete.

However the Duke's greatest delight was the *Endymion* commissioned directly from Canova. He again needed patience. Reports came from Gaspare Gabrielli, his agent in Rome; first, on 18 October, 1819 he had seen the clay model; then, three years later almost to the day, Canova had died. In Gabrielli's opinion the *Endymion* was not quite finished although the head was to the sculptor's entire satisfaction. However, after its installation, Chantrey wrote to the Duke 'It has the rare merit of being natural at the same time that it is classical, and its greatest

WOMAN SEATED BESIDE HER DAUGHTER
Marble. Height 63 ins. Roman. First century AD

– its only fault is that it is not ancient.' He declared that the Chatsworth Gallery would 'do more honour to the country than any collection we now possess'. The Duke scarcely needed such professional encouragement. 'The quality of marble is so fine,' he exulted, 'so hard, so crystalline, that Canova would not change it on account of the stain in the arm; that on the cheek he liked, and thought it represented the sunburnt hunter's face.' He enshrined the dead sculptor's tools in his Gallery, and commissioned Chantrey to produce a full-size copy of the *Endymion* in bronze as a garden ornament for the South Front.

The Duke's taste comprehended greyhounds from Gott, 'the Landseer of marble'; the *Discobolus* which was the last work of the short-lived Kessels; a statue and bas-reliefs from Schadow; and, in 1825, a dreadfully ponderous *Mars and Cupid* from Gibson, who had been introduced by Canova. Besides Canova he employed one other sculptor of real distinction, Thorwaldsen. The *Endymion* had reached Chatsworth intact; but unfortunately Thorwaldsen's *Venus* arrived broken in three. Nothing mars the cool perfection, however, of the reliefs of *Briseis Taken from Achilles* and *Priam Petitioning Achilles for the Body of Hector*, which the sixth Duke took over from their original purchaser, Agar-Ellis; or the roundels of *Night* and *Day*.

The sixth Duke liked Gott in animal sculpture, Landseer in painting. *Bolton Abbey in the Olden Time* is to our eyes a dull invention: but *Trial by Jury* is full of spirit, a canine caricature of the notables of the day. The poodle in the centre is Lord Lyndhurst, the Lord Chancellor; and from the study painted of two of the Duke's own dogs, *Boney and Var*, Boney is introduced to the Chancellor's left. Their master's voice can be heard describing the South East Sitting Room: 'Boney and Var are by Edwin Landseer. To speak of living dogs appears superfluous, and, in this case unnecessary, for surely their names are European. The head of Boney was the study for his introduction as a reporter in the picture at Chiswick, called the Poodle laying down the Law.' Boney might seem a strange name for a cur to be given by the inheritor of the *Napoleon, Opus Canovae*. Only an early nineteenth-century Duke, perhaps only that one, could make the combined ownership seem entirely natural.

He owns that he could not describe pictures; and he was not more than superficially attentive to painting. 'The Titian of three figures I bought at Mr Cholmondeley's sale' is a group of a man, woman, and a girl, apparently a family. They are exchanging, as love tokens, apples. Signed by Paris Bordone, it is perhaps the 'Paris Bordone, his wife and daughter, painted by himself exceptionally well and in a vigorous manner', which was Lot 2 in the Jan Six Sale at Amsterdam on 6 April, 1702. The sixth Duke is frank also about 'pictures by De la Hire and Carlo Cignani . . . also from Devonshire House, where I thought them

HEAD OF APOLLO *Bronze cast. Height 14 ins. Greek. Mid-fifth century BC. Found near Salamis, Cyprus in 1836. Now in the British Museum*

works of Guercino'. He had his own ideas about conservation and display. He unleashed the brothers Seguier on the work of restoring and re-christening paintings. Some thought in this kind was necessary: the Luca Giordano of *Sophonisba Accepting a Nuptial Gift from Masinissa* when moved from the Green Drawing Room at Devonshire House to Bolton Abbey had become, with at least the connivance of the sixth Duke, the *Story of Fair Rosamond*. He hung Old Master drawings in the Sketch Galleries. 'They hardly ever saw the light in my Father's time, nor in mine often, till I rescued them from portfolios, and placed them in the South Gallery below.' – 'Like keeping one's friends in a dungeon,' added the preposterous Leigh Hunt in the annotated copy of the *Handbook* at Chatsworth. This merciless process, nearly complete by Waagen's visit in 1858, was not reversed until after 1870.

Since the sixth Duke's day comparatively few things have been added to Chatsworth. Two cabinets in the Dining-Room display the Berlin service, once the property of Warren Hastings, which was bought by the present Duke. A bronze head commissioned by him and his Duchess from Epstein of their younger daughter stands in the Blue Drawing-Room. And the Duke's delight in fine books with large coloured illustrations has enriched this section of the Library with, for example, Thornton's *Temple of Flora*, Lawrence's *Roses*, and the splendid Wentworth copy of the *Hortii Amstelodamensis*. Much of great note besides the fifth century *Apollo* left the collection by the 1957 arrangement made in part settlement of the outstanding Death Duties. The

British Museum got in addition the *Benedictional of St Aethelwold*, the *Liber Veritatis*, Van Dyck's Italian Sketch-book and ninety printed books and bindings. Hardwick and its entire contents were handed over to the Treasury and are now in the care of the National Trust. The National Gallery gained at that time the Donne triptych, the only such work by Memling which had remained with the descendants of the donors, and the *Philosopher* by Rembrandt. Since then it has been able to buy the impressive double portrait by Jordaens. The cartoon by Holbein of *Henry VII and Henry VIII* went to the National Portrait Gallery. The Walker Art Gallery in Liverpool now has the Rubens *Holy Family with St John and St Elizabeth*, formerly in Devonshire House. Other paintings, plate, and books were sold at Christie's in 1959.

Generous loans to exhibitions, particularly since the last war, have enabled the story as well as the physical presence of some of the chief remaining treasures to be more widely known. The superb, pagan vision painted by Nicholas Poussin, *Et in Arcadia Ego*, which Louis XVI's minister, Comte Loménie de Brienne, inherited from 'L'avare Made du Hausset, ma parente, qui croyait que c'estoit un tableau de devotion et l'avait, pour cette raison, placé dans son oratoire'; the two splendid fifteenth-century Bruges manuscripts, the *Roman de Gillion de Trasignies*, and the *Vengeance de Notre-Seigneur* ordered by Philip the Good of Burgundy from the younger Yvonnet; the Perrault *Contes des Fées* printed on vellum for Georgiana; Rubens' drawing of a tree-trunk and brambles, these have all been exhibited outside Chatsworth and catalogued for the benefit of the interested public. Yet no external showing can match for pleasure and interest the chance to apprehend the wealth and range of the family collections at home. Concentrated now in one great house in Derbyshire, despite depletions which in sum would have been enough to have made another famous inheritance, are the cream of the contents of Devonshire House and Chiswick, Burlington House and Londesborough, besides whatever has been at Chatsworth since first coming into Devonshire ownership. Chatsworth, as a result, has never been more splendid nor more full of treasures than it is in the care of the eleventh Duke and Duchess at the present time.

The south-east corner of the Sculpture Gallery designed for the sixth Duke by Wyatville. Left to right: Endymion *and* Hebe *by Canova,* Tadolini's Ganymede, *and Gibson's* Mars and Cupid. *On the wall reliefs by Thorwaldsen*

The Princes
Fürstenberg

Altgraf Salm

The collections of the Fürstenberg family at Donaueschingen and Heiligenberg are outstanding among those assembled by German princely families. The emphasis is on things Germanic and works by artists from the area around Lake Constance feature largely. Many different types of objects and works of art are included, some made for members of the Fürstenberg family, some inherited and some purchased, dating from every period from the twelfth century until to-day. The earliest Fürstenbergs are represented by some fine pieces of German mediaeval (twelfth to fourteenth centuries) craftsmanship in bronze and gold made for secular as well as religious purposes. There is also a fascinating group of German Gothic wood carvings and an impressive collection of gold and silver objects for household use made in German workshops between the sixteenth and eighteenth centuries. The family's collection of paintings includes twelve panels by Hans Holbein the Elder, as well as works by Cranach, the Master of Messkirch and two grisaille panels from the Frankfurt Altarpiece by Grünewald, while among the drawings are great works by Dürer and Tobias Stimmer. The Library of over 130,000 books contains the finest private collection of Middle High German manuscripts, as well as hundreds of incunabula, and an important collection of early musical scores. A recent addition to the gallery of family portraits is Graham Sutherland's portrait of Prince Max Egon (1896–1959), who acquired many important pieces for the collection, particularly objects relating to the past history of the Fürstenberg family.

The Princes Fürstenberg

Altgraf Salm

The collections of the Princes Fürstenberg at Donaueschingen and Heiligenberg Castle near Lake Constance are typical of many which until recently were still in the possession of German princely families, irrespective of whether they had remained autonomous rulers down to 1918 or, like the Fürstenbergs, had lost their independence in 1806 by Napoleon's Act of Mediation. The creators of these collections were motivated more by a sense of obligation towards a community – prompted by considerations which might be religious or secular, practical or pedagogical – than by a pure collector's passion. A collection of this kind, composed of a wide range of objects collected for different reasons and of very diverse provenance, is obviously much more subject to change than the more specialized collections made during the nineteenth century; a change in its conception can mean that a

whole section is jettisoned to make room for something more in keeping with a revised plan.

The oldest pieces in such collections were usually acquired for ceremonial purposes, though some may have simply been valuable household objects. 'Art collecting' as such began in Central Europe only in the later sixteenth century, and reached its peak around 1600 when it became fashionable to have a so-called 'art cabinet'. The contents of these were mostly *curiosa*, often in elaborate settings, though some genuine works of art might be included, perhaps even paintings by great masters. The Thirty Years War (1618–48), whose ravages affected most of Central Europe, put an end to this development, but within a few decades the German princes had so far recovered their fortunes that they could reconstruct their residences in the Baroque style, and

Schloss Heiligenberg, built in 1510 and formerly the residence of the Counts of Werdenberg. It passed to the Fürstenberg family in 1534 following a marriage alliance between the two families

Portrait bust of Ferdinando de' Medici by G. B. Foggini. Marble. Height with stand 39 ins. Florentine. c. 1685

Opposite PRINCE MAX EGON ZU FÜRSTENBERG (1896–1959)
Graham Sutherland (b. 1903) oil on canvas 61 × 55 ins. 1958/9. Prince Max Egon made substantial additions to the collections

decorate them with paintings. The Baroque collections of the princes of this period were made with only one object in view: the embellishment of their houses in the contemporary style. Deliberate acquisition of a collection (often with intent to instruct) only became an end in itself once men had been taught by the Enlightenment to explore the classical past systematically and had been inspired by the Romantic movement to explore the traditions of their own people.

The Princes regarded it as a duty to provide culture and education for their subjects, and to this end they formed art collections, which were open to the public. Sometimes they pursued a particular interest and assembled smaller collections accommodated in their private apartments. However, we must not forget that music and drama played an equally important role in the cultural life of these princely courts. The house of Fürstenberg still has a place of honour because it has extended its patronage into our own times, notably in initiating the Donaueschingen Festival of Contemporary Music.

The house of Fürstenberg takes its name from the castle of Fürstenberg a few miles south of Donaueschingen in South Baden, near the borders of Germany and Switzerland. The Fürstenbergs are descended from a family of Frankish counts who settled in Central Swabia in Carolingian times. These counts of Urach acquired considerable importance under the Emperors of the eleventh and twelfth centuries, although they tended to favour the pro-papal party and became allied with the Dukes of Zähringen.

The original castle of Fürstenberg near Donaueschingen, which is now demolished, came into the family as part of the Zähringen inheritance. This was in the time of Count Henry, who was the first to call himself Count of Fürstenberg (about 1250); he was a loyal adherent of Rudolf, the first Habsburg king of Germany, and for the next seven hundred years the fortunes of the two dynasties remained closely intertwined. One might even say of the Fürstenbergs as it was said of the Habsburgs: *alii bella gerunt, tu felix Austria nube* (Other nations go to war, happy Austria conquers through marriage). For many of the territorial principalities allied with the house of Fürstenberg came under its jurisdiction through marriage and were acquired by the family when the lines died out. This is true, for example, of the castle of Heiligenberg, formerly the seat of the Counts of Werdenberg (1534), of the important territories ruled by the Counts of Zimmern and of Helfenstein at Messkirch (1637), and of the lands of the Marshals of Pappenheim at Stühlingen (1639).

The Fürstenberg family was distinguished for its loyalty to the Habsburgs, and many individual members rose to eminence in the imperial service. There was however one branch in the Heiligenberg line which supported the Wittelsbachs, and as a

result Franz Egon (1626–82) and his brother Wilhelm Egon (1629–1704), both bishops of Strasbourg, were caught up in the toils of French diplomacy, while the Stühlingen and Messkirch lines were strongly pro-Habsburg. When the Heiligenberg and Messkirch lines died out (in 1716 and 1744) the entire possessions of the house came together as the Principality of Fürstenberg under Prince Joseph Wilhelm Ernst (1699–1762). He married Maria Anna, Countess of Waldstein, who brought with her the substantial property of Pürglitz in Bohemia.

The numerous scattered Swabian properties united under Prince Joseph Wilhelm Ernst remained under the rule of his sons and grandsons until 1806, when they were divided between Baden, Württemberg, and Hohenzollern.

The history of the Fürstenbergs as hereditary Princes of the Empire goes back to 1664, when the Fürstenberg and Heiligenberg lines were raised to this rank. In 1804 the main line of hereditary Princes died out and the Swabian properties passed to the secondary Bohemian line, represented by Prince Karl Egon II (1796–1854), at that time a minor; his father, Prince Karl Aloys, had been killed fighting against Napoleon at the battle of Stockach while serving as Field-Marshal-Lieutenant in the imperial army. The mother of Karl Egon II was Princess of Thurn and Taxis; he himself married Amalie-Christine, Princess of Baden (-Hochberg) and thus became connected with the Grand Dukes of Baden. This marriage brought the family a number of sovereign rights which they retained down to 1918. The house of Fürstenberg has shown itself well able to meet the challenges of modern times, and through its great estates and economic enterprises still occupies an important position in Baden and beyond.

DONAUESCHINGEN

The castle at Donaueschingen stands on the site of a late medieval building, which in its time underwent repeated transformations. When Count Wolfgang von Fürstenberg acquired Donaueschingen from the Lords of Habsberg in 1488, he enlarged the existing fortified residence to meet the needs of a large court and household. A great feast was held there in 1499 in honour of the Emperor Maximilian I, who was entertained by an exuberant carnival held on the meadow where the Danube rises, only a stone's throw from the castle.

During the sixteenth and seventeenth centuries the castle was apparently somewhat neglected. The Donaueschingen branch of the house of Fürstenberg-Heiligenberg was never wealthy and suffered considerably from the ravages of the Thirty Years War. It was only when this subsidiary branch of the family died out and their properties passed to the main Heiligenberg line that

Processional Cross. Bronze, partly gilded. Height 12 ins. South-west Germany. Twelfth century

Opposite THE MADONNA IN GLORY *Master of Messkirch, identified as Pieter Strueb of Veringen (c. 1485–c. 1540). The fourteen saints surrounding the Madonna are guardians of the donor, Count Gottfried Werner von Zimmern. Central panel from an altarpiece originally commissioned for the chapel at Schloss Wildenstein, a castle owned by the Counts von Zimmern, whose territories passed to the Fürstenbergs in 1637*

Donaueschingen increased in importance. Anton Egon (1656–1716), the last prince of the Heiligenberg line, who acted as regent for King Augustus the Strong in Dresden, had ambitious plans for Donaueschingen and appears to have engaged the famous architect Pöppelmann to carry them out. But the project never advanced beyond its earliest stages, a fate which also overtook the plans drawn up by Carl De Feignet, a Strasbourg architect, for Prince Joseph Wilhelm Ernst. In the end this prince had to be satisfied with a huge but undistinguished four-storey building, which survived unchanged until 1892. Prince Joseph Wilhelm Ernst was chiefly concerned with his position as an autonomous Prince, so that anything he built was connected with the administration of his territory. In consequence Donaueschingen was never given the Baroque or Rococo embellishments which one would expect of such a powerful prince. The interior of the great house was undoubtedly grandly furnished in the eighteenth and nineteenth centuries, but practically nothing of this has survived, because old pieces were constantly being replaced or given away as dowries or legacies. By the time Prince Karl Egon IV and his wife Dolly, born Countess of Talleyrand, came to rebuild and refurnish the house in 1893 very little of value from previous periods still remained.

The present structure is the work of a Viennese architect named Bauqué. In executing his design he was influenced by the French tastes of the Princess, who was responsible for the international character of the furnishings and the interior décor. Thus we find above the main staircase two great wall tapestries designed by J. L. Berain and woven c. 1700, probably at Beauvais. This staircase gives access to the great hall, built about 1896 in a remarkable medley of English and Italian styles. The chimney-piece, settles and other furniture are to some extent sixteenth- and seventeenth-century originals. But the most interesting objects are two marble busts of Cosimo III Medici, Grand Duke of Tuscany, and of his son Ferdinand by the Florentine sculptor G. B. Foggini, executed c. 1685. A number of family treasures (acquired by inheritance or purchase) are on display in this room in glass cabinets. A massive silver jug, surmounted by a group of Europa and the bull, and its salver, are the work of the Augsburg goldsmith J. Lencker (c. 1630). This was purchased some ten years ago by Prince Max Egon (1896–1959), whose taste has left its imprint on many parts of the collection. Another of his acquisitions is displayed in the same cabinet: a carved ivory tankard by L. Kern, mounted in silver by the Ulm goldsmith E. Busch. The gold cup beside it was presented by the College of Swabian Counts to Prince Froben Ferdinand (of the Fürstenberg-Messkirch line) on the occasion of his golden wedding in 1740. The silver cup in the same cabinet, bearing the monogram of Prince Joseph Wilhelm Ernst (of the Swabian branch), was bought by

Prince Joachim, the present owner of the castle. The glass case opposite contains a collection of forty pocket-watches, some of them noteworthy, for example the enamel watch made by the Geneva master J. P. Huaut c. 1700. This particular group was acquired in the mid-nineteenth century by Prince Karl Egon III, who not only added to the collections but rearranged them, and had a passion for everyday objects, such as pocket-knives and pipe-bowls. In the hall are cases containing souvenirs of various other ruling houses, assembled between 1900 and 1940 by Prince Max Egon II, who enjoyed a uniquely influential position through owning lands in both Germany and Austria, as well as being on terms of close friendship with the Emperors of both countries. His friendship with Kaiser Wilhelm II was particularly close and is reflected at Donaueschingen in many pieces.

A corridor leading off the great hall is lined with two double rows of sporting guns, which represent only a part of the great family armoury, the important pieces of which are now kept at Heiligenberg.

An adjoining room is known as the *Kupferzimmer* because it once housed the collection of engravings. The drawings and engravings have since been transferred to the *Karlsbau*. In the Kupferzimmer, which is lined with French *boiseries*, there is now a display of medieval treasures, most of them inherited pieces. The earliest is a twelfth-century bronze crucifix which, like several other pieces, originally came from Heiligenberg. Notable among these is a unique onyx cameo of the thirteenth century, showing the Virgin enthroned; this was subsequently mounted and used to decorate a late Gothic chalice. There is no record of how this piece came to Heiligenberg, but it can be identified as one of the finest examples of late Hohenstaufen gem-cutting, and was probably executed in southern Italy in the time of Frederick II (c. 1240). Another piece from Heiligenberg is a marble crucifix (1482), which once belonged to Count Hugo of Werdenberg, and on which a fourteenth-century gold cross has been mounted. The most outstanding of the secular objects is the Fürstenberg fief-cup, from which the head of the house drank when a vassal was invested with his fief. This lidded goblet is made of silver and is partially enamelled and gilded. Recent research has shown it to be the work of a Nuremberg goldsmith of c. 1490. The letters W.G.Z.F. engraved on the base signify Wolfgang Graf zu Fürstenberg. A close friend of the Emperor Maximilian I, he revived the glory of the house of Fürstenberg after several decades of declining power, and thus prepared the way for its splendid achievements in the sixteenth and succeeding centuries. He may also have owned the fifteenth-century drinking vessel in ox-horn with silver mounts of the type known as 'gryphon's claw'.

There are also several rooms containing a rich variety of eighteenth-century French and German furniture. The walls are

Carved ivory tankard with silver mountings.
Carving by L. Kern c.1640; silver mounts by
E. Busch, Augsburg c.1703

The Fürstenberg fief cup. Silver, enamelled and
partly gilded. Height 15 ins. Nuremberg c.1490.
The initials of Count Wolfgang zu Fürstenberg
(1465–1509) are engraved on the base

Above left *Chamber pot (bourdalou)
of Napoleon I. Sèvres porcelain with
gilt bronze mounts. Height 7 ins.
c. 1810. The case of red morocco
leather is stamped with
the letter N and the imperial eagle*

Right *Ceremonial sword of the
diocese of Strasbourg. Made by the
Strasbourg goldsmith D. Harnischter for Prince Franz Egon zu
Fürstenberg, Bishop of Strasbourg.
Silver and steel. Length 52½ ins.
1652. The medallions on the scabbard display the arms of ancestors
of the Prince-Bishop. The hilt
(detail left) is in the form of an
eagle, the heraldic beast of the
Fürstenberg family*

hung with seventeenth- and eighteenth-century family portraits and paintings. One small room is reserved for mementoes of the Napoleonic period, including a miniature of the Emperor and one of his most unusual possessions, a Sèvres *bourdalou* (chamber-pot) in the form of an Etruscan bronze vessel. Its morocco leather case is stamped with a huge N and the imperial eagle. Another souvenir is a gold necklace with cameos, a gift from the Empress Josephine to Princess Amalie while she was still a child. The Second Empire is also represented by a charming oil sketch by Winterhalter for his famous group portrait of the Empress Eugénie with her ladies-in-waiting.

The former ballroom, hung with eighteenth-century French tapestries, is now the family museum and contains costumes and uniforms worn by members of the family during the past two centuries. Everyday objects are also included, such as umbrellas and belts and the rather more unusual field medicine kit which belonged to Prince Karl Aloys.

One item in the collection of outstanding interest is the huge ceremonial sword in silver made by the Strasbourg goldsmith D. Harnischter for Prince Franz Egon zu Fürstenberg-Heiligenberg, Bishop of Strasbourg (†1663). The hilt is in the form of an eagle, the heraldic beast of the family, while the scabbard is engraved with medallions bearing the arms of the Prince-Bishop's ancestors. The sword only came back into family ownership quite recently, when it was bought from a private owner by Prince Max Egon, who acquired many such objects of family interest, in addition to major works of art like the two panels by Grünewald. He was also a patron of the contemporary arts, initiating

Ceremonial jug and dish. Silver, partly gilded.
Height of jug 16 ins.; dish 29 × 24½ ins.
Augsburg c. 1630. The jug is in the form of
Europa and the bull

The Madonna and Child Enthroned. Onyx cameo. 1 × ¾ ins. Southern Italy c. 1230. Enlarged × 5½. The cameo is now mounted on a late fifteenth-century chalice

the Donaueschingen Festival of Contemporary Music, and in the last years of his life taking great interest in modern painting. Shortly before he died he commissioned a portrait of himself from Graham Sutherland. With this impressive portrait, a symbol of the international outlook of the Fürstenberg family in matters of culture, we must take leave of the treasures in Schloss Donaueschingen.

THE COLLECTIONS IN THE KARLSBAU

The building in Donaueschingen now known as the Karlsbau was originally erected in the eighteenth century as a tithe barn. The abolition of serfdom made it redundant, and in 1869 Prince Karl Egon III commissioned an architect named Diebold to convert it into a public museum. The collections first housed here were assembled during the first half of the nineteenth century by Prince Karl Egon III and his father and were designed to provide instruction in a wide range of subjects particularly interesting to schoolchildren. The extensive mineralogical and zoological collections now occupy the two lower floors of the Karlsbau. The pre-eminently nineteenth-century aspect of this section of the museum is not without a certain old-fashioned charm, which contrasts with the modern presentation of the collections relating to palaeontology and pre-history.

The main attraction of the Karlsbau, however, lies in the collections on the top storey, which houses a picture gallery and an important collection of Gothic wood carvings. The picture collection centres round a group of early German panel paintings purchased by Prince Karl Egon III from Baron Joseph von Lassberg in 1853, at the same time as the library. Lassberg (1770–1855) was among the most unusual and versatile personalities of the German Romantic movement. Employed in the Fürstenberg forestry service, he rose to become chief forestry official of the area. As confidential adviser to the widowed Princess Elisabeth, he had the opportunity to study international politics in action at the Congress of Vienna, while his journeys on this and other occasions brought him into frequent contact with international art dealers and also with smaller dealers in the area round Lake Constance. There was nothing hidebound about Lassberg's interests. On the contrary he was always expanding the range of his connoisseurship and it was due to his particular fondness for Middle High German manuscripts that the library at Donaueschingen acquired a collection unsurpassed by any other private owner.

The paintings include works by three great masters, Grünewald, Hans Holbein the Elder and the Master of Messkirch. The masterpiece of the collection is undoubtedly the pair of panels by

ST ELIZABETH AND ST LUCY *Matthias Grünewald (1470/80–1528) panel 38 × 17 ins. c. 1511. Panels from the lower parts of the fixed wings of the Heller altar from the Dominican church at Frankfurt am Main*

THE SCOURGING OF CHRIST
*Hans Holbein the Elder (1465–1524) panel $34\frac{1}{2} \times 34$ ins.
c. 1496. One of twelve panels of the Passion made for
the high altar of the church of St Ulrich and St Afra, Augsburg*

ST ANNE WITH THE VIRGIN AND
CHILD AND FEMALE SAINTS
*Master of Messkirch, identified as
Pieter Strueb of Vehringen (c. 1485–
1540) panel 20 × 26 ins. c. 1524.
Centre panel from the Falkenstein altar*

Below THE ADORATION OF THE
CHRIST CHILD *Hans Holbein the
Elder (1465–1524) panel 12½ × 8½ ins.
Probably begun in 1500, but left un-
finished and completed in 1514 by
Hans Holbein the Younger*

Grünewald, acquired by Prince Max Egon in 1950 from a private owner. The panels, showing St Elizabeth and St Lucy,
formed part of the stationary wings of the altar-piece commissioned from Dürer and Grünewald between 1509 and 1511 for
the Dominican church of Frankfurt by a city merchant, Jacob
Heller. The central panel by Dürer was destroyed by fire in
1729; the two movable wing-pieces are still in Frankfurt, as well
as the upper sections of Grünewald's panels showing St Lawrence
and St Cyriac. In these striking grisaille panels Grünewald has
achieved the final mastery, which found its greatest expression in
the Isenheim altar, painted a short time afterwards. Something
of Grünewald's genius has been captured in another picture in
the Donaueschingen Collection, the copy of his lost *Magdalen
at the Feet of the Crucified* made by C. Krafft in 1648. The same
room in the gallery also contains twelve panels of *The Passion*
by Hans Holbein the Elder (1465–1524). These were executed
c. 1496 and originally formed part of the high altar of the Bene-
dictine Abbey Church of St Ulrich and St Afra in Augsburg. The
panels composed the wings of the altar, one set of six being visible
when the altar was open and the other when it was shut. They
enclosed a centrepiece – probably a sculpture – of the crucifixion.
The predominant tone of the outer panels is stone grey, with
little additional colour; the inner panels are a natural wood

FAUN AND FAMILY *Lucas Cranach*
(1472–1553) panel 11 × 7 ins. c. 1527

Opposite THE TEMPTATION OF ST
ANTHONY *Master of the Violets (active in
Zürich c. 1500) panel 38 × 38 ins. c. 1500.
St Anthony is shown bargaining with the devil
for the cure of the donor, who is afflicted with
erysipelas, or St Anthony's fire*

colour, which suggests that the centrepiece was also of natural wood with some colouring.

Another treasure in the collection is a tiny panel showing the *Adoration of the Christ Child*. The full history of this piece is not known but the stylistic evidence, taken together with the inscription HAN HOLBAIN DER JUNG 19 IAR and the date 1514, suggests that this painting was begun by Hans Holbein the Elder, left unfinished for fifteen years and finished by his son. The original long tapering angel's wings are still clearly visible beneath the present cherub's wings.

The gallery possesses twenty-four panels by the Master of Messkirch, including the Wildenstein and Falkenstein altars and three wing-panels from the high altar of the abbey church at Messkirch. This representative of the late Gothic school of German painting can probably be identified with Pieter Strueb of Vehringen (*c.* 1485–1540). He worked most frequently in a small format, of which he was a master, and was a forerunner of German Mannerism. The colours of his panels glow with an enamel-like quality, yet avoid the glazed harshness of so many German Mannerist painters. Each of his figures seems to be taken from the life, despite the fact that most of his subjects are saints.

The Swiss masters of the period *c.* 1500 are also well represented, due to the fact that Lassberg lived in the Thurgau for many years and bought pictures on the spot. This group includes the Anthony Altar by the Zürich painter known as the Master of the Violets, which shows St Anthony bargaining with the devil for the restoration to health of the donor, who was a victim of erysipelas, or St Anthony's fire.

There is also a fine group of portraits and secular paintings by Lucas Cranach the Elder and his school, some of which have belonged to the Fürstenberg family for a very long time.

In addition to the paintings the gallery also contains some fourteenth- and fifteenth-century sculptures, which are interspersed among the pictures. One of the most outstanding pieces is a small figure of Christ *c.* 1320, a devotional sculpture for a monastery, originating either from the Upper Rhine (possibly Katherinental) or from Constance. It shows very clearly the influence of the great Dominican mystics Eckhart and Suso.

The period around 1600 is represented by an impressive *Assumption of the Virgin* by Hans Rottenhammer (1564–1625) and by several works by local masters. Unfortunately there are no works by any important painters of the seventeenth, eighteenth and early nineteenth centuries in the Fürstenberg Collection. There is, however, one painter who is of considerable historical interest, J. B. Seele (1774–1814). He was the son of a soldier attached to the Fürstenberg militia and his natural interest in military subjects found plenty of scope in the period of the Napoleonic Wars.

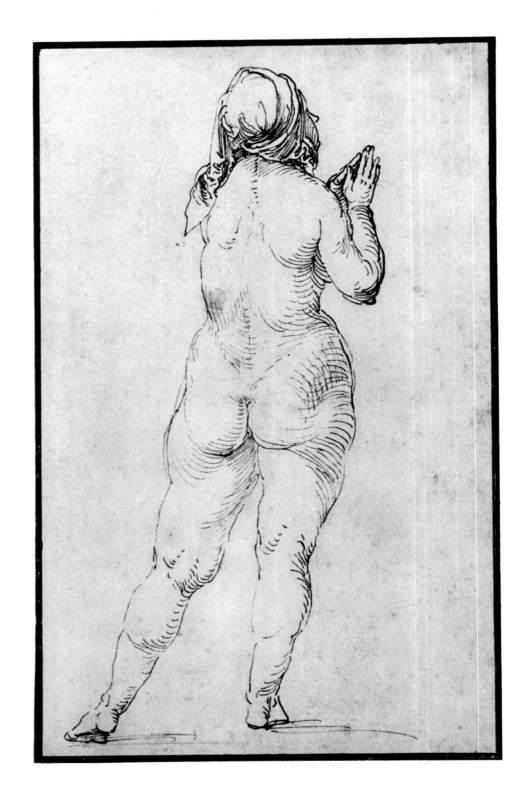

PORTRAIT OF A YOUNG WOMAN *Hans Holbein the Elder*
(1465–1524) Silverpoint 5¾ × 4 ins. c. 1510

Right FIGURE OF A WOMAN SEEN FROM BEHIND
Albrecht Dürer (1471–1528) pen and ink 8½ × 5½ ins. c. 1500

Among the collection of copper engravings mentioned earlier are a few portfolios of fine drawings, including one characteristic Dürer and a sheet from one of Hans Holbein the Elder's sketchbooks with portraits on both sides: on one side a pensive young woman, on the other a bearded man. Drawings by Swiss masters are well represented by engravings. However, the outstanding item in this particular group is certainly the self-portrait in watercolour by Tobias Stimmer, which is one of the masterpieces of German portraiture.

THE LIBRARY

The Haldenstrasse, the road leading from the castle of Donaueschingen to the famous Fürstenberg brewery, still looks much as it did in the eighteenth century, with its sober administrative offices and houses built by Prince Joseph Wilhelm Ernst. Two of these, reached by attractive flights of red sandstone steps, stand out from the rest and now house the library and the family archives.

The library building, erected between 1723 and 1735, was originally used by Prince Joseph Wilhelm Ernst as the administrative offices of his *Land* government. After the purchase of the Lassberg Library in 1853 there was not sufficient space for such an extensive collection in the archives building and Prince Karl Egon III therefore built new administrative offices and turned the old building into a library. This collection consists of about 130,000 volumes including some 600 medieval manuscripts and 500 incunabula. The music section containing manuscripts of orchestral and operatic works is a valuable source for musicologists. These came from the court theatre which was burned down in 1850. For nearly a hundred years until 1850 performances of the latest operas were put on there by members of the family and other amateurs. Mozart's *Marriage of Figaro* was produced there only a year after its first performance in Prague in 1785.

The archives are housed in the building next to the library which was erected by Prince Joseph Wilhelm Ernst between 1756 and 1768. The Prince assembled here all the records relating to his estates, arranged in categories and made easily accessible for reference. All the family and official papers were, and still are, systematically deposited here and can be consulted by the public. This unusually comprehensive collection of records is an important source for students of constitutional history and allied subjects relating to the period up to the 1806 Act of Mediation. The upper storey contains a room named after Prince Max Egon, who died in 1959, which is used for displaying some of the treasures from the library. The walls are lined with wooden cases richly decorated with inlay and carving, and similar cases stand

CHRIST CROWNED WITH THORNS
Polychrome wood sculpture.
Height 34 ins. Constance (?) c. 1320

The Max Egon Room in the Archives Building, where some of the treasures from the library are on display. The early eighteenth-century book-cases were originally made for the library of the Fürstenberg castle at Messkirch

Right *Gold ornamented pontifical MS 191 $12\frac{1}{2} \times 9\frac{1}{2}$ ins. Probably executed in Reichenau. Late ninth century*

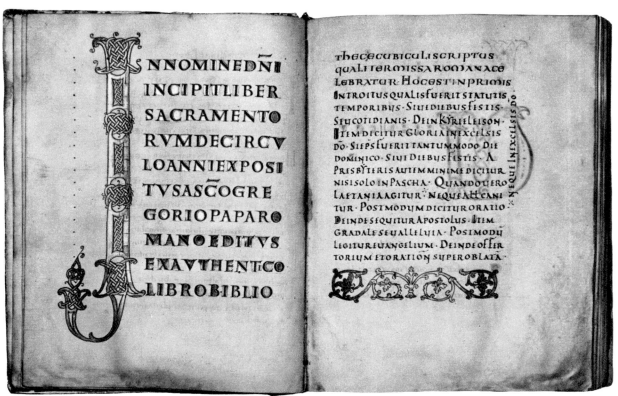

between the two pillars. These were originally made for the castle library at Messkirch, but were brought to Donaueschingen in 1765. Only a few sections had to be added to adapt them to their present setting.

The exhibition contains some of the finest examples of book-binding over the last six hundred years and manuscript books, opened to show the brilliant colours and the gold of the illuminations and miniatures, are displayed in glass cases. The first case contains MS 18 *Paulus Orosius* dating from the eighth century. There is also a Carolingian gold-ornamented pontifical, MS 191, with decoration that is still Anglo-Saxon in style. The two most valuable manuscripts, the Breviary, MS 309, and the Nibelung Manuscript C, MS 633, have a case to themselves. The breviary was inherited from the Werdenberg family and the Nibelung Manuscript was bought by Lassberg during his period at the Congress of Vienna. Part of Lassberg's collection of Middle High German manuscripts is on display here and the rest is kept in the library. This collection was inspired by Lassberg's interest in the Romantic movement; to-day it is an important source for students of philology and literary history.

Silver cover of the Breviary MS 309. Hildesheim c. 1260.
The arms of the Counts von Werdenberg are engraved on the clasps

HEILIGENBERG CASTLE

Heiligenberg stands on the east side of Lake Constance a few miles from the shore on a steep escarpment in the foothills of the Alps. The castle itself stands on a rocky crag, which is only accessible by a bridge. The large forecourt with its former farm buildings and clock-tower is on the site of the ancient fortress which protected the bridge. Nearly all the existing castle buildings date from the sixteenth century. They were erected by Count Friedrich II (1496–1559) and Count Joachim (1538–98), when Heiligenberg came into the possession of the house of Fürstenberg through Count Friedrich's marriage in 1534 to Anna, the last Countess of Werdenberg. The Werdenberg family had ruled the area east of Lake Constance for two hundred years following the death of the last Count of Heiligenberg in 1277.

From 1534 Heiligenberg was one of the most important and influential territorial possessions of the house of Fürstenberg and until 1716 the seat of a very powerful branch of the family. In the seventeenth century the members of this branch allied themselves with Bavaria and France and pursued an anti-Habsburg policy, while the other branches of the family remained loyal to the Habsburgs. As a result the *Egoniden* were expelled from the Empire by Leopold I. For all their love of art and ornament the only trace of their patronage that has survived is some stucco work. For example we know that Cardinal Wilhelm Egon had his portrait painted by Hyacinthe Rigaud and by several other

ST CHRISTOPHER *A miniature from the breviary*
MS 309. 8 × 5 ins. Hildesheim c. 1230

Stained glass windows from the chapel at Schloss Heiligenberg. c. 1320. Originally in the Dominican Abbey of Constance

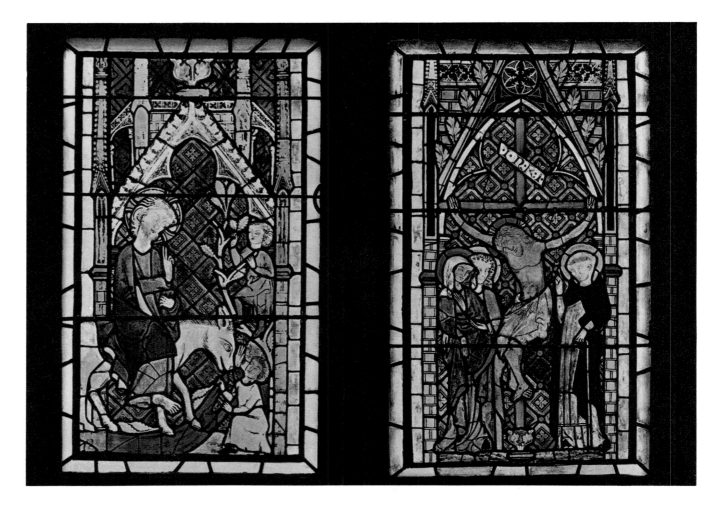

important painters from the court of Louis XIV. Prince Anton Egon, the last of the Heiligenbergs, was regent for Augustus the Strong in Dresden, where he played an important part in the cultural and artistic life of the city and was the virtual founder of the Meissen porcelain industry. None the less there is little evidence at Heiligenberg of these artistic interests.

The atmosphere at the castle of Heiligenberg is quite different from that of Donaueschingen, with its wide variety of collections. Heiligenberg is a typical castle of the German Renaissance and has been inhabited for centuries almost without a break, whereas the great house at Donaueschingen is a nineteenth-century reconstruction. This difference is emphasized by the approach to Schloss Heiligenberg by way of a long bridge and sombre gateway leading directly into the inner court. This is characteristic of the four-sided inner courtyards of many German castles, which have rows of open arcades one above the other, either on one side as at Heiligenberg, or more frequently on several sides. The arcades at Heiligenberg have richly moulded

pilaster decorations which must have been the work of Jörg Schwarzenberger, who was employed for many years at Messkirch. As with all Schwarzenberger's work, the arcades and the clock-tower in the forecourt show signs of Italianate French influence.

After passing an unusual well-room the visitor reaches the chapel, whose porch is decorated with much weathered sandstone carvings. The interior of the chapel gives the impression of great height and its dominant feature is a wealth of carvings on the galleries and ceiling, executed by H. Dürner in the last decade of the sixteenth century. The colouring on the carvings was adapted in keeping with late nineteenth-century romantic taste when the chapel was restored between 1878 and 1884. The magnificent windows *c.* 1320 from the church of the Dominican Abbey in Constance (Inselkloster) were also added during this restoration.

From the gallery a small door leads into the *Rittersaal*, or Knights' Hall, so called by the Romantics. This is the work of

Opposite SELF PORTRAIT *Tobias Stimmer* *(1539–84) pen and watercolour 8 × 6 ins. c. 1563*

Tobias Stimer
von Schaf-
hausen.

The Rittersaal, or Knights' Hall, designed by
Jörg Schwartzenberger. Family portraits from the sixteenth
century to the present day hang on the walls

Opposite *A detail of the ceiling in the Rittersaal at
Schloss Heiligenberg, designed by Jörg Schwartzenberger.
1575/76*

One of the heraldic insets in the windows of the
Rittersaal showing the arms of Count Wilhelm
Werner von Zimmern. Diameter 12 ins. 1541

Jörg Schwarzenberger and is one of the glories of the late German Renaissance, or Mannerist, style. Costly woods, such as mahogany, alternate with brightly painted carving, while light streams in through windows on all four sides, playing on the polished wood floor and on the ancestral portraits which hang on the walls. The quality of the light is further enhanced by the bulls-eye glass of the windows, with their bright heraldic insets. When open, the windows in the outside walls offer a breathtaking view over the smiling landscape round Lake Constance and the distant chain of the snow-covered Alps. After a while one comes to realise that the *Rittersaal* is not so much a hall as a vast loggia in which the splendour of the interior is balanced by the grandeur of the landscape.

Long passages and staircases lead to the remaining apartments, some of which contain seventeenth-century stucco work; others, as well as some of the passages, still have the beamed ceilings and painted decorations of the period *c.* 1570, so that it

takes little imagination to visualize how the castle must have looked in the sixteenth century.

Prince Max Egon had a special affection for Heiligenberg and during the period before and after the First World War he and his wife, Irma Countess Schönborn, acquired a number of objects that had formerly decorated the castle and put the inherited family treasures on display there. Both were keenly interested in family portraits and were fortunate enough to acquire the enchanting Schenk-Werdenberg double portrait (*c.* 1450).

No visit to Heiligenberg would be complete without going down into the crypt chapel, the burial place of the Fürstenbergs. Here the Heiligenberg Madonna and her apostle companions (*c.* 1500) look down in compassion from the altar and from the walls, while Hans Wimmer's bronze crucifix (1951), hanging above the vault of Prince Max Egon and Princess Irma, is a harsh admonition to reflect on the sufferings of mankind and the griefs of two world wars.

**WILHELM SCHENK VON SCHENKENSTEIN
AND AGNES VON WERDENBERG**
panel 6 × 6 ins. Constance (?) c. 1450

THE HEILIGENBERG MADONNA *Anonymous
pupil of Gregor Erhart. Height 45 ins. Ulm (?)
c. 1500. Originally from the Fürstenberg crypt
at Neudingen*

The Earls
Spencer

Kenneth Garlick

The collections at Althorp are rich in pictures, furniture and silver. They were begun by Robert, second Earl of Sunderland, who inherited the Althorp estate in 1643. He acquired most of the portraits by Lely, while from the family of his wife came the celebrated double portrait by Van Dyck. During Sunderland's travels and periods of residence in Europe he also built up a collection of old masters which included Holbein, Van Dyck, Rubens, Salvator Rosa, Bourdon and Lebrun. In 1747 the collection was further enriched following the death of Sarah, Duchess of Marlborough, who bequeathed the Marlborough ambassadorial plate and many pictures to her grandson the Hon John Spencer. His son and grandson, the first and second Earls Spencer, commissioned the portraits of members of the family by Sir Joshua Reynolds which now hang in the Marlborough Room, and subsequent holders of the title have made contributions of varying importance. The present Earl has added to the beauties of the house by recreating Lord Sunderland's Great Room on the first floor, which had been divided during Henry Holland's reconstruction at the end of the eighteenth century.

The Earls Spencer

Kenneth Garlick

Althorp, the home of the Spencer family, lies about seven miles north-west of the county town of Northampton. Its present appearance is due to Henry Holland who, between 1789 and 1791 encased in stone and white 'mathematical tiles' the old red brick of the Elizabethan mansion which the second Earl of Sunderland had incorporated in a new façade in 1666. It is a dignified, composed and very formal exterior, but Horace Walpole who knew the house before and after this major alteration, lamented the 'old simplicity' of what had been before. That 'old simplicity' is recorded in a painting by John Vorstermans of 1677 which hangs at Althorp to-day, and from this it would seem that Walpole exaggerated unless, as may well be, he was referring rather to the inside than the outside of the house. The design of the older façade was certainly controlled but it was not really simple. It was quiet but sophisticated, decidedly Italian, with a balustrade along the line of the roof and the window bays divided one from another by half-columns with Corinthian capitals. It had more variety of surface detail and more variety of colour than that which replaced it, and there must also have been a charm about the surrounding moat, which had been drained and 'turf'd with a sweet carpet,' for which no level gardens could quite compensate. Without and within it impressed the great diarist John Evelyn when he visited in 1688 as 'such as may become a greate Prince'. Nonetheless, despite the outside transformation, Holland did not wholly destroy the earlier character of the house. With some minor changes the outline ground plan remained very much the same. Since then there have been extensive alterations to the arrangement of the rooms within, especially on the ground floor, but as a whole the new house that has grown from Holland's time until to-day is still, in size and shape, basically the same as Lord Sunderland's. It has, even in very recent years, regained one of its first splendours, for the present Lord Spencer

The entrance front at Althorp, home of the Spencer family since 1508

ROBERT SPENCER, SECOND EARL OF SUNDERLAND
Sir Peter Lely (1617–80) oil on canvas 50 × 40 ins. c. 1666.
The founder of the family collection, responsible for acquiring
some of the finest Lelys and Van Dycks

SARAH JENNINGS, DUCHESS OF MARLBOROUGH
Sir Godfrey Kneller (1646–1723) oil on canvas 18¾ × 16½ ins.
c. 1690–95. On her death in 1744 she bequeathed her valuable collection
of paintings to her grandson, the Honourable John Spencer

has recreated Lord Sunderland's 'Great Room', a grand living-room on the *piano nobile* in the Italian style, which Holland had divided into three.

There is a sense of continuity at Althorp which many houses of its size no longer have because the changes that have taken place have been too fundamental. If this is true of the house, which we are to consider primarily as a setting for the collection, it is also true of the collection itself. From time to time, and inevitably, individual works have gone elsewhere, but the character of the collection, like the character of the house, has not changed radically. It remains remarkably rich both in quality and historical association.

The history of the collection is so closely bound up with the history of the family that some familiarity with the family story is essential to an understanding of it. The Althorp estate came into full possession of the Spencers in 1513 when the licence of Althorp Park was granted to John (later Sir John) Spencer by the King. The principal family residence was then Wormleighton in Warwickshire, but the house at Althorp must have been enlarged and aggrandized during the sixteenth century, for in 1603 the Queen, Anne of Denmark, Henry, Prince of Wales and the Princess Elizabeth were entertained there by Sir Robert Spencer, who was afterwards created Baron with the title of Spencer of Wormleighton. His grandson, Henry, third Baron Spencer, who was created Earl of Sunderland, was killed at the Battle of Newbury in 1643, and was succeeded by his son Robert, then only three years old; and it is with him, Robert, second Earl of Sunderland, that the history of the Althorp collection really begins. With him also begins the increased importance of Althorp itself, for Wormleighton was burnt down in the Civil War and from that time Althorp became the family home.

During the second Earl's minority his mother, who before her marriage was Lady Dorothy Sidney (the Sacharissa to whom Edmund Waller addressed a number of his poems), safeguarded the house and estates; but when he came of age he made great changes. About 1666 he began to alter the exterior of the house in the Italian style, as we have seen (the 'pretty outside' which Horace Walpole liked so much). Inside he built the great oak staircase stained with walnut which Evelyn found 'incomparable' and repanelled the long gallery as an appropriate setting for the portraits by Van Dyck and Lely which still hang there to-day – 'a gallery,' wrote Walpole, 'of all one's acquaintance by Vandyke and Lely'.

Sunderland was an able, ambitious and devious character, ambassador to Madrid in 1671 and to Paris in 1674, created a Knight of the Garter by King James II in 1687, but a supporter of the Revolution in 1688. For a time when he was out of favour he lived in Holland. As a young man he travelled in Italy. In

addition to remodelling the house he is said to have employed Le Nôtre to lay out the avenues in the park, and he bought pictures both at home and abroad. As Thomas Dibdin, librarian to the second Earl Spencer, wrote in 1822, 'It was at this period that Althorp began to be enriched by those paintings obtained chiefly from the continental travels of its noble proprietors.' No inventory of Sunderland's collection exists but a large part of it survives among the pictures which hang at Althorp to-day. Perhaps it would be proper to begin by a consideration of the portraits.

There are at Althorp thirty-four portraits by or from the studio of Sir Peter Lely, the majority of which were painted for Lord Sunderland, or were acquired during his time. Many of them, and almost all those that hang in the long gallery have ornate, deeply carved and scalloped frames in the full Italian Baroque style, a type that has become known as a 'Sunderland', but which though Italian in appearance may in fact have been designed in Spain. They form an imposing series, and the frames which with their full curves appropriately repeat the full-blown draperies of the sitters, give them a rather grand air of furnishing *en suite*. They express the taste of a man who was already familiar

The Staircase Hall seen from one of the galleries added by Henry Holland in 1790. On the walls are portraits of members of the Spencer family of various periods

199

*Lord Sunderland's Great Room, restored by the
present Earl Spencer. The mirrors and pier
tables were originally made for the ballroom at
Spencer House, London*

with some of the new palaces and mansions of Europe, and who was aware, as many Englishmen of his class were not, of developments in Flemish, French and Italian art, an awareness that was more precisely reflected in the European pictures which he bought. We may see Sunderland himself in a fine Lely of 1666, an assured and handsome young man who rests his hand possessively on a bust of Diana. Two years earlier, in 1664, he had been painted in Rome by Carlo Maratta, full-length in classical dress, and this portrait with its companion, *Wentworth Dillon, 4th Earl of Roscommon*, forms one of the early pictorial records of the English nobleman abroad, at least a generation before the Grand Tour had become an established part of his way of life. A hundred years later the Englishman in Rome would be painted quite explicitly in the role of visitor, in everyday dress, the more spectacular monuments of the city visible in the background, almost with guide-book in hand. Sunderland and Roscommon, quite to the contrary, are shown as 'ancients' come to life. Only the long hair and perhaps the full sleeve of the shirt betray the seventeenth century. In the case of Sunderland his left hand droops from the pedestal on which his arm is resting to point to a panel in low relief which represents Love overcoming Time, a very probable reference to the fact that he had fled from the threat of a union with Lady Anne Digby, the lady whom in fact he married in 1665.

Lady Anne was herself painted by Lely shortly after her marriage, a rather large and daunting lady, and the portrait now hangs on the great staircase beside that of her husband to which it is a pair. There is another version of it among the 'Windsor Beauties'. She was a daughter of the second Earl of Bristol, and she brought to Althorp the most celebrated of its Van Dycks and one of the finest of his English 'peeces', the double portrait of her father when Lord Digby, and her mother's brother, Lord Russell, later first Duke of Bedford. Venetian in its red and gold and silver, this picture looks most splendid hanging at the far end of the gallery. Its frame is even finer than the 'Sunderlands', more deeply carved, more boldly designed with dolphins, leaves and fruit, a piece of truly remarkable English craftsmanship contemporary with the portrait. This was not however the first Van Dyck to come to Althorp. Penelope, Lady Spencer, wife of the second Baron, Sunderland's grandmother, was painted by him at about the same time as the Digby and Russell group – at least before the death of her husband in 1636 – and her portrait is Van Dyck at his gentlest and most sensitive, predominately a soft blue, the colour of her dress, with a red rosette at the breast, a brown-gold curtain, and a large urn from which or on to which there sprouts or falls a spray of vine. The effect is that of an easy formality, so natural that it is almost an informality, a presentation and a mood which Van Dyck perfected if he did not invent, an interpretation no less natural for having been in the first place calculated.

A third and an important Van Dyck, rather later than the others, the half-length double portrait of Catherine, Countess Rivers and her sister, Lady Andover, attended by a Cupid, was bought by Sunderland at Sir Peter Lely's sale in 1682. A fourth, the whole-length of Rachel de Ruvigny, Countess of Southampton, as Queen of the World trampling on death, probably came to Althorp after the death of her sister-in-law Penelope, Lady Spencer, in 1667. It is not recorded in the house before 1732 when it was noted by Vertue. There are other portraits by Van Dyck, notably the whole-length of the Prince d'Arenberg.

In addition to the portraits there are seven more Van Dycks at Althorp, five heads of Apostles and a sketch for an *Adoration of the Magi*, all bought by Sunderland, and a *St Jerome in Penitence*. The Apostles which now hang with the *St Jerome* in the chapel, would appear to have formed part of a set, somewhat similar to the series painted by Rubens in 1603/4 which is now in the Prado; but if this is correct the others in the set have yet to be identified. They are smaller than the Rubens Apostles, rather more spontaneous in execution, lighter in touch, as one would expect of Van Dyck even at this early stage. The *St Matthew*, who is represented as a young man in contrast to the older figure of Rubens, has features not unlike those of Van Dyck himself.

The remaining pictures known to have been purchased by Lord Sunderland were of a varied character. They included primarily the Rubens sketch for one of the tapestries in the Eucharist series, *David Sacrificing Before the Ark*, which is now at Washington, the famous Holbein *Henry VIII* which now belongs to Baron Thyssen, the Sebastien Bourdon *Deposition*, now the altarpiece in the chapel at Althorp, and the Le Brun *Martyrdom of St Andrew*; but there were others of all kinds – among them a skating scene by Avercamp, a self-portrait attributed to Artemisia Gentileschi, a Bassano *Road to Calvary* which has the chalk mark *My Lord Sunderland £21* still visible on the back, a fine Fetti *The Angel Appearing to Hagar*, and a *Scène Galante* by Paris Bordone, all of these still in the collection. The Bourdon is an important and a rather surprising picture to find in an English country house. For whom it was commissioned and when Sunderland bought it are not known. Bourdon died in 1671 and it was perfectly possible for Sunderland to have bought it from him on a visit to Paris in the 60's before he became ambassador, but it would seem to belong to an earlier date, before the influence of Poussin on his style became so strong. It seems in fact to accord very well with Sir Anthony Blunt's description of another of his paintings, 'an ambitious Baroque composition with a Venetian looseness of handling'. The contrast between it and the more Poussinesque Le Brun is instructive, the contrast between the tenderly emotional

Above ST MATTHEW *Sir Anthony Van Dyck*
(1599–1641) panel $24\frac{1}{4} \times 18\frac{1}{4}$ *ins. c. 1620*

Opposite GEORGE DIGBY, SECOND EARL
OF BRISTOL AND WILLIAM RUSSELL,
FIRST DUKE OF BEDFORD *Sir Anthony Van
Dyck (1599–1641) oil on canvas* 97×62 *ins.
c. 1633*

Overleaf *The Marlborough Room, showing a
chimney-piece and part of the set of furniture
designed for the ballroom at Spencer House,
probably by James Stuart c. 1765. Gainsborough's
portrait of Lady Georgiana Spencer (1763)
hangs over the chimney-piece*

Left LADY PENELOPE WRIOTHESLEY, WIFE OF
WILLIAM, SECOND LORD SPENCER *Sir
Anthony Van Dyck (1599–1641) oil on canvas*
81×50 *ins. c. 1633–6*

Opposite LAVINIA, VISCOUNTESS
ALTHORP *Sir Joshua Reynolds (1723–92)*
oil on canvas 29½ × 24½ ins. 1782

THE MARTYRDOM OF ST ANDREW *Charles
Lebrun (1619–90) oil on canvas 39 × 32 ins. c. 1647*

and the sternly emotional interpretation of a scene of martyrdom, and there is little doubt that the Le Brun if the less moving is the more powerful picture. It is a replica or perhaps a finished study, one of two recorded 'tableaux en petit', for the altarpiece executed for Notre Dame, Paris, in 1647.

Sunderland died in 1702. He was succeeded as third Earl by his son Charles through whose second marriage, to a daughter of the first Duke of Marlborough, the collections at Althorp were eventually to receive a great enrichment. The history is complicated. The Duke of Marlborough had no surviving son. His elder daughter Henrietta, Countess of Godolphin, succeeded him as Duchess of Marlborough in her own right by special act of parliament, and in the ordinary way her son would have succeeded to the Marlborough title and estates on her death; but he predeceased her. At this point therefore the prospective heirs were the sons of her younger sister, Anne, Countess of Sunderland, who had died in 1716. The Sunderlands had three sons, but the eldest, Robert, having succeeded his father as fourth Earl, died before the Duchess, and it was the second son, Charles, fifth Earl, who on her death in 1733 ultimately became third Duke of Marlborough. Through all these vicissitudes however the widow of the first Duke, the celebrated Sarah, Duchess Dowager of Marlborough, was still alive, and she lived on until 1744. She did

not have the disposal of Blenheim or the settled estates, but she had a great deal of her own to bequeath, including the considerable collection of works of art at Marlborough House and her other houses at Wimbledon, Windsor and St Albans. Her heir, as it proved, was not the new Duke but his younger brother John. It was he who succeeded to Althorp when his brother succeeded to the Marlborough title and in this way the Duchess Sarah's pictures were eventually added to those already in the house. For many years however they remained mostly in the houses which had belonged to her and which the family retained.

The Duchess's pictures naturally included portraits of the Duke and herself. There were, among others, the Knellers, the lively half-length of the Duke in armour said to have been painted for her when he was sunburnt, and the well-known portrait of herself where she holds in her hand the locks of hair she severed after a quarrel with her husband. A sketch by Kneller, presumably done at the same time, as the hair appears to be cut short, she bequeathed to her waiting woman, Grace Ridley, and it only came to Althorp in the nineteenth century.

The pictures at Althorp to-day which are known to have belonged to the Duchess are as varied in kind as those collected by Lord Sunderland. She was a great buyer at auctions. The small Francesco Albano *Holy Family* for instance came from the Duke

CINCINNATUS CALLED FROM THE FARM
Salvator Rosa (1615–73) oil on canvas
91 × 102 ins. c. 1640–45

Right WILLIAM POYNTZ *Thomas Gains-*
borough (1727–88) oil on canvas 91 × 60 ins.
1762

Opposite *The Entrance Hall at Althorp, completed in*
1733. The hunting scenes by John Wootton were
commissioned as part of the original decoration

of Portland's sale in 1721, and the well-known self-portrait at the clavichord by Sofonisba Anguisciola from Lord Cadogan's sale in 1726. There are a large Hondecoeter, a large Snyders, and a Cornelis Bisschop *Old Lady* inevitably called *Rembrandt's Mother* in the Duchess's day. More interesting, more unexpected and of higher quality are three of the finest of the smaller pictures in the house, the portrait of *Anna Botzheim of Nuremberg* by Nicholas Lucidel, *A Lady as the Magdalen* (for long miscast as Lady Jane Grey) by the Master of the Female Half-lengths, and *G. B. Grimaldi of Genoa* by Joos van Cleve.

For a large part of the eighteenth century Althorp was used by the family comparatively little. They owned at this time and chiefly used Sunderland House on the site of what is now the Albany, and Wimbledon Park which had belonged to the Duchess Sarah, and later (1755–60) the first Earl Spencer built Spencer House, St James's. Althorp fell into some neglect and it was this which necessitated the repairs and alterations which Holland carried out around 1790. There was however one important series of acquisitions, the paintings by John Wootton which form an integral part of the decoration of the hall. Although the fifth Earl of Sunderland succeeded to the Marlborough title in 1733 he did not live at Blenheim until after the death of Duchess Sarah eleven years later, and in the intervening years he completed alterations which he had begun at Althorp.

Wootton's huge canvases, hunting scenes in which members of the family are presented, and horse portraits of a rather engaging kind – *Brisk* for instance drinking at a trough – are dated 1733. They make an unusual and unexpectedly successful decorative scheme in so grandly classical a setting. Wootton painted two other schemes of the kind, one at Longleat House, the home of the Marquess of Bath, and one at Badminton, the home of the Duke of Beaufort, but in neither do the canvases form so large a part of the architectural whole as here.

The Hon John Spencer died in 1746 only two years after inheriting his grandmother's wealth. He was himself a collector and the Carlo Dolci *Marriage of St Catherine* is one of his acquisi-

tions. His son John was created Viscount Spencer in 1761 and Earl in 1765, and it was he who, as a friend of Reynolds, began to commission from him portraits of members of the family, commissions which extended over nearly thirty years, and which now almost fill the Marlborough Room at Althorp. As a range of portraits going through from *Louisa Poyntz* of 1759 to *Viscount Althorp* of 1786, they present Sir Joshua at his most direct, familiar and intimate. Only the whole-length of the second Earl as a young man in Van Dyck costume, standing pensively with book in hand, illustrates the rather grander exhibition style which he adopted in the 1770's. Some of these portraits are among the best known of all Reynolds' works. *Lavinia, Countess Spencer*, the young

wife of the second Earl, standing in a landscape in a wide-brimmed straw hat, was engraved by Bartolozzi in 1787 two years after it was painted, and that of her sister, *Lady Anne Bingham*, in the actual year of painting, 1786. The lovely group of Georgiana, Countess Spencer with her daughter Georgiana, who afterwards became the Duchess of Devonshire, begun in 1759, was engraved by Watson in 1770, and the portrait of the Countess's second daughter, Harriet Frances, Countess of Bessborough, by Grozer in 1785. By this means they have been almost from the first among the most celebrated Reynolds portraits in the world. Others, like the whole-length of the third Earl, when Viscount Althorp, aged four, self-possessed in his smart clothes, and the second portrait of Lavinia, Countess Spencer, his mother, in a fur wrap, although less well-known from the en-

gravings, have been reproduced so many times that one has been familiar with them all one's life. Less familiar but among the most sympathetic of all Reynolds' female portraits is that of Georgiana, Countess Spencer's close friend, Madame Blanckart, later La Maréchale De Muys. Nearly all these portraits have been exhibited many times, from their first appearance at the Royal Academy in the years of their execution to the Old Master winter exhibitions in the later nineteenth century and the more frequent and varied exhibitions of to-day.

In the same room there are four Gainsboroughs, of the first Earl Spencer, Countess Spencer, Lady Georgiana Spencer, and the Countess's brother William Poyntz. The charming little picture of Lady Georgiana, painted in 1763, four years after the Reynolds group was begun, shows her looking not much older

(Reynolds did not complete his picture until 1763), and with a puckish mouth that one recognizes twenty-three years later in the famous Reynolds group at Chatsworth where she is now the mother and holds her own Georgiana in her lap. *William Poyntz* hangs in the centre of one wall balancing Reynolds' portrait of the second Earl at the other. He stands against a tree, resting but very much alert, gun in hand, bag slung over his shoulder, and his dog Amber resting at his feet. It is interesting that this was a commission from Countess Spencer while the Reynolds of herself and Lady Georgiana was a commission from William Poyntz for himself and did not come to Althorp until 1845. Several of the Reynolds series in fact did not come to Althorp in the first place and one must not think that what is now the Marlborough Room was designed by Holland to hold them. But as things have worked out and as they now hang together they form a most noble group, which vividly conveys to us to-day an understanding of the composure, the natural dignity, the unselfconsciously cultivated way of life of aristocratic society in England in the later eighteenth century. Their setting has recently been enriched by some of the furniture and fittings from Spencer House, which is now let on a long lease.

There are many other eighteenth and early nineteenth century portraits at Althorp, notably Knapton's large group of the Hon John Spencer and his son out shooting with their black servant, Caesar Shaw, Batoni's portrait of Georgiana, Countess Spencer, painted in Rome in 1764, and Hoppner's of Lady Caroline Lamb. In addition there are two portraits of horses and one of a Dutch barge dog, Mouton, by Stubbs. *Scape Flood – a Hunter* which is signed and dated 1777 is a particularly fresh and attractive picture with the stable boy in his pink striped jersey carefully holding the horse's reins.

The portraits in the Marlborough Room form the third and last group of pictures which like Lord Sunderland's and the Duchess of Marlborough's may be considered as making a major contribution to the collection as a whole; but they do not complete it. There are other pictures bought in Italy in the eighteenth century, and in the French and English salerooms in the nineteenth century, which are important and give added variety to the Althorp collection. It seems that the first Earl felt that large Italian paintings would be suitable, as indeed they no doubt were, to adorn the grander rooms in Spencer House. At the Henry Furnese sale in 1758 he bought for £2,200 a version of Guido Reni's *Liberality and Modesty* and Andrea Sacchi's *Apollo Rewarding Merit and Punishing Arrogance*, a picture which had only left Italy some thirty years before. Both of them are large fillers of wall-space. More important as works of art are the two Guercinos, *The Samian Sibyl* and *King David*, bought through the agency of Gavin Hamilton in 1768, which hang in the dining-

MADAME BLANCKART, AFTERWARDS LA MARÉCHALE DE MUYS *Sir Joshua Reynolds (1723–92) oil on canvas 29 × 24 ins. 1771*

GEORGIANA, COUNTESS SPENCER AND LADY GEORGIANA SPENCER *Sir Joshua Reynolds (1723–92) oil on canvas 48¾ × 45 ins. c. 1759–61*

ADMIRAL CORNELIS TROMP *Nicolas Maes*
(1632–93) oil on canvas 41 × 33 ins. 1677

SUPPOSED PORTRAIT OF ANDRÉ
LE NÔTRE *Nicolas de Largillière*
(1656–1746) oil on canvas 54 × 40 ins. 1689

SUPPOSED PORTRAIT OF ROBERT ARNAUD
D'ANDILLY *Philippe de Champaigne (1602–74)*
oil on canvas 35 × 28 ins.

A YOUNG LADY *Corneille de Lyon*
(d. 1574) panel 6¼ × 5½ ins. c. 1560

MARY ANNE WALTHAM *François Quesnel*
(1544?–1619) panel 22 × 17½ ins. 1572

A VENETIAN GENTLEMAN *attributed to Lorenzo Lotto*
(c. 1480–1556) canvas 37 × 34 ins. c. 1510–20

however is the fact that he bought in Rome in 1785 the so-called *Young Cornaro*, a fine Venetian portrait given to Titian at the time of the purchase, and now more convincingly ascribed to Lotto. It is a searching portrait, something of a psychological study of a much pre-occupied young patrician, composed in subdued browns, blacks and greys. The preoccupation of the painter with the fact that the sitter is pondering some problem is, apart from the actual style of the painting, a characteristic of one phase of Lotto's portraiture.

The second Earl seems to have been attracted to French painting. At the Duc d'Alberg sale in London in 1817 he bought Philippe de Champaigne's so-called portrait of Robert d'Andilly, the Jansenist divine, who lived for many years at Port Royal, which, whether d'Andilly or not, is a fine example of de Champaigne's austere and patently truthful portraiture. Three years later at the Quintin Crauford sale in Paris in 1820 he bought the whole-length Pourbus, *Claude de Lorraine, Duc de Chevreuse*, which now looks down the long length of the library, and in 1821 the *Young Lady*, now accepted as one of the few autograph works of Corneille de Lyon. But his main interest was in the collecting of books and he amassed a great and famous library which was sold as a whole to the John Rylands Library in Manchester in 1892. Gibbon who paid a visit to Althorp when the collection was still in the making describes how he 'exhausted a whole morning . . . among the first editions of Cicero'.

The attractive portrait of *Mary Anne Waltham*, one of the attendants of Mary, Queen of Scots, signed in monogram by François Quesnel and dated 1572, a picture which used to be accepted as a portrait of Mary, Queen of Scots herself, was bought by the 4th Earl in 1848. In 1850 he bought a Largillière, thought to be a portrait of André Le Nôtre, and a male portrait by Simon Vouet. It is acquisitions of this kind which provide surprises at Althorp and give unexpected pleasure to the visitor with a discerning eye. Such a visitor will also note with pleasure *Admiral Cornelis Tromp*, by Nicholas Maes, painted in 1676 to commemorate the successful relief of Copenhagen from the Swedish blockade, another of the second Earl's purchases from the d'Alberg sale.

The portraits commissioned by the family during the nineteenth century are also of interest, including a Watts and work by that under-rated artist H. T. Wells. Those of the present century rank as works of art in a great collection as twentieth-century family portraits very rarely do. There are, among others, four charcoal drawings by Sargent, the sixth Earl painted by Orpen at his academic liveliest in 1916, just before his work had set into the fluent similarity of his later style, the present Earl Spencer by Augustus John in 1930, and a beautifully reticent portrait of Countess Spencer by Sir William Nicholson.

room at Althorp with, on the same wall, the two large Salvator Rosas, *Cincinnatus Called from the Farm* and *Diogenes*, which also may have been bought through Hamilton. They form a pair, were painted in the 1640s, and must be reckoned among Salvator's most important works. His latest critic, Luigi Salerno, rates them 'fra i capolavori'.

There are three more Guercinos at Althorp. One, *The Tribute Money*, more important than the others, an early rather Caravaggesque work, has been recently cleaned and is now revealed in remarkably broad and rich tones of blue and red.

When the second Earl Spencer succeeded to the title in 1783 Spencer House was already furnished with pictures, and his own acquisitions perhaps reflect a more personal taste than that of his father. There were naturally more portraits of members of the family. In addition to the Reynolds portraits of his wife and son there are a full-length of himself in Garter robes by Copley and others by Hoppner, Phillips and Shee. Much more interesting

One of a pair of silver pilgrim bottles by John Goode.
Height 23½ ins. 1701

Silver wine fountain and cistern by Pierre Harache.
Height of fountain 23¾ ins. Overall
length of cistern 27 ins. 1700 and 1701

Opposite The Dining Room at Althorp with a display of pieces
from the Marlborough ambassadorial plate and other family silver.
In the foreground is the great wine cistern by Philip Rollo

If the paintings at Althorp form the major part of the collection of works of art, and are that part of it best known to the public, the silver is no less important in its own right. It has indeed been described by A. G. Grimwade as 'without question . . . one of the greatest surviving groups of English ancestral silver', and it has been discussed by him in detail in a recent series of articles published in *The Connoisseur* 1962–64. Its range extends from the Marlborough ambassadorial plate through an important series of pieces by Paul De Lamerie to fine examples of the later eighteenth century and the Regency. It includes, in Mr Grimwade's words, 'one of the most extensive and representative ranges of candlesticks and candelabra, if indeed not

unique, that one may expect to find surviving in one house'; and there are a small number of continental pieces of an equally high quality, among them the earliest in the collection, a silver-gilt *doppelpokal* of about 1600 by Hanss Beutmüller of Nuremberg.

The Marlborough ambassadorial plate became the personal property of the Duchess Sarah, and was a part of her bequest to the Hon John Spencer. It was made in 1701, the year of Marlborough's appointment as Commander-in-Chief of the English forces in Holland, and was a gift to him from King William, and it is for this reason described as 'the King's Plate' in the early plate lists at Althorp. Every piece is splendid. The great wine-cistern by Philip Rollos, an émigré Huguenot silversmith, im-

poses by sheer size (it has an overall measurement of 46 inches) but also, as one looks at it a little longer, by the grand simplicity of the ornament which is confined to the purely functional elements, to the massive scroll feet, the handles, and the boldly spaced gadrooning of the lip. Like all the other pieces of the Marlborough plate it bears the family coat of arms, most beautifully engraved. The fact that the arms are surmounted by the Ducal Coronet and the double-headed eagle of the Holy Roman Empire indicates that they were not engraved until after 1705 when Marlborough as a Prince of the Empire was granted the Principality of Mindelheim.

The Marlborough plate includes a second, rather more elaborately ornamented cistern with a wine fountain by Pierre Harache the younger, a pair of rose-water ewers and dishes by the same maker, and a fine pair of pilgrim bottles which appear from the design to be the work of one of the Huguenot silver-smiths, although they bear the maker's mark of John Goode. The number of fine, later pieces of silver in the collection is far too great to be considered or illustrated in any detail here.

In recent years Althorp has received some of the more important fittings and furniture from Spencer House, notably the chimney-piece in white marble by Athenian Stuart now in the centre of the long gallery, some splendidly ornate mirrors in the newly constructed Great Room and in the Yellow Drawing

Room, and a set of chairs and sofas designed for the ballroom (probably by Stuart) which now enhance the Marlborough Room. Of the other furniture only a table in marquetry and walnut remains from the days of the second Earl of Sunderland. The remainder belongs largely to the time of the first and second Earls Spencer. It includes a number of French pieces, notably by the *ébénistes* Criard, Saunier and Weisweiler. Of the Saunier pieces two mahogany commodes-servantes were ordered by Holland from Daguerre, Paris, for the piers of the dining-room at Spencer House in 1786. Others were purchased, also from Daguerre, in 1791, and one should mention in particular the black lacquer commode *à l'anglais* and the black and gold lacquer encoignures and commode *en suite* which are now in the Yellow Drawing Room.

Space does not allow for a proper consideration of the furniture but the illustrations of interiors give at least an indication of some of the sets and individual pieces. There is however one piece which because of its charm and its associations, and because it is unique, deserves to be mentioned separately; that is the Cabinet-Secretary veneered with harewood and satinwood and probably made by Tait in 1783, or the beginning of 1784. It was a present to Georgiana, Countess Spencer from her son, the second Earl, his wife Lavinia, and her daughters Georgiana, Duchess of Devonshire and Henrietta, Countess of Bessborough (then Lady Duncannon). On one door their initials are inlaid in ivory within an oval frame which surrounds the initials of the Countess and her coronet. On the other door, four M's are inlaid in the same way around the word *Vous*, which is to be interpreted *Les quatres vous aiment* [M] *autour de vous*, a sweet and an odd conceit.

This account of a collection that is large with a history that is long is necessarily restricted – there is no mention of the miniatures, the porcelain and the snuff-boxes which are all important – but one hopes that with the illustrations it may convey that intermingling of the arts and history which gives to Althorp and its collections an especial quality.

Cabinet-Secretary by Tait, veneered with harewood and satinwood. Height 53 ins. 1783–84

HOUGHTON ENGLAND

The Marquess of Cholmondeley

F. J. B. Watson

Houghton Hall in Norfolk was begun by Sir Robert Walpole, England's first Prime Minister, in 1722. With the help of his architect Colen Campbell, William Kent, who designed the interior and much of the furniture, and other such brilliant craftsmen as the sculptor Rysbrack and the Italian stuccatore Artari, he created the finest of the great Palladian country houses with which the Whig magnates filled the English countryside. Walpole also filled Houghton with one of the most remarkable collections of paintings ever assembled by an English collector, including amongst its many masterpieces, twenty Van Dycks, nineteen Rubens and eight Titians. Unhappily the greater part of this wonderful collection was sold by his eccentric grandson, the third Earl of Orford, to Catherine the Great of Russia, and now forms an important part of the Hermitage at Leningrad. At the end of the eighteenth century the house and its remaining contents (including the magnificent sculpture and furniture) descended to the fourth Earl of Cholmondeley, whose successors have added family portraits by Hogarth, Reynolds and others, a masterpiece by Holbein and other old-master paintings. The contribution of the present Marquess has been a fine group of Sèvres porcelain, whilst the collection has also been enhanced by some outstanding French and English eighteenth-century paintings, as well as French eighteenth-century furniture, Renaissance jewels and objects of art inherited by the present Marchioness of Cholmondeley from her brother, Sir Philip Sassoon.

The Marquess of Cholmondeley

F. J. B. Watson

Houghton Hall in the heart of Norfolk, almost mid-way between Norwich and King's Lynn, has a story which is as deeply woven into English history, architecture, art and collecting as any house in the land. It was probably in the summer of 1720 that Sir Robert Walpole, in spite of pressing public and private causes for worry, conceived the idea of pulling down the old-fashioned Jacobean house he had inherited from the long line of modest Norfolk squires who had been his forebears, and replacing it by a more grandiose and more up-to-date Palladian mansion. For his architect he chose Colen Campbell, the leader of the classical re-action against the heavy baroque of Vanbrugh and his school, and Thomas Ripley was to supervise the building work. William Kent was made responsible for the interior decoration and fur-nishing, whilst the large park was to be laid out by a follower of Bridgeman, a certain 'Mr Eyre', according to Sir Robert's son, Horace Walpole. The foundation stone was laid on 24th May,

1722 and work went ahead with such rapidity that the house was partly habitable by 1726 and completely so in 1729, when the small village of Houghton was demolished and its inhabitants rehoused in a series of model cottages outside the park gates. The furnishing, however, was probably not completed for a further five or six years.

The constellation of craftsmen whom Walpole employed – they included the sculptor Rysbrack and the Italian *stuccatore* Artari, in addition to those already mentioned – produced what is unquestionably the most richly decorated, even if it is not the largest, of all the great Palladian palaces with which the Whig aristocracy ornamented the English countryside in the first half of the eighteenth century, thus asserting their political ascen-dancy. It provided a fitting setting for the great art collection, the formation of which was one of the consuming passions of Sir Robert Walpole's full and vigorous life.

Houghton Hall built by Colen Campbell for
Sir Robert Walpole between 1722 and 1729

Below left SIR ROBERT WALPOLE IN THE UNIFORM OF MASTER OF THE ROYAL HOUNDS AND RANGER OF RICHMOND PARK AND WINDSOR FOREST *John Wootton (c. 1686–1765) oil on canvas 34 × 30 ins. c. 1716. The creator of Houghton and the founder of its collections*

Below right PORTRAIT OF HORACE WALPOLE *Rosalba Carriera (1675–1757) pastel 23¼ × 16⅞ ins. Probably executed in 1741 whilst Sir Robert Walpole's son was in Venice on the Grand Tour*

Sir Robert, whose spirit still broods over Houghton, was a most remarkable figure. This chubby, red-faced, 'engaging, ruthless and adroit' man was not only a politician and financial expert of outstanding ability, the first British Prime Minister in the modern sense, a passionate lover of hunting (as his portrait by Wootton shows), and a convivial country squire who 'laughed the heart's laugh', but a connoisseur of quite outstanding taste.

The striking contrast between the highly intelligent politician and financier, the Hogarthian squire for ever surrounded in the country by men who seemed to his son mere 'mountains of roast beef out of whom steamed gravy', and the connoisseur who formed the most remarkable art collection in the England of his day, appeared less curious in the eighteenth century than to-day. Lord Hervey (Pope's 'Lord Fanny' and no man of brawn himself) makes this plain enough in a letter written from Houghton in 1731. Although he speaks of 'a snug little party of about

thirty-odd up to the chin in beef, venison, geese, turkeys, etc and generally over the chin in claret, strong beer and punch', he goes on to add that 'in private we drew plans and cultivated the country'.

Well before the idea of creating Houghton entered his mind, Walpole was buying pictures. His houses in Downing Street and in Chelsea were still full of paintings even after he had hung the cream of the collection at Houghton. His personal interest in the collection is attested by the entries and attributions written in his own hand in the earliest manuscript catalogue of the collection, whilst in dedicating to his father the *Aedes Walpolianae*, the first *catalogue raisonné* of a private picture gallery to be printed in England, Horace Walpole wrote with justice, 'What I offer you . . . is a Work of your own, a plain description of the Effects of your Taste.'

The passion for art collecting grew on Sir Robert with the passing years. He had agents all over Europe buying pictures for him; diplomats and friends, too, sent them either as thank-offerings or to curry favour with so influential a politician. His own direct purchases in the art market bear striking witness to his enthusiasm. The prices he paid were often record ones for the period: £500 for Salvator Rosa's *Prodigal Son*, £700 for Guido Reni's *Consultation of the Fathers of the Church*, £320 for Poussin's *Holy Family* (a letter to Lord Waldegrave shows him to have been willing to go up to £400). When complete the collection totalled over four hundred paintings and included twenty Van Dycks, nineteen Rubens, eight Titians, a large number of Carlo Maratas, five Murillos, three each by Veronese and Reni, two Velasquez, and a Frans Hals (both singularly discerning purchases in that age), a Raphael, an outstanding Poussin and the works of dozens of other highly esteemed old masters.

The sad history of these wonderful paintings is too well-known to require more than a brief mention here. Rich as Sir Robert had become as the result of successful speculation in shares in the South Sea Company and in consequence of holding high political office for over a quarter of a century, the cost of creating Houghton outran even his purse and he left a much encumbered estate on his death in 1745. Although his eldest son who succeeded him at Houghton managed to stave off the apparently inevitable bankruptcy, the wanton extravagance and wayward behaviour of his successor George, 3rd Earl of Orford, lost the collection of paintings for England. In 1779 they were sold *en bloc* to Catherine the Great of Russia for a sum said to amount to £36,080. The sum, large as it was (it must be multiplied by at least twenty to relate it to to-day's prices), only slightly exceeded the valuation of £34,975 placed on the collection at Sir Robert's death and was probably below their market value at that time. It was based on an estimate drawn up on rather curious principles by Benjamin

West. The true tragedy lies in the fact that the sale was unnecessary; it took place at a moment when, according to Horace Walpole, there was real prospect of the estate being disencumbered of debt at last. To Horace, himself an art collector and connoisseur, his nephew's action came as an almost unbearable blow: 'It is the most signal mortification to my idolatry for my father's memory . . . the stripping of the temple of his glory and affection'. All that remains at Houghton to record this inglorious transaction is the portrait of the Empress by Roslin, sent by Catherine to Lord Orford after the sale was signed and sealed.

But if the cream of Sir Robert's collection of old master paintings is to-day absorbed into the Hermitage Museum (apart from the losses due to time and a few masterpieces sold by the impoverished Soviet government in 1929), much that he assembled still remains at Houghton. The family portraits at least were not sold to Catherine II. Wootton's vigorous portrait of Walpole himself in his uniform as Ranger of Windsor Forest and Richmond Park surrounded by his favourite hounds hangs in the great Stone Hall from which he must often have set out hunting. This is surely a most life-like representation of the Hogarthian side of the great minister's character. Then there is the group of pastels by Rosalba, an artist who enjoyed a reputation as a portraitist second to none in the early eighteenth century, showing his three sons, Robert, Edward and Horace, the youngest, who has gained a posthumous celebrity as a letter-writer even greater than his father's as a politician. There are portraits of Sir Robert's two wives by Dahl and Van Loo and a number of other representations of various relations and friends. But if these make a poor showing compared with what came to be known as the Houghton Gallery through the sumptuous albums of engravings published by Boydell, the furniture, sculpture and decorations with which Sir Robert filled the great house survive almost untouched.

No detailed accounts survive for either the building, the decoration or the furnishing of the interior of Houghton. It seems likely that Walpole destroyed them at the time of his fall in 1742, lest they be used by his enemies as evidence of peculation from public funds. As far as the furniture is concerned there is little more than a solitary bill dated 1729 from Thomas Roberts for an unspecified £1,420 8s 7½d. In spite of some difficulty in reconciling dates, this craftsman must surely be the same man who was supplying considerable quantities of furniture to the Crown under successive reigns from the time of James II onwards, until replaced by his successor Richard Roberts in 1714. The Roberts were apparently principally chair-makers (Richard is described as 'chairmaker to his Majesty' in a London newspaper of 1728). But it is not easy to associate any of the magnificent sets of chairs at Houghton with their name with any certainty, for the few identifiable pieces supplied by Roberts

Side table of gilded oak with a marble top and matching wall mirror, both designed by William Kent and carved with motifs of putti and shells. Height of table 34 ins. c. 1730. The chairs on each side are en suite with the sofa illustrated opposite

at Hampton Court, Knowle and Chatsworth are in an earlier style than anything here. Roberts may perhaps have furnished Sir Robert with the set of mahogany chairs and a settee parcel-gilt with simple splayed square feet and contemporary green velvet upholstery that stand in the Stone Hall. These are unlikely to be by William Kent, and there is a very similar chair by Roberts in the Victoria and Albert Museum dating from 1717. It is possible, too, that Roberts was responsible for the set of armchairs and two sofas with gilt walnut frames upholstered with green damask which are now to be found in the Drawing Room (sometimes referred to as the Green Drawing Room, a misnomer since Horace Walpole tells us that it was hung with 'Yellow Caffoy' in his day, and it still has a golden silk on the walls). These, with their arms terminating in splaying eagles' heads and claw and ball feet, seem to date from around 1725. This suite of chairs, too, is unquestionably earlier in date than most of Kent's furniture, which is one of the great glories of Houghton to-day. Fourteen hundred pounds was a lot of money to spend on chairs in the eighteenth century, and one more set of chairs at Houghton may conceivably have been supplied by Roberts. This is a suite not unlike the last with arms terminating in lions' heads, lions' masks above the knees and satyrs' masks on the apron below the front rail of the seat. It is, however, just possible that they are amongst the earliest known examples of Kent's work, though they differ strikingly from the somewhat ponderous classicising manner of his developed style.

William Kent was, however, certainly responsible for the design of the magnificent set of twelve armchairs, four stools and two small sofas of mahogany parcel-gilt and upholstered with a deep red cut-velvet matching the walls of the Saloon where they stand. The exceptional richness of their carving with the huge shell below the centre of the front rail of the seat, female masks below the knee, swags of foliage and double scrolls, distinctly recall the chair which appears as Plate 43 in Vardy's *Some Designs of Mr Inigo Jones and Mr William Kent*, issued in 1743 some years after the completion of Houghton. Kent, too, was certainly responsible for the design of the splendid gilt side-tables surmounted by huge over-mirrors which stand between the windows in the same room. Below the marble top is a life-sized *putto* seated in a shell, whilst another, holding up a swag of flowers and also seated in a shell, surmounts the cresting of the mirror.

The sources of Kent's style are puzzling. It is generally declared to derive from Venetian work of the eighteenth century, but the resemblance is of the slightest, though there is a vaguely Italianate note in its somewhat florid and monumental character. The whole style of these tables, and still more of another pair, also by Kent, whose marble tops are supported on the backs of two female sphinxes, is surely far more French than Italian.

Mahogany chair carved with lions' heads and satyrs' masks, and gilded. Probably designed by William Kent (1684–1748) height 35½ ins. c. 1730

Sofa of carved mahogany with gilt enrichments and upholstered with crimson Utrecht velvet. Designed by William Kent (1684–1748) for Houghton. Height 49 ins. c. 1730

Lebrun designed a number of side-tables of a similar character which were executed in silver for the furnishing of Versailles and survived there until melted down to pay for Louis XIV's vainglorious wars. Even though Kent can hardly have seen such things (the last were melted down in 1709), the magnificence of the silver furniture at Versailles made such an impression on contemporaries that he can hardly have been unaware of its character.

The superb bed hung with green Italian velvet which Kent designed for the State Bedchamber is of a far more purely classical design than the side-tables. Here again Kent's favourite shell-motive plays a prominent part in the decoration surmounting the bed-head, designed as a classical sarcophagus with a broken pediment. This simple but truly monumental piece of furniture owes its impressive effect as much to the magnificence of the material used as to the design, a rich green Italian silk-velvet, with appliqué decoration of gold passementerie. The lavish use of this material throughout the house contributed greatly to the sumptuous appearance of the interior which so struck contemporaries. Sir Thomas Robinson, himself an amateur architect of distinction, commenting on a visit to Houghton at just about the time the interior was completed, remarks not only on 'the vast quantity of mahoganie' (a very recent and costly furniture material in England) everywhere, but specifically singles out the 'Genoa velvet and damask' for praise: 'this one article is the price of a new house, for in one drawing-room there are to the value of £3,000'.

Throughout the house the textiles used are extraordinarily rich. Sir Robert Walpole clearly spared no expense. In the pure air of Norfolk they have remained in an amazing state of preservation. Green Italian velvet is used for many of the chairs. The walls of the Saloon are likewise hung with contemporary Utrecht cut-velvet of deep crimson colour, a material also used to upholster the seats of the parcel-gilt mahogany furniture in the same room; another set of chairs (by William Kent and in the Marble Parlour or dining-room) with gilt frames and a high back *en anse de panier* is covered with cut-wool velvet, this time crimson on a cream ground. Of an almost equally astonishing freshness are the Spitalfields silk wall-hangings in the White Drawing Room (once the 'Carlo Maratta' Room where Sir Robert Walpole's group of greatly admired paintings by this artist hung). They replace earlier hangings of green velvet and are woven with a neo-classic design of a very French character, closer in style to Salembier than to Robert Adam; they were presented to the First Marquess of Cholmondeley by the Prince Regent. Here time has faded the pure white of the original background to a delicate ivory, much to its advantage. This material is rather later in date than the Italian velvets. It was installed in

Above *The Stone Hall, originally the main entrance hall. The walls are faced with cream-coloured Whitby stone from Yorkshire. On stone brackets round the room are a series of classical marble busts obtained for Sir Robert Walpole in Rome. The writing table and matching cartonnier on the right of Rysbrack's chimneypiece are stamped by Martin Carlin* (maître *1766*)

Left *Bust of Sir Robert Walpole by John Michael Rysbrack (1693–1770) Height 25 ins. c. 1730*

Opposite top *The Green State Bed designed by William Kent. Height 16 feet. 1732*

Opposite bottom *Gilt-gesso table with mirror top of engraved* verre eglomisé *with interlacing Rs and Ws, the monogram of Sir Robert Walpole. Height 28 ins. c. 1735–40*

225

1797 at the same time as an azure-blue Chinese hand-painted wallpaper was put up in the Cabinet, where Sir Robert's wonderful group of Van Dyck's, purchased in 1725 from Lord Wharton, formerly hung, together with Rubens' portrait of his wife, Helena Fourmont (now in the Gulbenkian collection, Lisbon), perhaps the most famous old-master painting in all England in Sir Robert's day. These changes were carried out by the 3rd Earl of Cholmondeley shortly after he inherited Houghton and are, to this day, the only substantial alterations in Sir Robert's original decorative scheme. But of all the wall-hangings in the house the set of Mortlake portraits in the Gold Tapestry Room is the most interesting to-day. This consists of five life-size portraits in tapestry representing James I and his Queen after portraits by Van Somer; Charles I and Henrietta Maria after portraits by Van Dyck; and a portrait of Christian II of Denmark, James I's brother-in-law after Franz Cleyn. The tapestries are surrounded by splendid baroque borders incorporating medallion heads of the Royal Stuart children. This set, perhaps the last great set of tapestries to be woven in England, is dated 1672 and signed in the selvedge F. P. for Francis Poyntz, director of the Mortlake factory from 1670 onwards and self-styled King's tapestry-maker. The conception of the set, woven for Charles II, was perhaps due to Ralph Montagu, later Duke of Montagu, who had purchased the office of Master of the Great Wardrobe shortly before this date. The account for the tapestries amounted to the immense sum of £1,416 13s 11d, and was paid in 1675 presumably when the tapestries finally came off the looms. Beneath Kent's very Italianate gold and white ceiling with a hexagonal central compartment painted with arabesques surrounding a mythological scene, they tell with great effect. How the set left the Royal Collection to enter that of Sir Robert Walpole is not known; possibly it was presented to Walpole by George II who can hardly have wanted life-size Stuart portraits hanging on his walls.

The fact that the greater part of Walpole's collection of paintings has gone for ever gives heightened importance to his surviving sculpture. This falls into two distinct groups: the decorative sculpture forming part of the architecture of the house and the free-standing pieces assembled as part of his art collection. Rysbrack, one of the two leading sculptors working in England in the eighteenth century, appears to have been a favourite both of Sir Robert and his son Horace. No doubt Kent introduced him, for they were working together at Kensington Palace at the time when Houghton was begun. His marble bust of Sir Robert which surmounts the chimney-piece and dominates the Stone Hall, represents him in his political aspect. In spite of the presence of the Garter Star, he is depicted as a Roman Senator, thus taking his place amongst the imperial Roman portrait busts pur-

chased for him in Italy by Matthew Brettingham which stand on stone brackets around the other three sides of the room.

Rysbrack was perhaps the first sculptor in Europe to revive this Roman style for contemporary portraiture in 1723 with his bust of the Earl of Nottingham. Even a superficial glance shows that the bust is a good likeness of Walpole, and we have Vertue's word that it was 'modeld from the life' in 1726 and 'very much like him and approved of'. It stands in front of a large bas-relief of a classical sacrifice forming the overmantel. This is one of several such reliefs by Rysbrack in the house. Another, representing a *Sacrifice to Bacchus* is set above the chimney in the Marble Parlour, as Sir Robert's dining-room was known. The full-sized cartoon for the latter was given to the British Museum a few years ago and is the only thing of its kind to survive from the hand of an English sculptor, as well as being a remarkably fine piece of draughtsmanship.

Each door of the great cubical Stone Hall is surmounted by a pediment on which *putti* by Rysbrack are reclining. They represent such abstract conceptions as Time and Eternity, though their actual significance is not very apparent to-day. Surmounting the pediments of each door are rectangular bas-reliefs in the classical style, one of which, a 'Sacrifice of a Bull', is derived from an engraving in Montfaucon's *L'Antiquité Expliquée*. No doubt the others derive from similar sources, a witness to the awakening interest in classical sculpture which the growth of the Grand Tour brought in its train. Larger reclining figures symbolising Peace and Plenty also by Rysbrack, adorn the pediment surmounting the central window of the Stone Hall (originally the main entrance of the house) and correspond to two figures of Neptune and Britannia on the exterior pediment, flanking a cartouche carved, also probably by Rysbrack, with Sir Robert's arms surrounded with the Garter collar. All these sculptures (the terracottas for most of which were sold with the contents of the sculptor's studio in 1766) contribute greatly to the classical effect aimed at by architects of the Palladian school in what Shaftesbury called 'these splendid and exact piles'.

The only other sculptor to contribute to the architectural decoration of the house was the Italian (or rather Swiss, for he was born at Lugano) *stuccatore*, Giuseppe Artari, who came to England about 1720. Hitherto he had worked only for the architect James Gibbs, and generally in collaboration with another Italian *stuccatore*, Giovanni Bagutti. It was probably the fact that Campbell had employed Bagutti at Mereworth just at the time that he was beginning work on Houghton that determined him to employ his colleague Artari at Houghton, where he was engaged to execute the elaborate ceiling and deep cornice of the Stone Hall, around which the gayest and most Italianate of *putti* laugh and play amongst swags and pendants of leaves. At the

GLADIATOR *Hubert Le Sueur* (*c. 1580–1670*) *bronze, life-size. c. 1630. A cast after the 'Borghese Gladiator', a Roman bronze in the Vatican Museum. Presented to Sir Robert Walpole in 1722 by the eighth Earl of Pembroke, who removed it from the gardens at Wilton*

Below THE LAOCOON *A bronze cast of the famous Hellenistic bronze in the Vatican, made c. 1690 by the brothers Jean-Jacques (1635–1700) and Jean-Balthazar Keller (1638–1702) under the supervision of François Girardon (1628–1715) for the gardens at Versailles, but never put in position*

227

THE CHOLMONDELEY FAMILY *William Hogarth (1697–1764)*
oil on canvas 28 × 35¼ ins. Signed and dated 1732. On the left is
Mary Walpole, Viscountess Malpas, Sir Robert's daughter, who
married George, third Earl of Cholmondeley, seated in the centre.
Her eldest grandson, the fourth Earl (and subsequently first
Marquess of Cholmondeley), inherited Houghton

Opposite *The Gold Tapestry Room hung with Mortlake tapestries of*
royal portraits woven 1672–75. Visible are Charles I, Queen Henrietta
Maria, and, right, Christian IV of Denmark. Beneath the tapestries is a
Louis XIV Boulle commode of unusual design

centre of each side, are large medallions enclosing portraits in
relief of Sir Robert and members of his family.

Facing Rysbrack's chimneypiece is Sir Robert's most important single purchase in the way of sculpture, a full-size cast of the
Laocoon in bronze. Although the *Aedes Walpolianae* describe this
as 'a fine Cast in Bronze by *Giradon*' there can be little doubt that
it was, in fact, cast by Balthazar Keller and his brother, *fondeurs*
du Roi to Louis XIV, from the mould taken in Rome which is
listed (together with other moulds of classical sculpture) in the
inventory of their *atelier* at the Arsenal after their deaths. Bronzes
from these were cast under Girardon's supervision for the decoration of Versailles, but the appalling economic consequences of
Louis XIV's wars brought the scheme to an abrupt termination
before the eighteenth century was out. This no doubt was why
Sir Robert's eldest son was able to purchase the *Laocoon* for
£1,000 for his father in Paris, as a manuscript note by Horace
Walpole in the writer's copy of the *Aedes Walpolianae* tells us. A

Opposite PORTRAIT OF AN UNKNOWN WOMAN WITH A SQUIRREL AND A MAGPIE *Hans Holbein (1497–1543) panel 21¼ × 15¼ ins. c. 1727–28. The sitter was probably a member of the circle of Sir Thomas More*

Left SELF-PORTRAIT *Thomas Gainsborough (1727–88) oil on canvas 23 × 19½ ins. 1754*

Below PORTRAIT OF THE ARTIST WITH HIS WIFE AND DAUGHTER *Thomas Gainsborough (1727–88) oil on canvas 35½ × 27 ins. c. 1752*

further note asserts 'it is said that the Empress of Russia offered £5,000 for this'.

The most interesting piece of sculpture in the house, however, is a life-size cast of the Borghese *Gladiator* which stands in the well of the Great Staircase. It is supported at the level of the first floor on an exceptionally high pedestal consisting of four Doric columns of stone supporting a white marble podium, an adornment specially designed for it by William Kent who painted the surrounding walls in chiaroscuro with mythological subjects and panels of arabesque work. Horace Walpole described this as 'a fine Cast in Bronze of the Gladiator, by *John of Boulogne*, which was a present to *Sir Robert* from *Thomas*, Earl of Pembroke'. This attribution is certainly incorrect, for the cast is the work of Hubert Le Sueur, 'the most industrious and excellent Statuary in all materials that ever this country enjoyed', as Peacham somewhat exaggeratedly called him. The mistake, however, is easily understood, for Walpole and his contemporaries believed Le Sueur to be a pupil of Giovanni Bologna. The figure corresponds in every particular (e.g. such minor features as the shaped plate on which the right forefoot rests) with the version of the same subject cast for Charles I by Le Sueur around 1630 at the same

THE WHITE DUCK *Jean-Baptiste Oudry* (*1686–1755*)
oil on canvas 37½ × 27¾ ins. Signed and dated 1753

Opposite LA LECTURE DE MOLIÈRE
Jean-François de Troy (1679–1752)
oil on canvas 28½ × 35¼ ins.
Signed and dated 1728

time as a group of bronzes after other celebrated classical marbles. These once stood in the Privy Garden at St James's and the survivors now adorn the East Terrace Garden at Windsor Castle.

Philip, 4th Earl of Pembroke, was Lord Chamberlain to Charles I and on excellent terms both with his master (who gave him the Raphael *St George* in exchange for the wonderful series of Holbein drawings at Windsor) and with Le Sueur who had already cast an effigy of his father the 3rd Earl. Nothing is more probable than that he should have been permitted to acquire a duplicate of the *Gladiator* (the best of the series according to Vertue) when the sculptures were being cast for St James's. In 1722, one year before the gift to Sir Robert Walpole, Thomas, 8th Earl of Pembroke had presented another statue by Le Sueur, the life-size portrait of his ancestor William, Lord Pembroke to

Oxford, both of them removed from the garden at Wilton.

No question arises over the traditional authorship of the large bronze group of the *Rape of a Sabine* which stands on a table in the centre of the Stone Hall. This, a simplified version of Bologna's marble of the same subject in the Loggia dei Lanzi in Florence, is an exceptionally fine bronze casting, probably done under the artist's own supervision. It was a gift to Sir Robert from his younger son's close friend, Sir Horace Mann, who doubtless acquired it in Florence where he was British Resident.

The elderly Horace Walpole succeeded to Houghton as 4th Earl of Orford on the death of his nephew, who had wrought so much 'havoc and spoil' there. When he died a bachelor in 1797 the Earldom of Orford, granted to Sir Robert Walpole on his retirement in 1742, became extinct. The house passed to Horace Walpole's great-nephew, the 4th Earl of Cholmondeley, grand-

son of his sister Mary Walpole, who appears in Hogarth's painting of *The Cholmondeley Family*. Although the new owner renovated a few of the rooms at Houghton, as we have already seen, Cholmondeley Castle in Cheshire was his family seat and throughout the nineteenth century the great house in Norfolk was seldom occupied continuously for any length of time, until this century when the present Marquess and Marchioness made it their principal home.

The pictures they brought with them have done a great deal to fill the tragic gap caused by the sale to the Empress of Russia. They fall into three groups: Cholmondeley family portraits, a small number of old-master paintings from the same source, and others belonging to the present Marchioness of Cholmondeley.

By far the most important of the second of these groups is a *Portrait of an Unknown Woman with a Squirrel and a Magpie* by Hans

Holbein, a work worthy to be compared with the finest of Sir Robert's lost pictures. The sitter in this extraordinarily life-like portrait has been compared with the drawing at Windsor Castle of Margaret Siggs, Sir Thomas More's daughter, who wears a similar fur cap, but seems considerably older. Although she remains unidentified for the present, it appears likely that she was a member of the circle of Sir Thomas More. The picture seems to have come into the possession of the Cholmondeley family only during the late eighteenth century, having at one time been in the Six collection as well as those of Sir William Hamilton and an unidentified 'Mrs Hunter'. Other old-masters purchased by Lord Cholmondeley in the eighteenth century, and now at Houghton, included a splendid working sketch by Rubens, for the painting of the *Marriage of Marie de Médicis*, in the Louvre.

Undoubtedly the most attractive of the Cholmondeley family

portraits transferred from Cheshire is Hogarth's portrait group of *The Cholmondeley Family*. Painted in 1732 it shows Sir Robert Walpole's daughter Mary, Viscountess Malpas, with her husband (later the 3rd Earl of Cholmondeley) seated in a library with their children, and therefore provides an appropriate visual record of the way by which Houghton descended to its present owners.

All the male children in this painting died before their father, who was himself succeeded in the Earldom by his grandson George, 4th Earl of Cholmondeley and inheritor of the house, who was advanced to the Earldom of Rocksavage and Marquissate of Cholmondeley by George III in 1815. His portrait, in coronation robes, by Sir Joshua Reynolds, painted in 1780, hangs in the Saloon as a pendant to the same artist's full-length portrait of his mother-in-law, Mary, Duchess of Ancaster, executed rather earlier in 1764.

There are a number of other Walpole and Cholmondeley family portraits at Houghton (notably by Allan Ramsay, Hoppner and Pompeo Batoni) and the present generation has added to them Sargent's two fine portraits of the present Marchioness and a further splendid example of his work in a portrait of her mother, Lady Sassoon. But the most important addition to the picture collection in the present century has been the group of French and English eighteenth-century paintings inherited by the present Marchioness from her brother, Sir Philip Sassoon.

Notable amongst his collection of English paintings was a group of conversation pieces, a type of eighteenth-century portraiture then only beginning to awaken the interest of collectors through the enthusiasm of a few discerning amateurs like Sir Herbert Hughes-Stanton and Sir Philip himself. Amongst this group Gainsborough's appealing *Portrait of the Artist with his Wife and Daughter* is outstanding on both aesthetic and historical grounds. Painted early in the artist's career, about 1751/52, this represents the peculiarly English genre in its fully developed form. The genre, which had its roots in both Dutch and French painting, began to be fashionable in England in the first decade of George II's reign and Hogarth's *Cholmondeley Family* is an admirable example of the art in its early stages of development.

The Gainsborough, whose pedigree goes straight back to the artist's daughter Susanna, was acquired by Sir Philip in 1927. Three years later he purchased another Gainsborough 'conversation', *Mr and Mrs Brown of Tunstall and their Child*. Painted about 1754/55, it dates from shortly after his own family group. It was in 1754, too, that Gainsborough painted a third picture which was once in Sir Philip's collection and is now at Houghton. This *Self Portrait* is an extraordinarily fluent performance showing him head and shoulders in a tricorne hat, painted in subtly varying tones of brown. Gainsborough rarely achieved the note of informality in portraiture with greater success than in this, his earliest surviving representation of himself.

Opposite top *William Kent's chimney-piece in the Drawing Room. On either side are two French secrétaires à abattant in the Louis XVI style lacquered with* vernis Martin *in the Chinese style. The one on the left is stamped by Pierre Macret (*maître *c. 1758), and the one on the right by L. Boudin (*maître *1761)*

Far left *Drop-front secretaire (secrétaire à abattant) veneered with thuya wood. Stamped by Georges Jacob (*maître *1767) c. 1792. On it stands a Vincennes bowl filled with porcelain flowers from the same factory*

Left *Commode of black and gold* vernis Martin *in the Chinese style by Jacques Dubois (*maître *1742). Height 34½ ins. The mounts are stamped with the crowned C, a hallmark used between 1745 and 1749 when a tax was levied on gilt bronze. The green lacquered Louis XVI clock is in the style of Bernard II Van Risamburgh (*maître *before 1735). The wall hangings are of Spitalfields silk c. 1800*

Occasional table *(table à la Pompadour) lacquered with green* vernis Martin *and mounted with gilt bronze. Height 28¼ ins. Probably by Bernard II Van Risamburgh (*maître *before 1735)*

Opposite *English portrait miniatures. In the second row, miniatures of James I and Ann of Denmark by Nicholas Hilliard (1547–1618/19) flank a miniature of Robert Devereux, Earl of Essex by Isaac Oliver (c. 1568–1617). Top right, a portrait of Charles II as a boy by David des Granges (1611/13–c. 1675), and bottom left, a portrait of an unknown woman by Richard Cosway (1742?–1821)*

A group of Renaissance jewels. The necklace of gold and enamel is probably of German seventeenth-century workmanship. At the top left is a pendant of a merman, the body formed of a baroque pearl mounted with gold and enamel, perhaps Italian sixteenth century. The miniature of the future George IV framed with diamonds and pinned to a ribbon was presented to the first Marchioness of Cholmondeley by the Prince Regent in 1797

There are other English conversation pieces (by Devis for instance) at Houghton, but the French sources of inspiration of this type of picture could hardly be better illustrated than by De Troy's *La Lecture de Molière*, a more sophisticated and more psychologically subtle representation of a scene of daily life than most English examples of the genre. The date of this painting has usually been given as 1710 owing to the misreading of the somewhat rubbed signature. In fact it was painted in 1728, a date much more congruent with the period of the furniture and dresses shown. It thus falls into that short period from about 1725 to 1735 when, as an anonymous contemporary writer tells us, De Troy turned from large-scale history or religious paintings to produce what he calls the artist's *tableaux de mode*. *La Lecture* may even have been painted for the great financier, Samuel Bernard, for whom De Troy was working throughout that year. Later it was acquired by Frederick the Great (perhaps through his agent in Paris, Count Rothenberg) and hung as a pendant to the same artist's *Declaration de l'Amour* (dated 1731) in his palace of Sans Souci at Potsdam until the period of the French Revolution. In 1806 it passed into the collection of Baron Vivant-Denon, Napoleon's brilliant adviser on the arts, one of the first connoisseurs to appreciate French *dix-huitième* art after the reaction against it provoked by the Revolution. After the death of his nephew and heir, Brunet-Denon, in 1846, it was acquired like so many important French eighteenth-century paintings by the 2nd Earl of Lonsdale.

Another famous collector of French eighteenth-century painting, the Swedish count Tessin, once owned Oudry's remarkable still-life *The White Duck*. It was exhibited in the Salon of 1753 as item 23 of the catalogue:

Autre de trois pieds sur deux & demi, representant sur un fond blanc tous objets blancs, comme Cannard blanc, Serviette damassée, Porcelaine, Crême, Bougie, Chandelier d'argent & Papier.

In a discourse on colour delivered to the *Académie* on 24th June, 1749, Oudry describes a method of painting silver objects which he might well have intended to demonstrate practically with this very picture. In order to get a piece of silver in the correct tone of white, the artist, he writes, should place beside it 'plusieurs objets d'un autre blanc, comme linge, papier, satin, porcelaine. Ces différents blancs vous feront evaluer le ton précis qu'il faut pour rendre votre vase d'argent'. Elsewhere he tells how his master, Largillière, threw away a bouquet of gaily-coloured flowers that the young Oudry was painting and replaced them by 'un paquet de fleurs qui soient toutes blanches' putting beside them on the table 'deux ou trois autres objets blancs pour me servir de règle pour la justice de la couleur'. The masterly success of *The White Duck* is sufficient comment on the soundness of Largillière's teaching.

The important group of French eighteenth-century furniture at Houghton and at Lord Cholmondeley's London house in Kensington Palace Gardens (where the Oudry hangs) comes

mostly from Sir Philip Sassoon. The greater part of it is of the Louis XVI period, but there are a few examples dating from the age of Louis XIV and Louis XV also. Outstanding amongst the Louis XVI pieces at Houghton are two *secrétaires à abattant* standing one on each side of the chimney-piece in the White Drawing Room. Both are painted in bright reds, greens and creams, with Chinese scenes in *vernis Martin* imitating Oriental lacquer. The secretaire on the left, predominantly red in colour, is stamped by Pierre Macret (*maître c.* 1758) whilst that on the other side of the fireplace bears the signature of Léonard Boudin (*maître* 1761) and is lacquered green with Oriental figures on a cream ground. This colour scheme is repeated with variations, by two smaller pieces of furniture in the room mounted with Sèvres porcelain plaques. The one, a small *table en chiffonnière* also lacquered green, the most famous of the colours devised by the brothers Martin, has a white Sèvres top painted in a reserve with a scene in the style of Teniers within a bold Greek key border in blue. This piece, which is unstamped, appears to be by Bernard II Van Risamburgh (*maître* before 1735), the interpretation of whose mysterious signature B.V.R.B. puzzled scholars for so long. It is one of the type almost certainly known to contemporaries as a *table à la Pompadour*, for that lady possessed a number of similar tables, and was painted by Boucher with one at her side. The second piece, in the manner of Martin Carlin (*maître* 1766), is of the kind delightfully known as a *serviteur fidèle*. Its circular top which rests on a single wooden leg with splayed feet is mounted with a highly decorative plaque of green and blue Sèvres porcelain of 'Catherine wheel' design. Above this rises a pair of candle-holders on movable and extensible arms of gilt bronze.

A solitary, but particularly magnificent example of Louis XV furniture stands in the same room. This is a commode of bombé shape also lacquered in the oriental style in black and gold *vernis Martin* and bears the stamp of Jacques Dubois (*maître* 1742). The mounts are particularly fine examples of rococo gilt-bronze work and are all stamped with the crowned-C showing that the piece was made in the years between 1745 and 1749 when a tax was levied on this semi-precious metalwork.

Considerably later is a drop-front secretaire with thuya wood veneer and stamped by Georges Jacob (*maître* 1767) which stands in the drawing-room at Kensington Palace Gardens. This must have been made at the end of this *ébéniste*'s career, for the mounts, of exquisite quality, are of a design found on Riesener's furniture in the days when he was *ébéniste du Roi*. Other craftsmen are unlikely to have found these available for general use before the break-up of the guild system in 1791.

The many small objects of art (*objets de vitrine*, as our nineteenth-century ancestors preferred to call them) at Houghton,

PORTRAIT OF SYBIL, FIFTH MARCHIONESS OF CHOLMONDELEY
John Singer Sargent (1856–1925) oil on canvas 53½ × 35½ ins. Signed and dated 1922.

Opposite *A group of eighteenth-century Sèvres porcelain collected by the present Marquess of Cholmondeley*

include notable groups of Renaissance jewellery, rock crystal and portrait miniatures. The greater part of these came to Lady Cholmondeley, not from her brother, but from her mother's family, the Rothschilds. Space is insufficient to allow of a detailed description of these small objects here. The reader's attention can only be drawn to a few outstanding pieces from those chosen for illustration. Amongst the seventeenth-century miniatures, for instance, there are portraits of James I and his Queen by Nicolas Hilliard, a signed David de Granges of Charles II as a boy, and a splendid Cosway of an unknown lady of the eighteenth century. The early jewellery includes a remarkable enamelled badge of the Order of Saint-Michel which must date from the seventeenth century, a splendid enamelled gold chain probably of German seventeenth-century make, and a knotted blue ribbon to which a portrait miniature is attached, an object presented by the Prince Regent to the 1st Marchioness, on the occasion of his visit to Houghton in 1797. She was a daughter of the 3rd Duke of Ancaster and co-heir with her sister to the hereditary office of Lord Great Chamberlain which, since that time, has been held in alternate reigns by a Marquess of Cholmondeley and an Earl of Ancaster.

Each generation which has owned Houghton, with the exception of the 3rd Earl, who sold so many of the choicest gems of painting to the Empress of Russia, has added something to the family inheritance. The process is a continuing one and the present Marquess is an active collector of Sèvres porcelain, a striking array of which decorates the dining- and drawing-rooms at Kensington Palace Gardens, as well as being dispersed through the various rooms at Houghton. It will thus be seen that the Cholmondeley collection, unlike many which have descended from the past into the more circumscribed world of the later twentieth century, is not a dead 'museum' but a living, organic creation. The differing tastes of successive generations imposed one upon another, so far from producing an appearance of diversity achieve, by means which are both psychological and aesthetic, a remarkably unified effect.

When the great German art historian Waagen had completed his five month tour of the art collections of England in 1835, he wrote in the concluding letter of his invaluable study *Treasures of Art in Great Britain*:

You will now have been able to form an idea of the astonishing treasures of admirable works of art of all descriptions which this island contains . . . I often feel some apprehension of my being unable to master the whole. I am literally, therefore, in an *embarras de richesses* and frequently wish for the hundred eyes of Argus, all of which would find ample employment here. . . . I cannot refrain from again praising the refined taste of the English for thus adorning the rooms they daily occupy, by which means they enjoy from their youth upwards the silent and slow but sure influence of works of art.

Time, taxation, social change, the chances of inheritance and the displacement of this country by America as the wealthiest centre of the Western world have greatly altered the spectacle of English collecting which Dr Waagen studied to such effect. But, were he to return to-day, the great German art-historian would find at Houghton an art collection which would bring to his mind vivid memories of the sort of hereditary collection which impressed him so greatly wherever he went in England just over a century ago.

Four paintings from the collection of Sir Robert Walpole sold to Catherine the Great of Russia in 1779 by the third Earl of Orford.
Left to right: SIR THOMAS WHARTON *Van Dyck*;

THE HOLY FAMILY *Nicolas Poussin*; PORTRAIT OF HIS WIFE, HELÈNE FOURMENT *Peter Paul Rubens*; PORTRAIT OF CLEMENT IX *Carlo Maratta. Taken from engravings of* The Houghton Gallery *by Boydell*

The Princes de Condé and the Duc d'Aumale

Prince Raoul de Broglie

Chantilly represents the successive heritage of four great families: d'Orgemont (four-teenth century), Montmorency (fifteenth to seventeenth centuries), Condé (seventeenth to nineteenth centuries), and Orléans (nineteenth century). The Château as we see it is essentially a nineteenth-century creation, because everything earlier – except the mid-sixteenth-century Petit Château – was demolished during and after the French Revolution, when the vast collections it housed were also seized, pillaged and dispersed. The rebuilding and reassembling of family possessions was begun by the Prince de Condé in 1814, after his return from exile in England. The Duc d'Aumale (1822–97), who inherited Chantilly in 1830, carried this on, but through his own purchases built up anew in Chantilly one of the greatest collections of all time. French things are dominant: great ensembles of Clouet, Poussin, and eighteenth and nineteenth-century artists; forty miniatures by Fouquet; a 'Virgin' by Charonton; the 'Très Riches Heures du Duc de Berry' with illuminations by the Brothers Limbourg. But Italian art too is very strongly represented with works by Fra Angelico, Sassetta, Piero di Cosimo, Raphael, Titian, Reni and A. Carracci. There is also a group of drawings by Dürer. Classical antiquities figure largely, the collection of portraits is of unique historical interest, and there is a library of over 13,000 volumes.

The Princes de Condé and the Duc d'Aumale

Raoul de Broglie

The Château de Chantilly as we see it to-day derives from successive buildings erected by four different families: the d'Orgemont, the Montmorency, the Condé and the Orléans. The foundations of the original château built by the d'Orgemonts at the end of the fourteenth century, between 1386 and 1394, still exist and they were used again when the present building was put up. None of the furniture or works of art from the d'Orgemont château has survived.

In 1484 Pierre III, the last of the d'Orgemonts, gave the domain of Chantilly to his sister Marguerite, who married Guillaume de Montmorency, father of the Constable. In 1560 the Constable Anne de Montmorency employed Jean Bullant, the architect of his château at Ecouen, to build the Petit Château, the outside of which has survived untouched. In the Galerie de Batailles of this Petit Château one can still see the Vinestock Table, the central part of which, so tradition has it, was made from the trunk of a single vine. The four corners of this table bear the arms of Henri II, King of France, while the inscription *Dieu et mon grand Service* is inlaid in ivory in capital letters along each side. This is probably an allusion to the service rendered to the King by Anne de Montmorency, as Master of the Royal Household.

Until 1789 this table stood in the gallery of the chapel at the Château d'Ecouen, which, like Chantilly, passed first from the

The Château de Chantilly. The original Petit Château, built by Constable Anne de Montmorency in 1560, is on the right

Montmorencys to the Condé family and then to the Duc d'Aumale. Other valuable works of art of the Renaissance now at Chantilly also came from Ecouen. First in importance is the altarpiece in the chapel, with bas-reliefs attributed to Jean Goujon representing the cardinal virtues and the four evangelists. Above the altar in the centre, is a white marble bas-relief depicting the Sacrifice of Abraham. The chapel is lined with *boiseries* which are dated 1548; these are of walnut inlaid with panels of rare wood and are carved with the figures of the apostles. The stained-glass is of the same period and represents the five sons of the Constable on the left, and his five daughters on the right.

There are two beautiful bas-reliefs in the corridor leading to the picture gallery (known as the *Tribune*), which are also attributed to Jean Goujon, and depict Phaethon setting out in the sun-god's chariot and falling into the Eridanus. These bas-reliefs once served as over-door decorations on the first floor of the great staircase at Ecouen. In the Vestibule are two large panels

of enamelled tiles made at Rouen in 1542 by Masséot Abaquesne for the sacristy floor in the chapel at Ecouen; they illustrate two scenes from Roman history: *Marcus Curtius Leaping into a Chasm in the Forum to Appease the Anger of the Gods*, and *Mucius Scaevola Thrusting his Hand into a Brazier of Live Coals in Porsenna's Camp*.

One of the most important items is a set of forty-four stained-glass windows, made between 1542 and 1544 for the gallery leading to the chapel at Ecouen. The subject of these is the *Loves of Cupid and Psyche*, and they were inspired by Raphael's famous frescoes in the Villa Farnesina at Rome. The designs are believed to be by Michel Coxie, and they were reproduced in France in engravings by Jean Maugin, known as the Petit Angevin, and later by Léonard Gaultier. The windows at Chantilly are in grisaille with a few light touches of yellow and silver, and beneath each subject is a verse inscribed on a scroll held by children or satyrs.

The Musée de Chantilly also contains manuscripts executed

for the Constable Anne de Montmorency, among them being the works of Valerius Maximus translated by Nicolas de Mailly and Machiavelli's *Prince* translated by Jacques de Vintimille. In addition there are some twenty other manuscripts bought by the Constable and originally owned by Jean de Mas, Seigneur de l'Isle, who died in 1493, and by Jacques d'Armagnac, Duc de Nemours, who died in 1477. Among these is a copy of the romance of *Tristan* in three volumes illustrated with numerous miniatures painted by Evrard d'Espinques, a native of Cologne.

On 3rd March, 1609, Charlotte-Marguerite de Montmorency, a descendant of the Constable Anne, married Henri II de Bourbon, Prince de Condé, whose father was first cousin to King Henri IV. As a result of this alliance Chantilly passed to the Bourbon-Condés, a younger branch of the royal family. The

Chantilly porcelain animals. Heights (left to right) 4½ ins., 2 ins., 4 ins. c. 1740

Vinestock Table, inlaid with ivory. Height 33 ins. c. 1545. The inscription Dieu et mon grand Service *probably refers to Anne de Montmorency's service as Master of the Royal Household to Henri II*

Opposite *Museum Minéralogique Various woods, carved and gilt. Designed by Johann Erich Rehn, constructed by Georg Haupt. Height 87 ins. 1773–74. This cabinet contains a collection of Swedish minerals given to the Prince de Condé in 1774 by Gustavus III of Sweden*

Mausoleum of Henri II de Bourbon-Condé (1588–1646). Bronze statues and bas-reliefs by Jacques Sarazin (1588–1640) 1648–60. Originally in the Church of St Paul–St Louis, Paris

Condés made great changes to the d'Orgemont château, which had already been considerably embellished by the Montmorencys during the Renaissance period. They were responsible for the building of the mansard roofs and later employed Jean Aubert, architect of the Great Stables, to make further additions. The mausoleum of Henri II de Bourbon-Condé (1588–1646), with bronze statues and bas-reliefs by Jacques Sarazin, originally set up in the church of St Paul-St Louis, Paris, is now at Chantilly.

After the battle of Rocroi in 1643, Chantilly became the residence of the Great Condé (1621–86), and there are many portraits of him at Chantilly, as well as trophies and pictures of his battles. Besides paintings by David Teniers the Younger, Juste d'Egmont and Stella which belonged to him, there are sculptures by Coysevox including the extraordinary bust in terra-cotta painted to resemble bronze, now to be seen in the library, and the medallion which stood on his catafalque when Bossuet delivered the celebrated funeral oration in Notre-Dame.

In the Galerie des Batailles are eleven large panels on which Condé's victories (Rocroi, Fribourg, Nordlingen, Lens, Senef, etc.) are represented; these were painted between 1686 and 1692 by Sauveur Le Conte, an artist who died at the age of 35 and probably collaborated with Van der Meulen. With these panels

THE SACRIFICE OF ISAAC
White marble, 42 × 50 ins. c. 1545. Bas-relief from an altar-piece, originally in the Château d'Ecouen, and now in the chapel at Chantilly

hangs a canvas by Michel Corneille the Younger, commemorating Condé's six campaigns of the years 1652–57. Over the chimney-piece is a glass case containing one of the standards of the Holy Roman Empire, captured by the Great Condé, as well as swords, pistols and canes engraved with the Condé arms.

The hero of Rocroi added several masterpieces to the collection among which the following are still at Chantilly: two fine portraits of Comte Henri de Berghe and Princesse Marie de Brabançon by Van Dyck, a gouache of the Dam Square at Amsterdam in 1659 by Jacob van der Ulft, and a water-colour of the Château de Chantilly in 1680 by the Flemish priest Levinus Cruyl, known as Levin.

The grandson of the Great Condé, Louis-Henri, Duc de Bourbon (1692–1740), Prime Minister to Louis XV, was an important figure in the history of art collecting. He commissioned the Great Stables, built between 1719 and 1735, and decorated with fine sculptures by Rémy-François Bridault and his collaborators. Louis-Henri was also responsible for the marvellous white and gold panelling in the State Apartments, and in 1735 he commissioned from Christophe Huet ten large panels of animals in exotic landscapes, five of which are now to be seen in the Great Condé's bedchamber. The exotic decorations in the room known as the Grande Singerie, consisting of monkeys and orientals in a leafy decor of garlands, foliage and arabesques may also be the work of Christophe Huet. The Goncourts attributed these to Watteau, and experts have since suggested that they might be by Audran, Gillot or Christophe Huet, but no definite attribution can be made.

Only a few of the paintings acquired by the Duc de Bourbon have remained in the collection. The most important are the portraits of Mademoiselle de Clermont (Marie-Anne de Bourbon-Condé) taking the waters at Chantilly and of Louise-Henriette de Bourbon-Conti, Duchesse d'Orléans, as Hebe by Nattier, as well as some hunting pictures by Oudry and Desportes. One of the most interesting and original projects initiated by the Duc de Bourbon at Chantilly was the porcelain factory

A corner of the Chambre de Monsieur le Prince showing three panels of animals in landscapes commissioned by Louis-Henri Duc de Bourbon in 1735 from Christophe Huet. The Beauvais tapestry coverings of the sofa and chairs were woven after cartoons by Le Prince (1734–81). The writing table (centre) is attributed to Charles Cressent (1685–1751)

which he started in 1735, and some of its most important pieces can be seen in the museum to-day. Several of these were made for the Condé family, in particular two little snuff-boxes mounted in silver and silver-gilt and decorated with a recumbent stag. There are also some statuettes of deer, panthers and leopards modelled after animals in the Condé menagerie and a set of plates with the Condé arms in blue *camaïeu*.

The Duc de Bourbon died at Chantilly on 27th January, 1740, and was succeeded by his four-year-old son Louis-Joseph for whom his uncle the Comte de Clermont acted as guardian. During the lifetime of Louis-Joseph, Prince de Condé (1736–1818), the Jeu de Paume (1757), the Château d'Enghien (1770) and Le Hameau (1775) were built. Like Chantilly, these three buildings were filled with valuable furniture. One of the most remarkable additions dating from this period is the extraordinary 'Muséum Minéralogique' given to the Prince de Condé in 1774 by Gustavus III, King of Sweden. The cabinet containing this collection of Swedish minerals was designed in Stockholm by the architect Johann Erich Rehn and made in Paris in 1765 by the famous cabinet-maker Georg Haupt, who was employed in the workshop of Leleu. It has carved and gilt bronze decorations. Other objects dating from this period which are still to be found at Chantilly are a valuable collection of plans and contemporary views of Chantilly by Chambé, which were presented to the future Tsar Paul I in 1784, as well as paintings by Nattier, Ribou and Madame de Tott.

To complete the list of seventeenth- and eighteenth-century objects in the collection we must mention numerous manuscripts and books, twenty-four portrait miniatures, coat-buttons with views of Chantilly, ivory and tortoise-shell boxes, fans, counters, pendants and seals engraved with the Condé arms. These relics, however, represent only a small part of the treasures which could be seen at Chantilly before the French Revolution. In the introduction to his book *Le Mobilier Royal Français*, Pierre Verlet writes: 'No museum in the world can ever give us an idea of what the apartments at Versailles, Compiègne or Fontainebleau must have looked like before 1790.' The Château de Chantilly should certainly be added to this list.

After the capture of the Bastille the Prince de Condé left France with his son the Duc de Bourbon and his grandson the Duc d'Enghien. By the law passed on 9th February, 1792, their possessions were confiscated and during the month of August two companies of the National Guard came from Paris and removed several cartloads of statues, bronzes and other works of art. In May 1793, the revolutionary administrators of the Senlis district and the 'Commissioners entrusted with the sale of the émigré Condé's furniture' made an inventory of everything left at Chantilly. A special list was made of everything which was to be

Top MADEMOISELLE DE CLERMONT (MARIE-ANNE DE BOURBON-CONDÉ) TAKING THE WATERS AT CHANTILLY *Jean Marc Nattier (1685–1766) oil on canvas 77 × 63½ ins. 1729*

DÉJEUNER D'HUÎTRES (THE OYSTER LUNCHEON) *Jean François de Troy (1679–1752) oil on canvas 71 × 49½ ins. 1734*

Opposite *The Library at Chantilly. The desk and furniture was commissioned by the Duc d'Aumale. The bust of the Great Condé by Coysevox stands on the mantelpiece*

THE EMPEROR OTHO II RECEIVING THE HOMAGE OF THE NATIONS *9 × 7½ ins. Late tenth century. Miniature from the* Registrum Gregorii, *School of Trier*

removed to Paris; all the furniture was put up for auction and disposed of in a series of sales lasting several days. By the end of August the château was completely empty, and it was then turned into a prison to house suspects from the Oise department.

The next threat was to the château itself, for on 17th November, 1798, a law was passed ordering the seizure of all unsold property belonging to *émigrés*. On 17th July, 1799, the Château de Chantilly and the surrounding buildings were sold to two demolition contractors – Gérard Boulée and Pierre Damoye, who started work immediately. They began with the orangery, the theatre, a building known as 'Bucan' and the menagerie, after which they pulled down the entire château. Nothing was left except the foundations. The contractors would have gone on to demolish other buildings, from which they could have salvaged more valuable material, but they came into conflict with the troops of the second regiment of light cavalry who were quartered there. The officers appealed to the Executive of the Directory to enforce the law of 17th July, 1791, by which buildings in use by the army were not subject to confiscation. Damoye and Boulée were accused of illegal profiteering; the sale was invalidated, and thus the Petit Château, built by Anne de Montmorency, the Great Stables and the Château d'Enghien were saved from destruction.

In 1814 Chantilly was restored to the Prince de Condé, who took up residence in the Petit Château – the only part still standing – and set about trying to recover his furniture. He applied to the public depositories, but all he succeeded in recovering was the Swedish Mineralogical Collection (which had been transferred to the Natural History Museum in 1793) and the Vinestock Table from Ecouen which had been taken to Versailles. Much of the furniture from Chantilly that was sold or confiscated in 1793 can be seen nowadays in public or private collections, though it is not easily recognisable because, unlike other royal châteaux, Chantilly had no special mark. However a pale mahogany commode made by Leleu for the Prince de Condé at the end of 1772 has been identified in the Wallace Collection, as

well as two other commodes by Leleu in the Louvre and the Petit Trianon. Some chased bronze chandeliers are now in the Bibliothèque Mazarine.

Much the same is true of the paintings. The Prince de Condé did succeed in recovering those mentioned earlier, but many works which had been in his possession before 1789 were never returned to Chantilly. For example, two large drawings by Le Paon of hunts organized in honour of the King of Denmark and the future Tsar Paul I in 1768 and 1782 were confiscated during the Revolution but are now in the École Polytechnique.

Prince Louis-Joseph de Condé died at the Palais Bourbon in Paris on 13th May, 1818. His son, Louis-Henri-Joseph, Duc de Bourbon (1756–1830), added some portraits of himself by Danloux, busts by Louis-Pierre Deseine, and the Château de la Reine Blanche, as it is called, at the Etang de Commelles, which is furnished in the neo-gothic style with pieces made at the time of the Restoration. Finally, there is a charming portrait by Nanine Vallain of the sixteen-year-old Duc d'Enghien (1772–1804) son of the Duc de Bourbon and the last of the Condés, as well as some miniatures.

In 1830, the Duc de Bourbon, the last survivor of the Condé family, died tragically and left Chantilly to his great-nephew and godson, Henri d'Orléans, Duc d'Aumale (1822–97) fifth son of King Louis-Philippe. In 1844 the young prince married Marie-

Caroline de Bourbon of the Two Sicilies, daughter of the Prince of Salerno and younger sister of the Empress Marie-Louise, wife of Napoleon I. The newly-married couple bought several eighteenth-century paintings to decorate their apartments in the Petit Château, among others the portraits of *Mademoiselle Duclos* by Largillière and of the *Duc de Bourbon* by Danloux. In 1848, following the revolution and fall of Louis-Philippe, the Duc d'Aumale took refuge in England, where he lived for twenty-two years.

Louis-Philippe died on 26th August, 1850. In the following year, the Duc d'Aumale bought for 6,000 francs at the sale at the Château de Neuilly ten large Gobelins tapestries depicting the Emperor Maximilian's hunts near Brussels in the sixteenth century; these were seventeenth-century copies which had been given by Louis XIV to the Comte de Toulouse. A few months later, at the sale of the contents of the Château d'Eu, the Duc d'Aumale purchased two famous canvases which had once hung in Louis XV's private apartments, namely Nicolas Lancret's *Déjeuner de Jambon*, and de Troy's *Déjeuner d'Huîtres*, as well as two commodes by Riesener, one of which was made in 1775 for the king's bedroom at Versailles, and an important suite of furniture by Jean-Baptiste Sené (a sofa, six armchairs and a firescreen), which is upholstered in Beauvais tapestry with a design of bunches of flowers and garlands. It can be seen to-day in the Salon d'Angle.

Opposite JANUARY, *an illumination from* LES TRÈS RICHES HEURES DU DUC DE BERRY, *the Brothers Limbourg* $9\frac{1}{2} \times 6$ *ins. 1413–16. The Duke at his Table*

Left THE ADORATION OF THE MAGI *Jean Fouquet (c. 1420 – in or before 1481)* $6\frac{1}{2} \times 4\frac{1}{2}$ *ins. 1452–60. Miniature from Etienne Chevalier's Book of Hours*

On 10th March, 1851, the Duc d'Aumale's father-in-law, Léopold de Bourbon of the Two Sicilies, Duke of Salerno, died. Among his possessions were an important collection of antiques from Herculaneum, Stabia, Pompeii, Cumae and Paestum, as well as paintings, some of which he had inherited – for instance from the Farnese family (including some Carraccis) – others which he had bought from the Borgia, the Noja or the Albani families. A sale of his collection was due to be held on 19th April, 1852 and the catalogue had been printed when, to prevent its dispersal, the Duc d'Aumale offered 100,000 ducats for the 175 pictures involved. He kept seventy-two of them and re-sold the rest. Among the canvases now at Chantilly and coming from this transaction are four by Annibale Carracci, twelve by Salvator Rosa, Gérard van Honthorst's *Last Supper*, Hackert's *Hunt at Carditello*, *The Three Ages of Man* by Gérard, and *Francesca da Rimini* by Ingres. There are also two mosaics coming from the Prince of Salerno: *The Rape of Europa* from Herculaneum and a *Boar-hunt* discovered at Pompeii in 1809 – as well as Roman altars, marble statues, amphorae, pottery and coins.

During this period the Duc d'Aumale was also building up his library. In 1851, when the remainder of Louis-Philippe's estate was sold up, he bought some 3,000 volumes – including 340 incunabula – which had been bequeathed to the King by the English collector Frank Hall Standish. Early in 1856 the Duc d'Aumale acquired the famous manuscript known as the *Très Riches Heures du Duc de Berry*, still considered to be the most beautiful illuminated manuscript in the world. It is the work of Pol de Limbourg and his brothers Jean and Hermann, and dates from the beginning of the fifteenth century. In 1416 the three Limbourg brothers died, leaving the manuscript unfinished. Seventy years later it was completed by Jean Colombe at the request of Duke Charles I of Savoy, grandson of the Duc de Berry. Duke Charles died in 1489 leaving no direct descendants; his heir was his cousin Philibert le Beau, and after him his widow, Margaret of Austria, daughter of the Emperor Maximilian. The *Très Riches Heures* passed in turn to the Genoese Spinola family, the Serra family, and the Baron de Margherita, from whom the Duc d'Aumale bought it.

A few years later the Duc d'Aumale bought up the complete library of Armand Cigongne (1790–1859), a broker turned industrialist; it consisted of 2,910 works collected with unusual discrimination, including 200 Elzeviers, 860 volumes of poetry, 339 volumes of plays, and ten volumes handwritten by Jarry.

In 1854 the Duc d'Aumale bought Poussin's famous painting of *The Massacre of the Innocents* from the London dealer Colnaghi; in 1859 he acquired at Lord Northwick's sale another Poussin, *The Childhood of Bacchus* and a fine fifteenth-century primitive of the Sienese school representing *Angels Dancing Before the Sun*. In

1860 the Prince bought yet another Poussin at the Higginson sale: *Theseus Discovering his Father's Sword*, and from Nieuwenhuys, Giorgione's *Adulteress* and Annibale Carracci's *Martyrdom of St Stephen*. In the same year Ary Scheffer's extraordinary portrait of *Talleyrand at the age of seventy-four* was bequeathed to the Duc d'Aumale by Lord Holland.

At this period there were no drawings at Chantilly. But in 1861 a collection made with exceptional skill and taste by Frédéric Reiset, curator of the Louvre, was to be put up for sale and the Duc d'Aumale succeeded in buying the complete collection by private treaty for 140,000 francs. There were 38 drawings by masters of the Florentine and Roman schools (eight leaves from a sketch-book of Verrocchio's, two drawings by Leonardo da Vinci and two by Michelangelo). The Lombard and Venetian schools were represented by drawings by Titian, Veronese and Annibale Carracci; the German school by four famous portraits by Albrecht Dürer made during his visit to Holland. The French school include no less than 92 drawings either by Poussin, or attributed to him.

On April 8th of the same year, the Duc d'Aumale bought, for 54,000 francs at Prince Soltykoff's sale, four large enamels by Léonard Limosin (at present in the Salle des Gardes) representing the two Kings of Navarre, Henri d'Albret and Antoine de Bourbon, Louis de Bourbon, the Duc de Montpensier (signed and dated on the back: LL 1550), and his wife Catherine of Lorraine. A large silver processional cross dating from the end of the fifteenth century was also bought at the same sale. This was wrongly described in the catalogue as coming from the treasury of Basle cathedral; there is every reason to believe that it is the work of a north Italian silversmith, probably from Milan.

During the next few years the Duc d'Aumale made several important single acquisitions, some in public sales, others in bookshops. In 1862 he bought Leonardo da Vinci's drawing of the *Nude Gioconda* from a Parisian collector, named Thibault, and in 1863 he acquired at Prince Demidoff's sale Ingres's famous painting commissioned by the Duc d'Orléans, brother of the Duc d'Aumale, representing *The Illness of Antiochus* or *Antiochus and Stratonice*. The following year Rosa Bonheur's *Shepherd in the Pyrenees* and Gérôme's *Duel after the Masked Ball* were added to the collection. In 1865 at the Comte de Pourtalès's sale an opening bid of 100 francs resulted in a very fine red-figure Greek amphora, known as the *Nola Vase* being knocked down to the Duc d'Aumale for 10,400 francs, in face of opposition from Thiers, the Louvre and the British Museum. The marvellous little bronze of Minerva dating from the fifth century BC was bought at the same sale.

In the same year, 1865, the Duc d'Aumale bought from the London bookseller Boone a sacramentary with beautiful gold

THE DEATH OF THE VIRGIN *Giotto* (*c. 1276–1337*) *panel*
17½ × 18 ins.

THE VIRGIN AND CHILD ENTHRONED BETWEEN
ST JEROME AND ST PETER *Perugino* (*c. 1445/50–1523*)
oil on canvas 57 × 50 ins. c. 1475

THE MASSACRE OF THE INNOCENTS
Nicolas Poussin (1593/4–1665) oil on canvas
58 × 67½ ins. 1632

Opposite VIRGIN AND CHILD *Raphael*
(1483–1520) panel 11½ × 8 ins. c. 1506.
Known as the 'Madonna of the House of
Orléans'

uncial and minuscule lettering on purple parchment, made by the monks of the Abbey of Lorsch in the diocese of Worms. The following year, at Prince Sigismond Radziwill's sale, the Prince bought a unique copy of one of the most beautiful of eighteenth-century illustrated books – Laborde's *Chansons*: four volumes printed on vellum in which the engravings were replaced by the original drawings by Moreau the Younger and other artists.

On 24th March, 1866, Queen Marie-Amélie died and the Duc d'Aumale's share of the inheritance included Van Dyck's portrait of *Gaston d'Orléans* and Madame Vigée-Lebrun's of Queen Maria Carolina of Naples and her two daughters, as well as miniatures, family portraits, jewels and valuable ornaments.

With 1868 began a period when various large collections were acquired. In February the Duc d'Aumale bought that of the Marquis Maison, which included four Greuzes, two paintings and twelve drawings by Prud'hon, eight paintings by Decamps and four panels by Watteau: *Country Pleasures, Love Disarmed, The Serenader* and *The Anxious Mistress*. In 1869 he bought for 160,000 francs at the sale of the Galerie Delessert, Raphael's famous *Madonna of the House of Orléans*, so called because it once formed part of the Duc d'Orléans's collection at the Palais Royal before the Revolution. In 1873 the Duke acquired Eugène Delacroix's painting of the Doge Foscari condemning his own son to perpetual banishment because the Council of Ten had found him guilty of secret communication with the enemy.

In 1876 the Duc d'Aumale acquired a very important collection of two hundred portraits formed towards the end of the eighteenth century by the archaeologist Alexandre Lenoir (1761–1839), whose diplomacy and courage saved innumerable works of art from destruction during the Revolution. He assembled a Musée des Monuments Français in the Convent of the Petits-Augustins, now the École des Beaux Arts, where statues, bronzes and paintings from churches, monasteries and châteaux were kept undamaged. He was also responsible for the preservation of the façade of the Château d'Anet, the work of Philibert Delorme and Jean Goujon.

Alexandre Lenoir's own collection was of portraits, nearly all of them French. It is unfortunately impossible to describe each of the paintings; we can only mention the portraits of François I, Henri II and Charles IX by Clouet and Corneille de Lyon, of Jean Bugenhagen attributed to Holbein, and of Henri IV by Porbus, the extraordinary panel portrait of the Bastard of Burgundy, a masterpiece of the fifteenth-century Flemish school, and the touching portrait of Molière by Mignard. The 130 drawings by Quesnel, Dumonstier and Nanteuil in this same collection are all of very great interest.

In the following year the Duc d'Aumale had 450 drawings by Carmontelle sent from Scotland to Chantilly. This artist was

celebrated for his drawing-room comedies, or 'Dramatic Proverbs,' in which he painted lifelike portraits of his contemporaries. Carmontelle, who was employed by the Orléans family in about 1765 as reader to the future Philippe-Egalité, gave free rein to his talent as a draughtsman and executed portraits of the princes, officers, ecclesiastics, great ladies, writers and artists he happened to meet. Thanks to the Duc d'Aumale, two-thirds of his work can be seen at Chantilly, and constitutes documentary evidence of the first importance about French society in the second half of the eighteenth century.

Finally, in April 1879, the Duc d'Aumale bought all the forty pictures which Frédéric Reiset had decided to put up for sale and for which he had already prepared a catalogue. Among the examples from the French school were: *The Virgin of Pity*, one of Enguerrand Charonton's most important works, four canvases by Poussin, a *Self-portrait* and *Madame Devauçay* by Ingres; from the Italian school: *The Death of the Virgin* by a follower of Giotto, two panels by Fra Angelico, Sassetta's *Mystic Marriage of St Francis of Assisi*, Lorenzo di Niccolo's *Coronation of the Virgin*, Botticelli's *Autumn*, the famous portrait of the beautiful *Simonetta Vespucci* (mistress of Giuliano de Medici and reigning beauty of Florence) by Piero di Cosimo, and three panels by Luini; from the Flemish school: two admirable *Portraits of a Man and a Woman* by the Master of St Gilles and the *Translation of a Saint's Relics* by a painter of the second half of the fifteenth century.

In 1880 the Duc d'Aumale bought six hundred drawings of officers and soldiers taking part in the conquest of Algeria, by Raffet, and the following year he acquired fourteen more drawings by Prud'hon. In 1885 he paid 92,500 francs for a diptych, possibly painted by Memling for Jeanne de France, daughter of Charles VII, and 625,000 francs for a little panel of the *Three Graces* by Raphael.

Meissonier's painting of *Cuirassiers of 1805* was bought in 1889 for 190,000 francs; a few months later the Duc d'Aumale bought for the same sum the Earl of Carlisle's astonishing collection of 311 sixteenth-century portraits of the most famous personalities of the reigns of François I, Henri II and Charles IX by Jean and François Clouet.

But his interest in works of art did not mean that the Prince neglected his library. In October 1891 he bought at Frankfurt forty miniatures from *Etienne Chevalier's Book of Hours* by Fouquet, and in the following year the *Psalter of Ingeburge of Denmark*, dating from the beginning of the thirteenth century and comprising fifty-one scenes from the Old and New Testaments framed in gold-leaf. In 1894 he acquired the second volume of Jeanne d'Evreux's little *Breviary*. Until his death on 7th May, 1897, the Duc d'Aumale continued to buy pictures and manuscripts from every country and school, guided only by his own eclectic taste.

PORTRAIT OF ANTOINE WATTEAU *Attributed to François Boucher (1703–70) red chalk heightened with crayon 9½ × 8½ ins.*

Opposite SELF-PORTRAIT *Jean Auguste Dominique Ingres (1780–1867) oil on canvas 30 × 24 ins. 1804*

The Duc d'Aumale had been able to return to the Petit Château at Chantilly in June 1871, but it was rapidly becoming too small to house such important collections. The duke and his architect, named Daumet, decided to add to the château a museum built in a style that would harmonise with it. This was the period when neo-Renaissance architecture was in fashion. In 1799 the large château at Chantilly had been razed to the level of the terrace, but the fifteenth-century foundations were still in existence. Daumet decided to preserve the triangular shape of the original substructure, and to erect on these foundations a building in the Renaissance style round a courtyard closed at the east end by a portico. Three towers which would abut onto the north façade were rebuilt; the apse of the chapel was built against the eastern tower, and the whole structure dominated by the charming statue of St Louis over the gabled entrance to the chapel.

On entering the Château the visitor is impressed by the proportions of the *Grand Vestibule*, the brilliance of the marbles and the variety of their colours. Opposite the glazed front door is another door, flanked by marble busts of the Duc de Bourbon and Madame Adelaide, godfather and godmother to the Duc d'Aumale, which leads to what were once the apartments of the Princes de Condé.

In the first room, which is furnished as an *Antechamber*, is the Swedish Mineralogical Cabinet given by King Gustavus III to the Prince de Condé, two fine cases of Chinese, Sèvres and Chantilly porcelain, portraits of the Duc d'Enghien and the Prince de Conti wearing the Condé hunting dress (fawn with purple facings) and a series of small equestrian portraits of the kings of France from François I to Henri IV. On the left of the antechamber as one leaves is the Duc d'Aumale's *Library*, containing 13,330 volumes, including 760 manuscripts and 670 incunabula. Seven hundred and fifty more manuscripts are in store.

The Antechamber leads into the *Salle des Gardes*, which has an ornamental chimney-piece in the Renaissance style by Daumet. Above it is the mosaic of the Rape of Europa found at Herculaneum. There are paintings by Van Dyck and Juste d'Egmont, enamels by Léonard Limosin, and glass cases full of old weapons and military relics belonging to the Duc d'Aumale.

The next room is the *Chambre de Monsieur le Prince*, occupied by the Princes de Condé during the eighteenth century. The Duc de Bourbon had it lined with beautiful white and gold panelling; the Duc d'Aumale added the animal-paintings by Christophe Huet, two commodes by Riesener from the Château d'Eu, a table by Cressent bought at Blois, and a set of chairs upholstered in Beauvais tapestry.

Immediately adjacent are the *Grand Cabinet de Monsieur le*

One end of the Tribune, the octagonal picture gallery. Top centre
The Coronation of the Virgin, *a triptych by Lorenzo di Niccolo*
(c. 1420); below it The Virgin and Child Enthroned between
St Jerome and St Peter *by Perugino; left* Gaston d'Orléans
by Van Dyck, and far right Botticelli's Autumn

Opposite top PORTRAIT OF SIMONETTA VESPUCCI
Piero di Cosimo (c. 1462–?1521) tempera on panel
22½ × 16½ ins. c. 1500

Opposite THE MYSTIC MARRIAGE OF ST FRANCIS
Sassetta (c. 1400–50) panel 37½ × 23 ins. One wing of an altarpiece
of which the other five wings are in the National Gallery, London

MARIE DE BOURGOGNE *Flemish School panel* $10\frac{1}{2} \times 9$ *ins.
Second half of fifteenth century*

Below ELIZABETH OF AUSTRIA *François Clouet (d. 1572)
panel* $14\frac{1}{2} \times 10$ *ins. 1571*

Prince, with Choiseul's writing-desk and furniture signed by J. B. Sené; and the *Salon des Singes*, containing four chairs which belonged to Marie-Antoinette.

The *Galerie de Batailles* is a vast ball-room hung with eleven pictures by Sauveur le Conte commemorating Condé's victories. The Vinestock Table from Ecouen has been placed here, and also a writing-desk by Leleu. Finally there is the beautifully panelled *Music-room* containing a show-case full of Chantilly porcelain.

The museum built by the Duc d'Aumale between 1875 and 1881 is reached by a short flight of steps on the left of the Vestibule. The first room, the *Galerie des Cerfs*, was used as a dining-room on the occasion of Queen Amélie of Portugal's betrothal celebrations in 1886, and also in 1895 for those of the Duchess of Aosta. It is hung with the marvellous late seventeenth-century Gobelins tapestries representing the Emperor Maximilian hunting near Brussels; these tapestries are copies of originals made in Flanders in the sixteenth century from Van Orley's cartoons (at present in the Louvre).

All the neighbouring rooms are picture galleries, in which the works of art are arranged according to the Duc d'Aumale's personal taste and late nineteenth-century fashion. This is the home of an enlightened patron of the arts, whose wide-ranging interests brought together the paintings he loved most.

The *Picture Gallery* contains seven Poussins, eight Carraccis, paintings by Titian, Andrea del Sarto, Guido Reni, Pulzone and Salvator Rosa. The French school is represented by numerrous works by Poussin, as well as paintings by Philippe de Cham-

Left PORTRAIT OF MOLIÈRE *Pierre Mignard (1612–95)*
oil on canvas 23 × 19 ins. c. 1670

Below THE ORANGE SELLER *Nicolaes Maes (1634–93) red chalk*
10 × 9 ins.

paigne, Lancret, de Troy, Nattier, Gérard, Delacroix, Corot, Decamps, Fromentin, Meissonier, Alphonse de Neuville and Rosa Bonheur.

The *Salle Caroline* contains a group of eighteenth-century portraits by Largillière, Watteau, Duplessis, Greuze, Vernet and Danloux. In the *Cabinet Clouet* are famous portraits of Henry II by Primaticcio after Jean Clouet, of Marguerite d'Angoulème, Elisabeth of Austria, Charles IX and the Duc de Nemours by François Clouet, and a great many other masterpieces by sixteenth-century painters.

The *Salon d'Orléans* contains the collection of drawings, including 362 sixteenth-century pencil portraits, 484 by Carmontelle and 102 attributed to Poussin, not to mention others of the Florentine, Roman, Lombard, Venetian, Flemish, German and Dutch schools. The *Salle Isabelle* is hung with seascapes by Ruysdaël and Van de Velde, an Ingres, a Boilly, and paintings by Decamps and Marilhat. The *Cabinet du Giotto*, which owes its name to a painting of the *Death of the Virgin* by an artist of the school of Giotto, also contains works by Fra Angelico, Filippo Lippi, and Mazzolino, and the *Virgin of Pity* painted in 1452 by Enguerrand Charonton.

The *Minerva Gallery* and the gallery next to it are devoted to Greek and Roman antiquities, including a marvellous little bronze statuette of Minerva dating from the fifth century BC, a red figure vase found at Nola in the south of Italy, some Tanagra figures and a fragment of a sarcophagus. Next we enter the *Salle de la Smalah*, full of material connected with Algeria and the

Detail of the VIRGIN OF PITY
Enguerrand Charonton (c. 1410–61)
oil on canvas 26 × 73 ins. 1452

Orléans family, followed by the *Vestibule du Logis*, which contains fragments of cartoons for tapestries by Raphael, representing the heads of the apostles, and a drawing of the nude Gioconda by Leonardo da Vinci. Finally, the *Galerie du Logis* contains a collection of fifty-two portraits, mostly sixteenth century, presented to the museum in 1939 by the Vicomtesse de Montaigne de Poncins.

On the left, the *Picture Gallery* leads into the *Galerie de Psyché*, which has stained-glass windows illustrating the history of the loves of Cupid and Psyche. Drawings by the Clouets are on exhibition here. In the middle of this gallery is the door into the *Santuario*, a cabinet hung with velvet in which the Duc d'Aumale arranged the forty miniatures painted by Fouquet in about 1455 for Etienne Chevalier's Book of Hours, two paintings by Raphael (the *Madonna of the House of Orleans* and *The Three Graces*), and a panel of *Esther and Ahasuerus* by Filippo Lippi.

At the far end of the gallery is the *Tour des Gemmes*, beautifully decorated with cases of miniatures, precious objects, weapons and porcelain. Next is the *Tribune*, an octagonal room of original design containing paintings by masters of every school and period. Every one of the sixty-two works in this room deserves description, but we can only mention some of the more famous: *The Mystic Marriage of St Francis of Assisi* by Sassetta, Piero di Cosimo's *Portrait of Simonetta Vespucci*, the diptych painted for Jeanne de France by Memling, the *Portrait of the Bastard of*

Burgundy, the *Portrait of Molière* by Mignard, and an Ingres *Self-portrait*.

The *Chapel*, built by the Duc d'Aumale in 1882, contains the Renaissance altar, wood-carvings and stained-glass windows from the chapel of the Château d'Ecouen, and also the funeral monument (1662) to Henri II de Bourbon, Prince de Condé, by Jacques Sarazin.

The arrangement of the works of art in the Château de Chantilly to-day is exactly as it was in the time of the Duc d'Aumale; he himself arranged the books on the shelves and decided exactly where the pictures were to be hung. The Duke wanted to preserve Chantilly and its magnificent treasures unchanged and since his two sons, neither of whom had married, had predeceased him he decided to entrust his collections to a distinguished body, whose independence and expert knowledge would ensure that they were kept intact. On 3rd June, 1884, he made a will leaving the Château de Chantilly to the Institut de France; on 25th October, 1886, this bequest was altered to an outright gift, reserving a life interest. The Duc d'Aumale died on 7th May, 1897, and since then the five academies composing the Institut de France (the Académie Française, and the Academies of Fine Arts, Sciences, Letters, and Moral and Political Sciences) have taken over responsibility for the upkeep of the Château de Chantilly and its collections.

MADRID SPAIN

The Dukes of Alba

José M. Pita Andrade

Much of the history of Spain and the Spanish grandee families is mirrored in the archives and art collections belonging to the Dukes of Alba. The present Duchess of Alba has inherited a collection which reflects the manifold activities of her forebears, who were patrons of the arts, courtiers and great warriors through many generations. The beginnings of the collection can be traced back to the first Duke, who in the late fifteenth century acquired an 'Annunciation' by the Master of the Virgin inter Virgines, and a set of Tournai tapestries. Inevitably, there are many pieces connected with the Grand Duke of Alba (1507–82), the victor of Mühlberg and a patron of Titian. Later major additions to the collection were made by the twelfth Duke, Ambassador in Paris in the mid-eighteenth century; by the thirteenth Duchess, a friend of Goya; and especially by the fourteenth Duke (d. 1835) who bought Italian and Dutch old masters. The late Duke (1874–1953) and his daughter, the present Duchess, have made interesting additions in the form of eighteenth-century English and nineteenth-century French paintings. Besides these, the Alba collections have been greatly enriched over the centuries through inheritances resulting from marriages with the Dukes of Berwick, of Stuart descent, and with the family of the Count-Duke of Olivares (Marquis of El Carpio), one of the greatest Spanish art collectors of the seventeenth century. Finally – as a result of the marriage of the fifteenth Duke with her sister – the Empress Eugénie, who died in the Palacio Liria, bequeathed many of her personal possessions to the Alba family. Apart from paintings and works of art the Alba collections consist of a superb library and private archive which includes the will of Philip II, papers signed by Christopher Columbus, and a first edition of 'Don Quixote'.

The Dukes of Alba

José M. Pita Andrade

The House of Alba is outstanding among the great Spanish noble families. Its history can be traced back for eight hundred years and members of the family have played an important part in Spanish history. Many of them were also distinguished patrons of literature and the arts, and the history of the House of Alba is echoed in its rich and varied art collections. These, and the documents housed in the archives of the Palacio Liria, are the most important sources of information about the family history. It is a complex story, made more intricate by the eminence of the families whose destinies were interwoven with the House of Alba to produce the greatest concentration of titles known in our day. The present Duchess of Alba, Doña Cayetana Stuart y Silva (her other surnames are omitted for the sake of brevity), has inherited nine titles of Duchess, sixteen of Marchioness, twenty-two of Countess, as well as inheriting by nineteen different lines of descent the title of Grandee of Spain.

Her titles, though many and important, give little hint of the distinctive elements of the family. The Duchess is a descendant of the ancient Kings of Navarre as heiress of the Counts of Lerin, and of the Stuart Kings through the Dukes of Berwick. She is also descended in direct line from Christopher Columbus. In her veins flow the blood of the Grand Duke of Alba, Philip II's famous and hated general; of the Count Duke of Olivares, Philip IV's Prime Minister; of the seventh Count of Lemos, patron of Cervantes; of the seventh Marquis of El Carpio, owner of one of the greatest art collections of the seventeenth century; of many Viceroys who governed in Italy and America in the name of the Spanish monarchs; and of Eugenia de Montijo, Empress of France through her marriage with Napoleon III.

Among the Duchess's ancestors are many famous personalities, eminent in politics, art and literature, whose characters can be evoked from the priceless records which have survived in the

The Palacio Liria, Madrid, built (1770–80)
by the third Duke of Berwick and Liria

The Spanish Room containing the collection of paintings by Spanish
artists. Velasquez's Infanta Margarita *is on the left wall and*
Francisco Rizi's The King's Wolfhound *in the centre*
of the right wall. The furniture is seventeenth-century Spanish

Palacio Liria, despite the many losses that have been incurred. A fine portrait of Mary Queen of Scots, bequeathed by the Cardinal of York, grandson of James II, hangs in the vestibule, while the first map of America drawn by Christopher Columbus is exhibited in the library. One room is devoted entirely to portraits, tapestries and other items connected with the Grand Duke of Alba. Another contains the armour of the Count Duke of Olivares, probably the same armour which he wears in the equestrian portrait by Velasquez. In the library there is a copy of the first edition of *Don Quixote*, dedicated to the Count of Lemos, who was a great patron of the arts. The Room of the Duchess of Alba contains paintings and objects which recall the close relationship of an earlier Duchess Cayetana with Goya. And in another room is a small painting of the Empress Eugénie in her salon in the Tuileries, in which can be distinguished a number of paintings and sculpture now in the Palacio Liria. All of these serve to emphasize how intimately the many objects forming the Alba Collection to-day are linked with the family history.

The origins of the House of Alba can be traced back to a certain Count Don Pedro in the eleventh century, who was connected by marriage to the Emperors of Byzantium. Between the twelfth and fifteenth centuries other members of the family achieved distinction in Toledo. They were ancestors of the first Duke of Alba, Don Garcia Alvarez de Toledo, who died in 1488 and was lord of the castle of Alba de Tormes near Salamanca. This fortress is now in ruins, but one tower has survived and contains some magnificent sixteenth-century paintings which have recently been restored.

Two items which belonged to the first Duke of Alba are exhibited in the Palacio Liria: *The Annunciation*, a panel by the Master of the Virgin inter Virgines, incorporating the figure of Don Garcia at prayer, and a tapestry with a scene from the Trojan War, one of a series of eleven woven at Tournai. Both works demonstrate the influences that were dominant in Spain towards the end of the fifteenth century. At that time Spain had recently achieved political, territorial and religious unity under Ferdinand and Isabella and was on the eve of great colonial expansion, but in the arts it was subject to influences from Flanders and Holland.

The House of Alba also owns a number of medieval castles – Monterrey, Andrade and Monforte de Lemos in Galicia, the castle of El Carpio in Andalusia and the fortress of Alba de Tormes and the Castro Nuevo in Castile and León. Some years ago the Duke and Duchess gave the castle of Coca, one of the most beautiful buildings in the Peninsula, to the state. This has now been restored and is a centre for agricultural studies.

Little is known about the second Duke, Don Fadrique Alvarez de Toledo, though it has been established that he was the patron of poets and musicians and that theatrical performances took place at his castle in the presence of Prince Don Juan, the ill-starred son of Ferdinand and Isabella. The Duke, who died in 1531, employed two famous architects, Enrique Egas and Juan Guas, who worked in a flamboyant gothic style. Portraits of Don Fadrique and his wife, attributed to Christoph Amberger, can be seen in the Palacio Liria.

Don Fadrique was succeeded by his grandson, Don Fernando Alvarez de Toledo, known as the Grand Duke of Alba. He showed a keen interest in literature and the arts – notably, he employed Titian – and his advisers and friends included some of the most eminent poets and humanists of his time. Although he spent much of his long life (1507–82) away from Alba de Tormes in the service of the Emperor Charles V and Philip II in Italy, Flanders and Portugal, he made a number of major improvements both to the castle, for which he commissioned frescoes of the Battle of Mühlberg, and to his country house La Abadía in Extremadura.

The Grand Duke's portrait was painted many times by artists of different nationalities – Titian, Antonio Moro, Alonzo Sánchez Coello and Key. These portraits, and other works which belonged to him or are associated with him, have been assembled in one room in the Palacio Liria. The walls are hung with three tapestries illustrating the Duke's 'Jornada de Alemania' (expedition to Germany) which are mentioned in a document of 1575. They were woven by Pannemaker in Brussels, of wool, silk and gold thread, and show three incidents from the battle of Guemmingen in 1568: the attack, the crossing of the river Ems and the victory of the Duke's army. These tapestries are of great documentary interest for the information they give about the weapons and uniforms of the period. Three portraits of the Duke show him at different ages. Rubens' copy after a lost original by Titian, showing him as he was in 1550, was made during Rubens' second visit to Spain in 1628. A second portrait, probably by Titian himself, shows the Duke some fifteen years later, while a third, by an unknown artist, shows him at the age of 74. Two busts of the Duke, which were once owned by the family, are now at Windsor and in the Frick Collection in New York. A half suit of armour worn by the Duke, one of his banners, and several historic documents have been preserved. A more recent addition to the collection is a caricatural polychrome wood carving which represents the Grand Duke, looking rather like Don Quixote, trampling on a three-headed hydra with the features of his three enemies, Elizabeth of England, Pope Paul IV and the Elector of Saxony.

The sixteenth century witnessed the rise of many noble families who were later to be linked with the House of Alba. Two of these, Monterrey and Villanueva del Río, possessed magnificent

THE GRAND DUKE OF ALBA (1507–82)
*Titian (c. 1488–1576) oil on canvas 39 × 32 ins.
c. 1565*

THE GRAND DUKE OF ALBA *Polychrome
wood sculpture. Height 11½ ins. 1680. The
Duke is trampling on a three-headed hydra with
the features of Queen Elizabeth I of England,
Pope Paul IV and the Elector of Saxony*

The Grand Staircase of the Palacio Liria, redesigned by Sir Edwin Lutyens after its destruction in 1936. Over the stairs hang a seventeenth-century Flemish tapestry woven with the arms of the seventh Duke of Veragua, Don Pedro Colón de Portugal, and an equestrian portrait of Don Francisco de Moncada, third Marquis of Aytona, attributed to Van Dyck. c. 1632. The Sedan chair is seventeenth-century Spanish

Opposite The Room of the Duchess of Alba containing paintings and objects associated with Doña Cayetana. Goya's full-length portrait of the Duchess hangs on the far wall

Renaissance palaces in Salamanca and Seville, which are now, together with the Palacio Liria in Madrid, the residences most frequently used by the family.

No spectacular additions were made to the Alba Collections in the seventeenth century by the family itself, but important works of this period were inherited later from families who intermarried with the House of Alba. Particular mention must be made of one of the most extraordinary figures of the time – Don Gaspar de Haro y Guzmán, seventh Marquis of El Carpio and fifth Count Duke of Olivares, who held high posts during the reign of Charles II. He had a boundless enthusiasm for collecting and in 1651, at the age of twenty-two, already owned about 300 paintings, among them Velasquez's *Venus at the Mirror* (the Rokeby Venus). When he died in 1687, his collection had grown to about 2,000 paintings, some inherited, but a large number bought in Italy where he had been Ambassador in Rome and Viceroy of Naples. If this collection had not been largely dispersed, the Alba collections of which it would have formed part would now rival the Prado. But on Olivares' death many of his possessions were auctioned to pay his debts, and later still the collection was even more reduced. However, some magnificent canvases which belonged to him do still hang in the Palacio Liria, notably the *Portrait of the Infanta Margarita* by Velasquez. This is probably the earliest in date of the paintings coming from the Olivares collection, and appears to be a preparatory study for the portrait in the Kunsthistorisches Museum, Vienna.

Opposite THE THIRTEENTH DUCHESS OF ALBA
*(1762–1802) Goya (1746–1828) oil on canvas
75 × 46 ins. Signed and inscribed
'To the Duchess of Alba, Frco de Goya 1795'*

LA MARQUESA DE LAZÁN *Goya (1746–1828)
oil on canvas 75½ × 44½ ins. c. 1800*

PORTRAIT OF THE INFANTA MARGARITA
*Studio of Velasquez oil on canvas 45 × 35 ins.
1654*

Opposite PHILIP V OF SPAIN INVESTING
THE FIRST DUKE OF BERWICK WITH THE
ORDER OF THE GOLDEN FLEECE AFTER
THE BATTLE OF ALAMANZA
*Jean-Auguste Dominique Ingres (1780–1867)
oil on canvas 32 × 41 ins.
Signed and dated 1818. Commissioned by
Don Carlos Miguel, fourteenth Duke of Alba*

THE FIRST DUKE OF BERWICK (*1670–1734*)
*Attributed to Sir Godfrey Kneller (1646/49–1723)
or Benedetto Gennari (1632–1715) oil on
canvas 45½ × 38 ins. c. 1705*

Below DON CARLOS MIGUEL, SEVENTH
DUKE OF BERWICK AND FOURTEENTH
DUKE OF ALBA (*1794–1835*) *Antonio Calliano
(active 1800–30) oil on canvas 29½ × 25 ins.
Signed and dated 1823*

Philip IV's unfortunate daughter is portrayed here at the age of
about three; she died at the age of twenty-two, having been
married for seven years to the Emperor Leopold, just before her
seventh child was due to be born. Among other works coming
from Olivares is *The King's Wolfhound* by Francisco Rizi, a
painter of Italian origins, who contributed to the development of
the Baroque in Spanish painting after Velasquez. An equestrian
portrait of the Marquis of Aytona by Van Dyck also comes from
the same source.

The marriage of the tenth Duke of Alba to Olivares' daughter
in 1688 opens a new chapter in the history of the Alba Collections. The pictures included in her dowry formed an important
addition to the existing collection, which was still further en-

riched during the eighteenth century by the acquisitions of the twelfth Duke, who bought a number of works by French artists during his time as Ambassador in Paris.

One of the most attractive figures in the history of the Alba family is the thirteenth Duchess, Doña María del Pilar Teresa Cayetana de Silva y Alvarez de Toledo. A woman of unusual beauty and charm, the Duchess Cayetana is perhaps best known for her great friendship with Goya. There is very little reliable evidence about the nature of her relationship with Goya and the whole story is now mixed up with legend. There is certainly no basis for the claim that *La Maja Desnuda* represents the Duchess. On the other hand there is no doubt that there was some sort of 'romance' between them, which probably began during the painting of the full length portrait which now hangs in the Palacio Liria. The Duchess is shown standing, with a small dog, and pointing to an inscription which reads 'To the Duchess of Alba, Frco de Goya 1795'. Some months after this was painted the Duke died and she retired to a large estate at Sanlúcar on the banks of the Guadalquivir near Seville. Goya followed her there and made numerous sketches of her. At the same time he painted the magnificent second portrait which is now owned by the Hispanic Society of New York. On it can be read the affectionate inscription 'Solo Goya' (Only Goya). Goya was probably more infatuated than the Duchess and the liaison was certainly brief.

FUNERAL OF A HOLY MONK *Attributed to*
Fra Angelico (c. 1387–1455) panel 7½ × 11 ins.
1430–40. Probably from a predella

A crystal goblet in a leather case, which she presented to Goya, can be seen in the Palacio Liria. The Duchess Cayetana died in mysterious circumstances (it has been suggested that she was poisoned) in 1802 at the age of forty, leaving no heir. The title therefore passed to her cousin, the seventh Duke of Berwick and thus the two great houses were united.

The history of the Dukes of Berwick goes back to the first Duke, James Fitz-James Stuart, illegitimate son of James II of England and Arabella Churchill, sister of the Duke of Marlborough. Following the accession of William and Mary, he went into exile and entered the service of Louis XIV, playing an important part in the War of the Spanish Succession which put Philip V, grandson of Louis XIV, on the throne of Spain. As a reward the new king bestowed on him the title of Duke of Liria. The second Duke of Berwick and Liria took up permanent residence in Spain and in 1716 married Catalina Colón of Portugal, Duchess of Veragua and a direct descendant of Christopher Columbus. Doña Catalina brought to the collection a set of tapestries woven with her family coat of arms and views of cities of the New World, as well as a magnificent landscape *Road to the Market* by Rubens.

The third Duke of Berwick, called James like his father and grandfather, married Maria Teresa de Silva y Alvarez de Toledo, sister of the twelfth Duke of Alba, and was thus responsible for uniting the two great families. It was he who began the construction of the Palacio Liria.

This palace, one of the finest buildings erected (1770–80) in Madrid during the eighteenth century, was inspired by the royal palaces of La Granja and Madrid, which had been built by the Bourbons in a classical style quite unlike the exuberant Baroque which dominated Spanish architecture at the time. Its plan was rectangular, columns and pilasters of the Tuscan order, with an Ionic entablature, being incorporated in the two principal façades. Both the architect Don Ventura Rodriguez and the third Duke died in 1785, not long after the building was completed, but the full splendour of the palace was not revealed until the time of Don Carlos Miguel Fitz-James Stuart, seventh Duke of Berwick and fourteenth Duke of Alba. He inherited the first title at the age of three and was eight years old when the Duchess Cayetana died in 1802. It would have been natural to expect that with the uniting of the two families their collections of works of art would also have been merged, but this did not happen immediately. The Berwick Collection was not particularly important. It contained family portraits of great historical value, such as the *Portrait of Mary Queen of Scots* mentioned earlier, but it could not stand comparison, either in quantity or quality, with the Alba Collection, which had been enriched by over two thousand paintings belonging to the seventh Marquis of El Carpio.

THE VIRGIN OF THE POMEGRANATE
Attributed to Fra Angelico (c. 1387–1455)
panel 32½ × 23 ins. c. 1444

ADORATION OF THE INFANT CHRIST
Perugino (c. 1445/50–1523) panel.
Diameter 48 ins. c. 1491

Right VIRGIN AND CHILD *Attributed to Fra Bartolomeo*
(c. 1474–c. 1517) drawing on yellow paper pasted on board
49 × 72½ ins. c. 1510

Unfortunately a large part of the Alba Collections was dispersed on the death of the Duchess Cayetana, so that Duke Carlos Miguel inherited only thirty-two paintings of real value, and these not among the best. Charles IV's Prime Minister Godoy illegally appropriated many outstanding works, including the Rokeby Venus (now in the National Gallery, London) and Raphael's 'Alba Madonna', later bought by the National Gallery of Washington for $1,500,000.

The new Duke of Alba, who showed a passion for art collecting early in life and acted as patron to many painters and sculptors, did his best to compensate for these great losses. But he nearly ruined himself in the process because of his ambitious projects. He was unfortunate in his choice of friends and advisers, who were largely to blame for his economic misfortunes. However it was his idea to build a gallery adjacent to the Palacio Liria which would be open to the public.

The works acquired by Don Carlos Miguel, especially in Italy, form a substantial part of the collections now distributed through the various Alba palaces. But when he died in 1835, he left his son, who married the seventh Countess of Montijo, sister of the Empress Eugénie, to face a period of grave economic crisis. Many valuable pieces, notably tapestries, had to be sacrificed and were sold in Paris in 1877, but fortunately none of the pictures were included. These losses were partly offset by the works inherited from the Empress Eugénie, which included Goya's *La Marquesa de Lazán*. The sixteenth Duke (1849–1901) made few additions to the collections. On the other hand his wife, Doña Rosario Falcó, initiated a period of restoration which has continued to the present day. The last Duke Don James (1874–1953), added a number of important works, chiefly connected with the family's history, and also filled gaps in the scope of the collection, by acquiring, for example, works of the English School.

Opposite THE ANNUNCIATION *Master of the Virgin inter Virgines (active 1470–1500) panel 36 × 27 ins. c. 1480. The donor, Don Garcia Alvarez de Toledo, first Duke of Alba is shown kneeling. Above* *his head is a shield displaying Moslem standards captured by his father, Don Fernando. The castle seen through the window is probably Alba de Tormes. On the reverse is an* Adoration of the Kings

SUMMER *Rubens* (*1577–1640*) *panel 55 × 85 ins.
c. 1630. A copy of the landscape in the British
royal collection*

LANDSCAPE WITH A DRAWBRIDGE *Rembrandt
(1606–69) panel 16½ × 23½ ins. c. 1640*

Opposite CHARLES V AND ISABELLA OF
PORTUGAL *Rubens (1577–1640)
oil on canvas 45 × 64½ ins. c. 1628–29.
A copy of a lost original by Titian formerly in
the Royal Palace, Madrid*

THE KING'S WOLFHOUND *Francisco Rizi*
(1608–85) oil on canvas 66 × 44 ins. c. 1670

Above right MRS PORTER *Sir Joshua Reynolds*
(1723–92) oil on canvas 30 × 24½ ins. c. 1757

Right SELF-PORTRAIT *Anton Rafael Mengs*
(1728–79) oil on canvas 53 × 38 ins. 1760

During the Spanish Civil War (1936–39) the Palacio Liria was bombed and much of the house and its contents was destroyed by fire. Fortunately many of the paintings and other treasures were saved. Reconstruction of the interior of the building was started very soon after the war was over (the eighteenth-century façades had not been damaged), and at this time modifications were made to the arrangement of certain rooms, as well as to the main staircase and chapel, following designs prepared by Sir Edwin Lutyens, who approved the plans in 1942, a few months before his death. By the time the seventh Duke died in 1953, the reconstruction was well advanced. His daughter, the present Duchess, opened the new building in 1956.

The collection of paintings, in which many different schools are represented, consists of more than 800 works. The most important hang in the Palacio Liria, but others are in the palaces of Las Dueñas in Seville, Monterrey in Salamanca, and Epila near Saragossa.

The Italian schools of the fifteenth and sixteenth centuries are very strongly represented. Thus there are two panels by Fra Angelico, *The Virgin of the Pomegranate* and the *Funeral of a Holy Monk*, which probably formed part of a predella, an *Adoration of the Infant Christ* by Perugino and another painting with a similar theme which is a copy of a lost work by Raphael. This last cannot of course compensate for the departure in the early nineteenth century of the 'Alba Madonna' by Raphael (now in the National Gallery, Washington) which had been in the Alba Collection for over a hundred years. The collection also contains a *Virgin and Child* by Andrea del Sarto and a large drawing of the *Virgin and Child* attributed to Fra Bartolomeo.

Works by Venetian painters include such splendid examples as Cima da Conegliano's *Virgin with the Dead Christ between Saints and Donors*, Antonio Previtali's *Virgin and Child between St Peter and St Jerome*, Palma Vecchio's *Portrait of an Unknown Youth*, and several important works by Titian: the *Portrait of the Grand Duke of Alba* mentioned earlier, a *Portrait of Federico Gonzaga, Duke of Mantua* (a curious painting incorporating an 'Allegory of Love Triumphing over Force'), and finally a *Last Supper*, whose composition resembles that of a similar painting in the Escorial. There are many other works by sixteenth and seventeenth-century Italian painters, including Cesare da Sesto, Luca Cambiaso, the Bassanos, Pordenone, Guercino, Guido Reni, Allori and Carlo Maratta, whose *Virgin and Child* is outstanding. Two paintings by Panini showing monuments of ancient Rome and an exceptional *Roman Ruins* by Francesco Guardi are among a number of works by eighteenth-century Italian artists.

The Northern schools too are well represented. The most important sixteenth-century work is a *Portrait of the Grand Duke of Alba*, attributed to Key, but which Max Friedlander considers to be the work of Antonio Moro. The works by Rubens and his school merit special attention. *Charles V and Isabella of Portugal*, a copy by Rubens of a lost original by Titian, is of particular artistic and iconographic value, while his *Portrait of Philip IV* is interesting for its bold use of colour. Other works by Rubens include a fine landscape *Road to the Market*, *Artemis the Widow of Mausolus*, *The Battle of the Amazons* (related to the similar canvas in Munich), and a *Supper at Emmaus*. The *Bathsheba* (a version of the Dresden painting) is probably by a pupil of Rubens. To these we can add an *Allegory of Human Vanity* by Velvet Brueghel, *Artemis the Inconsolable Widow of Mausolus* by Jordaens and *Portrait of a Child* attributed to Van Dyck.

Dutch painting is well represented in the Palacio Liria, which is fortunate in view of its limited representation in the Prado. Apart from a number of small genre scenes, there is an important group of landscapes by Ruysdael, Wynants, Van de Velde and Van Goyen. The most important work, however, is undoubtedly Rembrandt's *Landscape* of 1640.

The only representative of the German school is Anton Rafael Mengs, who lived and worked in Spain for almost twenty years (1763–79) and had a great influence in the period immediately preceding the rise of Goya. Among portraits by Mengs, are those of the *Empress Maria Theresa*, *Marie Louise de Bourbon*, *The Twelfth Duke of Alba*, *The Duchess of Huescar* (mother of Cayetana), and a magnificent *Self Portrait*.

The English School is principally represented by portraits of the Stuarts: the *Portrait of Mary Queen of Scots* by an unknown sixteenth-century Anglo-Flemish painter, portraits of Charles II and James II attributed to Sir Peter Lely, and portraits of the Marshal of Berwick and his first wife, Honoria de Burg, by Kneller. To make up for the lack of English eighteenth-century paintings the last Duke of Alba and the present Duchess have acquired works by Reynolds, Gainsborough, Romney and Raeburn.

French painting is represented by several eighteenth and nineteenth-century works many of which belonged to the Empress Eugénie. The most typical eighteenth-century painting is *The Children of the Second Duke of Berwick* by Louis Michel van Loo, depicting them in Roman costume. There is also a curious painting by Ingres signed and dated 1818 of *Philip V of Spain Investing the First Duke of Berwick with the Order of the Golden Fleece*. Most of the works coming from the Empress Eugénie are by artists who achieved success at the Salon, but are practically unknown today. In addition there are a number of portraits of the family of Napoleon III, including some by Winterhalter. The Empress, who died in the Palacio Liria aged ninety-four, also bequeathed to the Dukes of Alba some fine pieces of French furniture. The present Duchess has selected works by Courbet, Corot, Fantin-Latour, Boudin and other nineteenth-century French painters.

Spanish painting is perhaps not as fully or grandly represented as one would expect, but it was this element which suffered the most severe losses when the various sales occurred. The most important sixteenth-century work is of course El Greco's *Crucifixion*. Seventeenth-century paintings include Velasquez's *Infanta Margarita* and Francisco Rizi's *The King's Wolfhound*, mentioned earlier, Ribera's *The Anchorite* and Zurbaran's *Santo Domingo de Guzman*. There is also a *Portrait of an Ecclesiastic* by Murillo. A number of eighteenth-century paintings show the development of Spanish painting in a period dominated by French influence, but the most outstanding later works are of course the two magnificent portraits by Goya, *The Duchess of Alba* and *The Marquesa de Lazán*. There are many examples of nineteenth and twentieth-century Spanish painting, and the present Duchess has shown an enthusiasm for the work of contemporary artists, which has resulted in a considerable increase in this aspect of the collection.

The Palacio Liria used to house an important collection of engravings, but unfortunately some six thousand were burnt during the Civil War. To-day some fifty sheets are on view, among those that were saved being eleven by Dürer, including *Death the Rider, Adam and Eve, Head of an Old Man*, and *Portrait of the Emperor Maximilian*, an *Entry of Christ into Purgatory* by Mantegna and six engravings by Rembrandt, including *The Burgomaster* and *The Hundred Guilders Print*. There are other engravings by Lucas van Leyden, Matheus Zasinger, Robetta, Van Dyck and Goya.

Opposite *The Ballroom decorated with paintings, sculpture and tapestries which belonged to the Empress Eugénie.* Right, *a marble bust of the Empress Eugénie by Alexandre Lequien (1796–1881). On the far wall a Gobelins tapestry woven in 1861 after a portrait of the Empress by Winterhalter*

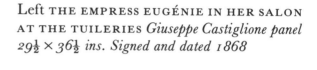

Left THE EMPRESS EUGÉNIE IN HER SALON AT THE TUILERIES *Giuseppe Castiglione panel* $29\frac{1}{2} \times 36\frac{1}{2}$ *ins. Signed and dated 1868*

PORTRAIT OF THE EMPRESS EUGÉNIE
Franz-Xavier Winterhalter (1806–73)
oil on canvas $90 \times 57\frac{1}{2}$ *ins.*
Signed and dated 1862

ST DOMINIC *Francisco de Zurbarán (1598–1664)*
oil on canvas 41 × 30 ins. c. 1634

Right PORTRAIT OF AN ECCLESIASTIC
Bartolomé Estebán Murillo (1617–82) oil on
canvas 77½ × 47 ins. 1680. Probably a portrait
of Don Juan de Miranda, a Canon of Seville

Female Head.
Marble.
Height 10 ins. Greek.
Fifth century BC

The collection of tapestries was greatly reduced as a result of the sales in the nineteenth century. However, there are still outstanding pieces in the Palacio Liria and at Seville and Epila. The most interesting of those in the Palacio Liria is one which is recorded as belonging to the first Duke of Alba in 1485. It is the only survivor out of a series of eleven and represents the *Battle between the Greeks and Amazons and the Death of Queen Penthesilea.* Next in order of time are three panels showing the victories of the Grand Duke of Alba, and twelve panels woven with the arms of the House of Veragua commissioned at the end of the seventeenth century by Don Pedro Colón de Portugal. There is also a beautiful specimen of the *Psyche* series taken from a painting by Giulio Romano in the Palazzo del Té at Mantua. Finally there are two important sets woven at the Gobelins factory in the late eighteenth century. The first, *The Indies,* consists of four panels based on cartoons by Desportes commemorating the expedition made by Prince Johann Moritz of Nassau to Africa and Brazil. It bears the name of the weaver Cozette and is dated 1789. The second set, of which only three pieces have survived, is entitled *The Loves of the Gods* and represents *Aurora and Cephalus, Neptune and the Danaid Aminona,* and *Vulcan and Venus.* The cartoons for these were prepared by Boucher and one carries the inscription 'Cozette fils à 1791'.

The small collection of Greek and Roman antiquities includes a fifth-century BC Female Head, possibly from the Temple of Niobe, and an *Aphrodite Genetrix*, probably Roman, though based

APHRODITE GENETRIX *Marble, probably Pentelic. Height 59 ins. Roman, probably based on a Greek original of the fifth century BC*

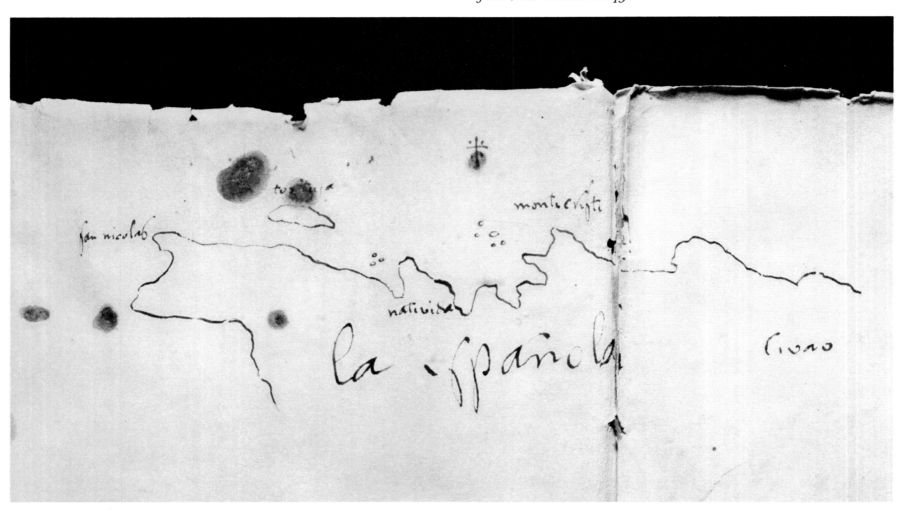

on a Greek original of the fifth century BC. There is also a Roman herm of Dionysius which imitates the style of a Greek original, and a group of Etruscan vases.

With the exception of a few medieval, Renaissance and Baroque pieces, the majority of the sculpture is nineteenth century. Duke Carlos Miguel commissioned a large number of busts of members of the Alba family, especially from José Alvarez Cubero, including a reclining figure of the Marquesa de Ariza, mother of the fourteenth Duke.

There is a valuable collection of porcelain. An outstanding piece of Meissen by Kaendler represents the Tailor Riding the Buck – a satire on one of the Ministers of Augustus III of Poland. A group of Sèvres urns comes from the collection of the Empress Eugénie.

No detailed description of the furniture is either necessary or possible here. Suffice it to say that there are fine pieces dating from the sixteenth century to the present day, especially of the eighteenth and early nineteenth centuries, including the Spanish version of the Louis XVI style, known in Spain as Charles IV.

The furniture bequeathed by the Empress Eugénie is of course French Second Empire.

The collections in the archives and library are still of great interest despite the losses suffered in the fire of 1936. The 'Bible of the House of Alba', dated 1430 and the work of a Jew, consists of the Old Testament only and contains some fine miniatures. There is a mass of documents covering the fifteenth to the nineteenth centuries, which from a historical, artistic and literary point of view is a mine of precious source material. Some of these documents, for example the wills of Ferdinand the Catholic and Philip II, papers signed by Columbus, and the marriage contract of Prince Don Juan and Margarita of Austria are on display. There are many rare books and incunabula, such as the first edition of *Don Quixote*, patents of nobility, and old maps.

The Palacio Liria represents the accumulated treasures of one family over many centuries. The rehabilitation of the collections in recent years symbolises respect for a great tradition of art collecting and a new desire to make these works of art more readily available to the general public.

The Princes
de Beauvau-Craon

R. A. Cecil

The collections of the Prince de Beauvau-Craon are housed mainly at the Château de Craon at Haroué, a few miles south of Nancy. This is the principal seat of the family, dating in its present form from the early eighteenth century, and built on the site of two former fortified castles by Marc, Marquis de Beauvau, prince de Craon (1679–1757), chancellor of Lorraine, and later viceroy of Tuscany. The works of art owned by the present prince consist mainly of furniture, tapestries and objects of art inherited by him from his own forebears, and from the families into which they have married since the middle of the eighteenth century. They represent an ensemble which is essentially French in character, and include many pieces of fine quality, some with historical associations, which are enhanced by the architecture of the château where they are to be found.

The Princes de Beauvau-Craon

R. A. Cecil

The early history of the family and collections of the princes of Beauvau-Craon is bound up with their possession since the late seventeenth century of the fief of Haroué, and of the château which lies within it. The property commands a ford over the river Madon, which flows into the Moselle a few miles to the north of Haroué, and lies on the main route from Germany to France, about twenty miles south of Nancy, the old capital of the Duchy of Lorraine.

The original fortified château was inherited through marriage by the family of Bassompierre about the middle of the fifteenth century, and it was they who subsequently built a new fortified château – parts of which are still extant – on the exact site of the present building. In 1596 the property was inherited by François, the celebrated Maréchal de Bassompierre, who was born at Haroué in 1579, and under him it was raised to a marquisate in 1623. By the time of his death in 1646, however, the château and estate were in a ruinous condition, owing to the wars of the Fronde. But when Duke Leopold of Lorraine was restored to the estates of his father under the terms of the Peace of Ryswick in 1697, a new brief period of peace and stability began within the duchy, and it so happened that the *grand écuyer* at the ducal court at that moment was the great friend, childhood companion and exact contemporary of the duke: Marc, Marquis de Beauvau, the main branch of whose family had transplanted themselves from Anjou to Lorraine in the fifteenth century.

Marc was the son of Louis, Marquis de Beauvau, and his second wife, Anne de Ligny. His grandfather was Henri de Beauvau, who had been tutor to the Duke Charles V of Lorraine, father of Duke Leopold, to whose son Marc himself was to become tutor. Both his own sister, Cathérine Diane de Beauvau, and also his half-sister, Marie Louise (daughter of his father by his first wife) were married to grandsons of Georges Affrican, the

The Château de Haroué (detail) by Claude Jacquart (1683–1736),
a Nancy artist. Executed after the rebuilding of the château by Boffrand

The forecourt at Haroué, as redesigned by Boffrand. The wrought iron gates are surmounted by the Beauvau-Craon arms

younger brother of the Maréchal de Bassompierre. It will be seen therefore that not only were the de Beauvau family in high favour at the court of the Duke of Lorraine, but they were also closely related by marriage to the family who still held, though tenuously, the *marquisat* and fief of Haroué. Marc had been appointed tutor to his nephew and nieces from 1709, and was therefore in a strong position to observe the final stages of a prolonged contest for possession of the fief between the Bassompierres and their creditors. He was also able to appreciate the immense potential value of the property, despite years of devastation and neglect, and in 1720 secured possession of it through purchase.

Marc de Beauvau-Craon is the central figure in the history of the family, although the circumstances of his distinguished career explain why the château at Haroué, which he rebuilt, not only failed to be completed but was often subsequently abandoned by the main branch of the family. Born in 1679, he was the same age and was educated with Leopold, son of Duke Charles V of Lorraine, who himself became duke in 1697. As a result of their friendship, Duke Leopold appointed Marc de Beauvau his *grand écuyer*, thus enabling him to become chief adviser on matters of state, and eventually tutor to his son Francis, later the Emperor Francis I. In 1722 the Emperor Charles VI created him Prince de Craon, and in 1729 he was made a Grandee of Spain by Philip V. Duke Leopold of Lorraine died in 1729, and was succeeded by his son Francis III, Marc de Beauvau's pupil, then aged twenty-one. When, however, he became betrothed to the Archduchess Maria Theresa, daughter of the Emperor Charles VI, in 1735, the objections of France to a union between Lorraine and the Empire, forced him to accept the dukedom of Tuscany instead, his place as Duke of Lorraine being taken by Stanislas Lesczinski, the deposed King of Poland, and King Louis XV's father-in-law. As a result of these political and dynastic manoeuvres, in which the Prince de Craon played an important part, Marc followed his former sovereign to Vienna, and was then appointed Viceroy of Tuscany in 1737.

As Viceroy of Tuscany, the Prince de Craon was compelled to spend a large part of his time in Florence, where he became famous as a patron of the arts and letters. In 1747 he returned to Lorraine, but he then lived mainly in the Hôtel de Craon in Nancy, which Boffrand had built for him. It seems that he did not often visit Haroué, which was still partly unfinished, though he did in fact die there on 10th March, 1754 and is buried in the parish church. His portrait by an unknown artist hangs at Haroué, and shows him in late middle age wearing the robes and insignia of the order of the Golden Fleece, bestowed on him by the Emperor Charles VI at the time of the marriage of Francis I and Maria Theresa.

In 1704 Marc had married Anne Marguerite de Lignéville,

The garden, or south façade at Haroué. The corner towers and moat of the medieval château were incorporated by Boffrand into his design

PORTRAIT OF MARC DE BEAUVAU, PRINCE DE CRAON
*(1679–1754) unknown artist, oil on canvas 50 × 38 in. c. 1740–45.
The first Prince, who wears the robes and insignia of the Golden Fleece,
acquired Haroué in 1720*

PORTRAIT OF CHARLES JUST, PRINCE DE BEAUVAU
*(1793–1864) François Gérard (1770–1837) oil on canvas
29½ × 23½ in. In 1848 Prince Charles Just returned to
live at Haroué which had been uninhabited since the death
of Prince Marc in 1754*

ALEXANDER AND PORUS, *one of the set of tapestries* L'HISTOIRE
D'ALEXANDRE, *designed by Charles Le Brun and bearing the arms of
the Prince and Princesse de Craon. Flemish, or possibly Lorrain. Width
71 ins. c. 1700. Below the tapestry is a Louis XIV gilt-wood console
table and two Louis XIV gilt-wood chairs upholstered in red silk*

Opposite *A corner of the Saloon showing another of the* HISTOIRE
D'ALEXANDRE *tapestries and, on the table, arms and armour belonging
to various Princes de Beauvau*

and their eldest son, Charles Just de Beauvau, born in 1720,
became a distinguished soldier and a Marshal of France. Yet
although he inherited all the possessions of his father at Haroué,
he chose to live at the Château de Val near Saint Germain,
which was given to him by Louis XV, and to this residence he
transported all the rich furnishings from his parents' château. He
died in 1793 leaving a widow and an only daughter, who became
the Princesse de Poix. It was as a result of the various *successions*
following their deaths that the original furnishings and objects
from Haroué became dispersed, leaving only the tapestries of
L'Histoire d'Alexandre which can for certain be identified as being
part of the original furnishings.

The Maréchal de Beauvau was succeeded in the title by his
younger brother, Ferdinand, and it is from him that the present
line descends. The latter's grandson, Charles Just, was born in
1793, and married in 1815 Lucie Marie de Praslin. His portrait
by Gérard is reproduced here. Neither his father Marc, nor his
grandfather, lived at Haroué, but he himself came back to live
there in 1848, and contrived to spend part of the year there until
his death in 1864. It was after this that a sale was held in Paris in
1865 consisting of valuable furniture, and a few pictures. His son
Marc (1816–83) chose to live at his house at Sainte Assise in the
Sarthe, for which department he was *député*, and ceded the
château at Haroué to his aunt, the Princesse de Craon. Prince
Marc died in 1883 leaving a son aged five, and two daughters.
This son, Charles Louis, decided after marriage in 1920 to move
back to Haroué, and to repair what he could of the damage
wrought by time and neglect. He was succeeded in 1942 by his
only child, the present Prince de Beauvau-Craon, who nobly
maintains his father's interests.

THE CHÂTEAU DE CRAON

Soon after taking possession of the château in 1720, Marc de
Beauvau appointed two expert architects to report on the state of
the various buildings, and recommend what should be preserved
and what restored. It was almost certainly as a result of this report that he made the decision to rebuild the château completely,
and not unnaturally he resorted to Germain Boffrand, the architect who had just completed the château at Lunéville, for Duke
Leopold of Lorraine, as well as his own *hôtel particulier* on the
Place Carrière at Nancy. The great originality of Boffrand's
plans, which are fully engraved in his *Livre d'Architecture*, published in 1745, lies in the fact that he preserved so much of the
Bassompierre fortress-château. The site is the same, including the
moat. The corner towers were incorporated and the outer eleva-
tions preserved, both almost complete. The main innovations
were the replacement of the former *donjon* or keep by a forecourt,
the exquisite colonnading of this forecourt, and the erection of

the splendid classical façade in soft grey stone, an elevation which is repeated with variations in the centre of the garden façade, and there combined with a very graceful flight of steps and a bridge over the moat. The work must have been begun soon after 1720, and was well advanced by the time that Marc de Beauvau left for Vienna in 1735. The roof, as it appears to-day, was restored to the design envisaged in Germain Boffrand's original plans by Prince Charles Louis de Beauvau-Craon. Both he and his son, the present prince, have continued the work of restoration.

The interior is and presumably always has been austere in style. The ground floor contains the principal state-rooms which, apart from the fine stone-faced entrance hall, are mainly panelled, some, like the library, being redecorated during the nineteenth century. Above the mantelpieces in the principal reception rooms are pier-glasses set in stucco and decorated with eighteenth-century bas-reliefs. There is little plaster work, and

Opposite *The Green Empire Saloon containing a suite of furniture originally designed c. 1815 by Belanger for Louis XVIII. On the left is a* Portrait of Louis XVIII in his Study at the Tuileries *by François Gérard c. 1816 and on the other wall* The Comtesse du Cayla and her Children, *also by Gérard c. 1826*

Below left *Louis XV mantelpiece in the Library at Haroué, with a Louis XVI clock and candelabra of gilt and patinated bronze. Above is a full-length portrait of the young Louis XV after Jean Baptiste Van Loo*

Below right *Chinoiserie wall painting c. 1750 in the style of Jean Pillement in one of the tower rooms at Haroué. The panels below are of later date*

practically no *boiserie* in the Louis XV style, which might perhaps be expected in a building of this date and style of architecture. Two of the corner towers (those facing the garden) contain
circular rooms on the ground-floor level, and these are decorated
with rococo plaster work on the ceilings, and charming paintings
on the lower walls in the style of Jean Pillement.

THE COLLECTIONS

The art collections owned by the present Prince de Beauvau-
Craon are, in effect, an accumulation of family possessions and
furnishings which have come down to him from various branches
of his family, and from those into whom they have married. They
present, therefore, a picture of aristocratic taste through three
hundred years, and the combination of the splendid architecture
of the château at Haroué, with the fine furniture which it contains can be seen to be essentially French in character, without
however deriving anything very particular from the land of Lorraine, where it is situated.

The circumstances through which the château and desmesne
of Haroué have passed, and its complete rebuilding by Marc de
Beauvau at the beginning of the eighteenth century, make it
plain that virtually nothing has survived from the seventeenth-
century owners, or from the *succession* of the Maréchal de Bassompierre. But owing to the French laws of inheritance, by which
possessions are divided and subdivided among co-heirs of each
successive generation, there is also virtually nothing beyond the
château itself, and its interior decoration, which dates from the
time of Marc de Beauvau. The most important item which can
safely be said to have belonged to the builder of the present château, however, is the fine set of tapestries representing *L'Histoire
d'Alexandre*, after the celebrated designs of Charles Le Brun, and
bearing the arms of the Prince and Princesse de Craon. But it is
clear that they were not woven at the Gobelins where the royal
sets were made. They may conceivably be Flemish, though the
style of weaving and the colouring suggest rather that they were
woven locally in Lorraine. Their quality is good, and they provide a fine and appropriate background to the furnishings of the
ground-floor rooms of the château. They are also of exactly the

right style and period for the rather austere panelled interior, even though they have to be stretched round corners because of their size. They also appear to have been cut at various times, and the borders separated from the actual panels, which may mean that they had to be adapted to their positions at different times and in different places. It is also possible that some or all of them once hung in the Hôtel de Craon in Nancy, or even accompanied the Prince de Craon to Tuscany. Their condition varies considerably, but of those illustrated here the colours are good and relatively unfaded.

It is probable, though not certain, that some of the fine chairs and console tables in the Louis XIV or early Louis XV style may also have belonged to Marc de Beauvau, in particular the two armchairs and console, and the lacquer cabinet and stand reproduced here. This furniture is mostly of the date of the rebuilding of the château, or just subsequently, but much of it may have come to the house later from other branches of the family.

The chest of drawers is interesting as it is said to be part of the original furnishings of the present château. It is veneered with

Below left *Chinese black lacquer cabinet and gilt-wood stand. Height of cabinet 34 ins. c. 1710*

Below right *Drop-front secretaire (secrétaire à abattant) veneered with floral marquetry of various woods. Stamped by J. G. Schlichtig (active 1765–82). Height 35 ins.*

lacquer in conventional designs and lavishly mounted in the rococo manner with gilt bronze of fine quality. Although not signed, it can be said to correspond to the style of the great cabinet-maker of the Louis XV period, Bernard van Risenburgh (who stamped his furniture B.V.R.B.), though it may not actually be by him. The fine pair of *meubles à hauteur d'appui* veneered with Boulle marquetry of brass and tortoiseshell are of a well-known design, but they seem not to have been part of the early furnishings of Boffrand's château and probably entered the family possession later. The commode veneered with the lacquer known as *vernis Martin* is interesting because the style of decoration is unusual. It is on a red ground which has darkened in the course of time, being now a deep maroon in colour. The subject represented is that of an oriental potentate leaving his house in a palanquin attended by horsemen carrying banners, and the design spreads over the whole of the front surface of both drawers, with details rendered polychromatically. The sides are decorated in the same manner, and show ladies in garden landscapes. The commode is late Louis XV in style, and is slightly un-French in feeling. It has the same provenance as the set of

black and gold lacquered furniture by Molitor mentioned below.

From the later eighteenth and early nineteenth century there are in many ways more valuable and interesting pieces of furniture. The fine set of chairs and sofas in the Louis XVI style reproduced here are carved in the manner associated with Georges Jacob, and upholstered with a floral tapestry which has kept its colour well. They are stamped by Claude Chevigny, a well-known maker of chairs in the second half of the eighteenth century. He became a *maître-menuisier* in 1768 and is known to have supplied furniture for the Duc de Choiseul at the Château de Chanteloup.

More striking because rarer and forming a set intended to be more or less *en suite*, is the splendid series of lacquer furniture in the late Louis XVI style, by or in the manner of Bernard Molitor. This group of pieces is known to have come into the possession of the Beauvau-Craon family through the marriage in 1840 of Marc, fifth Prince de Beauvau-Craon, to Mlle d'Aubusson de la Feuillade, and consists in the main of a chest of drawers, two low cupboards, and (though possibly not *en suite*) a console with three shelves. They are all in the very austere style of the immediate

Opposite Louis XVI sofa and chair upholstered in Aubusson tapestry. Part of a set stamped by Claude Chevigny. Height of both 40½ ins. c. 1770–80

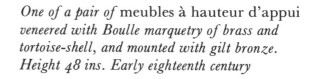

One of a pair of meubles à hauteur d'appui *veneered with Boulle marquetry of brass and tortoise-shell, and mounted with gilt bronze. Height 48 ins. Early eighteenth century*

Commode lacquered in the oriental style with red vernis Martin. *Height 35 ins. French, mid-eighteenth century*

Black and gold lacquered cabinet attributed to Bernard Molitor (c. 1730– after 1810) Height 37½ ins. c. 1790. Standing on it are a set of blue Chinese vases with late Louis XV gilt-bronze mounts

Below Black and gold lacquered cupboard from the same suite, attributed to Molitor. Height 37½ ins. c. 1790

pre-Revolution period, which is characteristic of Molitor's work, and their decoration consists almost exclusively of the fine lacquered landscapes, with the minimum mounting of gilt bronze. The tops of Siena marble are also most harmonious and of good quality.

The beautiful little table also reproduced here does not seem to belong strictly to this group, but from the point of view of quality is the finest piece of French eighteenth-century furniture in the collection. It is not signed, but the top, sides and drawer fronts are all covered with lacquer of the finest order, and the tapering legs are gracefully designed and mounted.

The upright secretaire (*secrétaire à abattant*) is a good example of a fairly common type made in the second half of the eighteenth century. It is signed by J. G. Schlichtig, the floral marquetry is of good quality, and it has practically no gilt-bronze mounts.

The *bronzes d'ameublement* in the collection include a fine clock, the case of gilt and patinated bronze, and a pair of candelabra of the same materials, the figures being those of Cupid (*l'Amour menaçant*) and Psyche, after models by Falconet. The gilt bronze chandelier reproduced here is also particularly fine, and is of a

Two pieces from the suite of furniture designed by Belanger for the Château de Saint Ouen. Gilt wood upholstered with green figured silk. Height 39½ ins. c. 1815

Black lacquer table with gilt-bronze mounts. Height 29 ins. c. 1785

rare design. All these pieces date from the second half of the eighteenth century, but from a slightly earlier period are the magnificent set of blue Chinese vases mounted with gilt bronze in the style of the late Louis XV period. The mounts are exceptional, and those of the central vase with its female terminal figures are unusually lavish, and of rare design.

It seems that the collection of French furniture of this period especially, was at one time somewhat larger and contained some very important pieces, but a sale of furniture and a few pictures took place in Paris on 21st April, 1865, after the death of Charles Just, the fourth prince. It comprised a number of pieces said to have been made for, or to have belonged to, Queen Marie Antoinette, including the lacquer *table à écrire* delivered by Daguerre and Weisweiler in 1784 for the *Cabinet de la Reine* at Saint Cloud, now in the Louvre, and the perfume-burner of jasper and gilt bronze by Gouthière, which was bought at the sale by the fourth Marquess of Hertford and is now in the Wallace Collection.

Numerically by far the most extensive section of the furnishings of the Château de Haroué are two large suites of furniture of the

Restoration period, one gilt and upholstered with green figured silk designed by Belanger, the other of mahogany carved, ungilt and still in use in the main dining-room at Haroué. These, and indeed all the furniture of this period at Haroué, came from the Château de Saint Ouen, and were made for Louis XVIII when he reconstructed it in about 1815. After the king's death, Saint Ouen passed to Zoe Victoire, wife of Achille, Comte du Cayla, who had exercised a great influence over him from 1820 onwards. Madame du Cayla bequeathed these sets of furniture to her daughter, the Princesse de Craon, who had married a younger brother of Charles Just, fourth Prince de Beauvau, and it was she who brought the furniture to Haroué, which had been ceded to her by her nephew Marc, fifth Prince. Since her death it has remained in the château.

Among the pieces is also the fine Empire-style bed and a marble bust of Madame du Cayla by Pigalle *fils*. The two large pictures by Baron Gérard of the king in his study at the Tuileries, and of Madame du Cayla and her children, came from the same source.

It would appear that none of the Princes de Beauvau-Craon were collectors of pictures, and the absence within the present collections of any important paintings, other than family portraits of various dates, is noticeable. The one exception is a series of decorative canvases by Hubert Robert with landscapes in the romantic manner. This series is let into the walls of a room on the ground floor of the Château de Haroué. A very few pictures were sold after the death of Prince Charles Just in 1865, including a *Head of a Boy* by Greuze, which is now in the Wallace Collection.

Mahogany bed and furniture en suite *by Belanger from the Château de Saint Ouen. Bed 47 × 69 ins. c. 1815*